THE
GOURMAN
REPORT

THE GOURMAN REPORT

A Rating of Graduate and Professional Programs in American and International Universities

EIGHTH EDITION
Revised

Dr. Jack Gourman

Random House, Inc. 1997

Princeton Review Publishing, L.L.C.
2315 Broadway
New York, NY 10024
E-mail: info@review.com

ISBN 0-679-78374-1

Editor: Jennifer Rothblatt
Production Editor: Bruno Blumenfeld
Design: Meher Khambata and Carmine Raspaolo

Manufactured in the United States of America on partially recycled paper.

9 8 7 6 5 4 3 2 1

Eighth Edition

This book is dedicated to the memory of
Blanka Gourman,
a kind and generous spirit.

PREFACE TO THE EIGHTH EDITION

As with previous editions, *The Gourman Report: A Rating of Graduate and Professional Programs in American and International Universities* addresses the need for a qualitative evaluation of higher-level education in the United States, Canada, and International universities. I have tried to organize the data so that educators, administrators, corporations, students, and others can quickly and efficiently locate the material of interest to them. To this end, several new programs have been added, in fields deemed important to our nation's economic and technical development. Universities in former Soviet-bloc countries have been excluded because of political instability.

As always, the greatest, most important change is in the ratings themselves. I regret that, in all too many cases, readers will turn to the ranking for their own programs and discover a lower score than in the last book. Let me be blunt: Higher education is in ill health today. Years of fiscal malnutrition have taken their toll. Public indifference, irresponsible actions and statements from elected officials, and growing cynicism on the part of faculty and administrators have compounded the symptoms. And, while the "patient" is the institution, those most aggrieved are the students themselves. Perhaps naively, young men and women still look to higher education for the knowledge and understanding that they will need later in life. At many of today's schools, their chances of finding what they seek are not good.

Even among established schools, many institutions again scored poorly based on one or more of the following shortcomings:

1. Objectives of the program are ill defined.
2. The present program is not constituted to meet the needs and problems of the students and faculty.
3. Institutional reports are not evaluated and beneficial changes are not recommended.
4. Administrators are reluctant to reveal the programs' weaknesses.
5. The public relations of the institution provide a false image to cover up deficiencies in programs.
6. Requisite improvements are not made in the quality of administrators, faculty instruction, curriculum, library resources, and the physical plant.
7. Graduate training is offered by institutions with inferior undergraduate programs.
8. Students suffer from poor counseling.
9. Funds for the improvement of faculty, curriculum, library resources, and the physical plant are misused.
10. Teacher education programs and training are below average.[1]
11. Graduate schools of education are below average.[2]
12. Criminal Justice/Criminology Correction programs are below average.[3]
13. Special interest pressure is exerted by administrators to the detriment of the faculty and the learning experience.
14. Student grants and scholarships are inadequate or nonexistent.
15. Faculty salaries are inadequate.
16. Funds for faculty research are inadequate.
17. Computer facility is not sufficient to support current research activities for both faculty and students.
18. Funding insufficient is for research equipment and infrastructure.
19. The number of teaching and research assistantships is inadequate.
20. Major research laboratories are inadequate.

[1]Credential Note: A student with a baccalaureate degree or higher with a 3.5 grade point average in the major (excluding education majors) and an overall 3.3 grade point average is eligible for a teaching credential. In addition, the candidate must submit two letters from faculty who can assess her professional potential. Prospective candidates should apply to the state board of education for a teaching credential. I strongly recommend credential programs be *discontinued* by the educational institution.

[2]The Graduate Schools of Education are not approved by *The Gourman Report* and should be discontinued by the educational institution.

[3]Criminal Justice/Criminology Correction programs are not approved by *The Gourman Report.*

Jack Gourman, Ph. D.

Los Angeles, California

August 1997

TABLE OF CONTENTS

Part I

THE GOURMAN REPORT GRADUATE PROGRAMS

Aerospace Engineering
Agricultural Economics
Agricultural Engineering
Agricultural Sciences
Agronomy/Soil Sciences
Anthropology
Applied Mathematics
Applied Physics
Architecture
Art History
Astronomy
Biochemistry
Biomedical Engineering
Botany
Cell Biology
Ceramic Sciences and Engineering
Chemical Engineering
Chemistry
City/Regional Planning
Civil Engineering
Classics
Comparative Literature
Computer Science
Drama/Theatre
Economics
Electrical Engineering
English
Entomology
Environmental Engineering
Forestry
French
Geography
Geosciences
German
History
Horticulture
Industrial Engineering
Industrial/Labor Relations
Inorganic Chemistry
Journalism
Landscape Architecture
Library Science
Linguistics

Materials Science
Mathematics
Mechanical Engineering
Microbiology
Molecular Genetics
Music
Near and Middle Eastern Studies
Neurosciences
Nuclear Engineering
Nutrition
Occupational Therapy
Oceanography
Organic Chemistry
Petroleum Engineering
Pharmacology
Philosophy
Physical Chemistry
Physical Therapy
Physics
Physiology
Plant Pathology
Political Science
Psychology
Psychology—Child Development
Psychology—Clinical
Psychology—Cognitive
Psychology—Developmental
Psychology—Experimental (General)
Psychology—Industrial/Organizational
Psychology—Personality
Psychology—Sensation and Perception
Psychology—Social
Public Administration
Radio/TV/Film
Russian
Slavic Languages
Social Welfare/Social Work
Sociology
Spanish
Speech Pathology/Audiology
Statistics
Toxicology

AEROSPACE ENGINEERING

LEADING INSTITUTIONS—RATING OF GRADUATE PROGRAMS

INSTITUTION	RANK	SCORE
CALIFORNIA INSTITUTE OF TECHNOLOGY	1	4.93
MASSACHUSETTS INSTITUTE OF TECHNOLOGY	2	4.92
STANFORD UNIVERSITY	3	4.91
PRINCETON UNIVERSITY	4	4.90
UNIVERSITY OF MICHIGAN—ANN ARBOR	5	4.89
CORNELL UNIVERSITY	6	4.88
PURDUE UNIVERSITY—WEST LAFAYETTE	7	4.86
UNIVERSITY OF TEXAS—AUSTIN	8	4.84
GEORGIA INSTITUTE OF TECHNOLOGY	9	4.82
UNIVERSITY OF CALIFORNIA—SAN DIEGO	10	4.81
UNIVERSITY OF CALIFORNIA—LOS ANGELES	11	4.80
UNIVERSITY OF MINNESOTA—TWIN CITIES	12	4.78
UNIVERSITY OF COLORADO—BOULDER	13	4.76
UNIVERSITY OF ILLINOIS—URBANA-CHAMPAIGN	14	4.74
VIRGINIA POLYTECHNIC INSTITUTE AND STATE UNIVERSITY	15	4.73
NORTH CAROLINA STATE UNIVERSITY	16	4.72
TEXAS A&M UNIVERSITY—COLLEGE STATION	17	4.70
PENNSYLVANIA STATE UNIVERSITY—UNIVERSITY PARK	18	4.69
UNIVERSITY OF WASHINGTON	19	4.65
UNIVERSITY OF MARYLAND—COLLEGE PARK	20	4.64
IOWA STATE UNIVERSITY	21	4.63
RENSSELAER POLYTECHNIC INSTITUTE	22	4.61
UNIVERSITY OF CINCINNATI	23	4.60
UNIVERSITY OF NOTRE DAME	24	4.59
OHIO STATE UNIVERSITY—COLUMBUS	25	4.57
UNIVERSITY OF KANSAS	26	4.53
UNIVERSITY OF FLORIDA	27	4.50
STATE UNIVERSITY OF NEW YORK AT BUFFALO	28	4.48
UNIVERSITY OF TENNESSEE—KNOXVILLE	29	4.45
AUBURN UNIVERSITY	30	4.42

AGRICULTURAL ECONOMICS
LEADING INSTITUTIONS—RATING OF GRADUATE PROGRAMS

INSTITUTION	RANK	SCORE
CORNELL UNIVERSITY	1	4.92
MICHIGAN STATE UNIVERSITY	2	4.91
UNIVERSITY OF ILLINOIS—URBANA-CHAMPAIGN	3	4.90
UNIVERSITY OF MINNESOTA—TWIN CITIES	4	4.87
UNIVERSITY OF CALIFORNIA—DAVIS	5	4.86
PURDUE UNIVERSITY—WEST LAFAYETTE	6	4.84
UNIVERSITY OF WISCONSIN—MADISON	7	4.80
UNIVERSITY OF CALIFORNIA—BERKELEY	8	4.76
STANFORD UNIVERSITY	9	4.73
PENNSYLVANIA STATE UNIVERSITY—UNIVERSITY PARK	10	4.72
UNIVERSITY OF MISSOURI—COLUMBIA	11	4.71
UNIVERSITY OF FLORIDA	12	4.66
TEXAS A&M UNIVERSITY—COLLEGE STATION	13	4.64
IOWA STATE UNIVERSITY	14	4.63
OHIO STATE UNIVERSITY—COLUMBUS	15	4.61
OREGON STATE UNIVERSITY	16	4.54
UNIVERSITY OF CONNECTICUT	17	4.53
UNIVERSITY OF MARYLAND—COLLEGE PARK	18	4.51
KANSAS STATE UNIVERSITY	19	4.48
VIRGINIA POLYTECHNIC INSTITUTE AND STATE UNIVERSITY	20	4.45
WASHINGTON STATE UNIVERSITY	21	4.40
UNIVERSITY OF NEBRASKA—LINCOLN	22	4.38
UNIVERSITY OF KENTUCKY	23	4.33
UNIVERSITY OF MASSACHUSETTS—AMHERST	24	4.31
NORTH CAROLINA STATE UNIVERSITY	25	4.29
AUBURN UNIVERSITY	26	4.27
LOUISIANA STATE UNIVERSITY—BATON ROUGE	27	4.23
COLORADO STATE UNIVERSITY	28	4.19
UNIVERSITY OF GEORGIA	29	4.17
OKLAHOMA STATE UNIVERSITY	30	4.15
MISSISSIPPI STATE UNIVERSITY	31	4.14
UNIVERSITY OF TENNESSEE—KNOXVILLE	32	4.12
TEXAS TECH UNIVERSITY	33	4.11
UNIVERSITY OF HAWAII—MANOA	34	4.10

AGRICULTURAL ENGINEERING

Leading Institutions—Rating of Graduate Programs

INSTITUTION	RANK	SCORE
CORNELL UNIVERSITY	1	4.92
MICHIGAN STATE UNIVERSITY	2	4.91
IOWA STATE UNIVERSITY	3	4.90
UNIVERSITY OF ILLINOIS—URBANA-CHAMPAIGN	4	4.88
PURDUE UNIVERSITY—WEST LAFAYETTE	5	4.87
UNIVERSITY OF MINNESOTA—TWIN CITIES	6	4.84
OHIO STATE UNIVERSITY—COLUMBUS	7	4.82
TEXAS A&M UNIVERSITY—COLLEGE STATION	8	4.81
PENNSYLVANIA STATE UNIVERSITY—UNIVERSITY PARK	9	4.79
UNIVERSITY OF WISCONSIN—MADISON	10	4.76
UNIVERSITY OF CALIFORNIA—DAVIS	11	4.74
UNIVERSITY OF MARYLAND—COLLEGE PARK	12	4.70
UNIVERSITY OF MISSOURI—COLUMBIA	13	4.66
COLORADO STATE UNIVERSITY	14	4.64
NORTH CAROLINA STATE UNIVERSITY	15	4.62
UNIVERSITY OF TENNESSEE—KNOXVILLE	16	4.59
WASHINGTON STATE UNIVERSITY	17	4.54
UNIVERSITY OF FLORIDA	18	4.52
KANSAS STATE UNIVERSITY	19	4.50
CLEMSON UNIVERSITY	20	4.46
VIRGINIA POLYTECHNIC INSTITUTE AND STATE UNIVERSITY	21	4.44
UNIVERSITY OF NEBRASKA—LINCOLN	22	4.40
OKLAHOMA STATE UNIVERSITY	23	4.33
OREGON STATE UNIVERSITY	24	4.32
UNIVERSITY OF KENTUCKY	25	4.28
UTAH STATE UNIVERSITY	26	4.26
LOUISIANA STATE UNIVERSITY—BATON ROUGE	27	4.22
AUBURN UNIVERSITY	28	4.21
TEXAS TECH UNIVERSITY	29	4.18
UNIVERSITY OF IDAHO	30	4.16
NORTH DAKOTA STATE UNIVERSITY	31	4.15
UNIVERSITY OF MAINE	32	4.12

AGRICULTURAL SCIENCES
Leading Institutions—Rating of Graduate Programs

INSTITUTION	RANK	SCORE
CORNELL UNIVERSITY	1	4.91
TEXAS A&M UNIVERSITY—COLLEGE STATION	2	4.89
UNIVERSITY OF ILLINOIS—URBANA-CHAMPAIGN	3	4.87
PURDUE UNIVERSITY—WEST LAFAYETTE	4	4.85
IOWA STATE UNIVERSITY	5	4.81
MICHIGAN STATE UNIVERSITY	6	4.80
UNIVERSITY OF CALIFORNIA—DAVIS	7	4.76
UNIVERSITY OF WISCONSIN—MADISON	8	4.73
UNIVERSITY OF MINNESOTA—TWIN CITIES	9	4.69
OHIO STATE UNIVERSITY—COLUMBUS	10	4.65
KANSAS STATE UNIVERSITY	11	4.62
UNIVERSITY OF MISSOURI—COLUMBIA	12	4.59
PENNSYLVANIA STATE UNIVERSITY—UNIVERSITY PARK	13	4.57
LOUISIANA STATE UNIVERSITY—BATON ROUGE	14	4.55
UNIVERSITY OF NEBRASKA—LINCOLN	15	4.51
UNIVERSITY OF MARYLAND—COLLEGE PARK	16	4.49
NORTH CAROLINA STATE UNIVERSITY	17	4.47
OKLAHOMA STATE UNIVERSITY	18	4.43
UNIVERSITY OF GEORGIA	19	4.40
OREGON STATE UNIVERSITY	20	4.37
UNIVERSITY OF TENNESSEE—KNOXVILLE	21	4.35
COLORADO STATE UNIVERSITY	22	4.33
UNIVERSITY OF MASSACHUSETTS—AMHERST	23	4.31
UTAH STATE UNIVERSITY	24	4.27
UNIVERSITY OF ARIZONA	25	4.22
TEXAS TECH UNIVERSITY	26	4.20
UNIVERSITY OF FLORIDA	27	4.17
AUBURN UNIVERSITY	28	4.15
CLEMSON UNIVERSITY	29	4.14
UNIVERSITY OF CONNECTICUT	30	4.12
WASHINGTON STATE UNIVERSITY	31	4.09
UNIVERSITY OF MAINE	32	4.07

AGRONOMY/SOIL SCIENCES

INSTITUTION	RANK	SCORE
CORNELL UNIVERSITY	1	4.87
TEXAS A&M UNIVERSITY—COLLEGE STATION	2	4.85
UNIVERSITY OF WISCONSIN—MADISON	3	4.81
UNIVERSITY OF CALIFORNIA—DAVIS	4	4.80
UNIVERSITY OF MINNESOTA—TWIN CITIES	5	4.78
UNIVERSITY OF ILLINOIS—URBANA-CHAMPAIGN	6	4.75
OHIO STATE UNIVERSITY—COLUMBUS	7	4.72
PENNSYLVANIA STATE UNIVERSITY—UNIVERSITY PARK	8	4.69
PURDUE UNIVERSITY—WEST LAFAYETTE	9	4.68
IOWA STATE UNIVERSITY	10	4.66
KANSAS STATE UNIVERSITY	11	4.62
MICHIGAN STATE UNIVERSITY	12	4.58
UNIVERSITY OF GEORGIA	13	4.55
UNIVERSITY OF FLORIDA	14	4.51
UNIVERSITY OF NEBRASKA—LINCOLN	15	4.50
LOUISIANA STATE UNIVERSITY—BATON ROUGE	16	4.46
VIRGINIA POLYTECHNIC INSTITUTE AND STATE UNIVERSITY	17	4.43
OREGON STATE UNIVERSITY	18	4.40
UNIVERSITY OF MARYLAND—COLLEGE PARK	19	4.38
UNIVERSITY OF ARKANSAS	20	4.37
NORTH CAROLINA STATE UNIVERSITY	21	4.33
OKLAHOMA STATE UNIVERSITY	22	4.31
UNIVERSITY OF CALIFORNIA—RIVERSIDE	23	4.26
UNIVERSITY OF MASSACHUSETTS—AMHERST	24	4.24
UTAH STATE UNIVERSITY	25	4.21
UNIVERSITY OF ARIZONA	26	4.19

ANTHROPOLOGY
Leading Institutions—Rating of Graduate Programs

INSTITUTION	RANK	SCORE
UNIVERSITY OF MICHIGAN—ANN ARBOR	1	4.92
UNIVERSITY OF CALIFORNIA—BERKELEY	2	4.91
UNIVERSITY OF CHICAGO	3	4.90
HARVARD UNIVERSITY	4	4.89
UNIVERSITY OF ARIZONA	5	4.86
UNIVERSITY OF PENNSYLVANIA	6	4.84
STANFORD UNIVERSITY	7	4.82
UNIVERSITY OF CALIFORNIA—LOS ANGELES	8	4.81
YALE UNIVERSITY	9	4.80
UNIVERSITY OF CALIFORNIA—SAN DIEGO	10	4.79
UNIVERSITY OF TEXAS—AUSTIN	11	4.78
UNIVERSITY OF FLORIDA	12	4.76
NEW YORK UNIVERSITY	13	4.75
UNIVERSITY OF ILLINOIS—URBANA-CHAMPAIGN	14	4.72
UNIVERSITY OF CALIFORNIA—DAVIS	15	4.71
COLUMBIA UNIVERSITY	16	4.68
WASHINGTON UNIVERSITY	17	4.66
DUKE UNIVERSITY	18	4.64
UNIVERSITY OF WISCONSIN—MADISON	19	4.63
UNIVERSITY OF CALIFORNIA—SANTA BARBARA	20	4.62
JOHNS HOPKINS UNIVERSITY	21	4.61
CITY UNIVERSITY OF NEW YORK GRADUATE SCHOOL	22	4.59
UNIVERSITY OF VIRGINIA	23	4.55
RUTGERS UNIVERSITY	24	4.53
UNIVERSITY OF PITTSBURGH	25	4.50
ARIZONA STATE UNIVERSITY	26	4.48
PRINCETON UNIVERSITY	27	4.46
INDIANA UNIVERSITY—BLOOMINGTON	28	4.44
UNIVERSITY OF WASHINGTON	29	4.40
UNIVERSITY OF NORTH CAROLINA—CHAPEL HILL	30	4.37
CORNELL UNIVERSITY	31	4.36

APPLIED MATHEMATICS
Leading Institutions—Rating of Graduate Programs

INSTITUTION	RANK	SCORE
HARVARD UNIVERSITY	1	4.88
PRINCETON UNIVERSITY	2	4.84
UNIVERSITY OF CHICAGO	3	4.82
MASSACHUSETTS INSTITUTE OF TECHNOLOGY	4	4.81
YALE UNIVERSITY	5	4.76
UNIVERSITY OF WISCONSIN—MADISON	6	4.73
COLUMBIA UNIVERSITY	7	4.69
CALIFORNIA INSTITUTE OF TECHNOLOGY	8	4.66
CORNELL UNIVERSITY	9	4.64
BROWN UNIVERSITY	10	4.60
RICE UNIVERSITY	11	4.57
UNIVERSITY OF WASHINGTON	12	4.53
NORTHWESTERN UNIVERSITY	13	4.50
UNIVERSITY OF MARYLAND—COLLEGE PARK	14	4.48
PURDUE UNIVERSITY—WEST LAFAYETTE	15	4.41
JOHNS HOPKINS UNIVERSITY	16	4.33
INDIANA UNIVERSITY—BLOOMINGTON	17	4.29
UNIVERSITY OF VIRGINIA	18	4.25
PENNSYLVANIA STATE UNIVERSITY—UNIVERSITY PARK	19	4.20
UNIVERSITY OF COLORADO—BOULDER	20	4.18
MICHIGAN STATE UNIVERSITY	21	4.16
UNIVERSITY OF IOWA	22	4.14
UNIVERSITY OF FLORIDA	23	4.10
UNIVERSITY OF KANSAS	24	4.09

APPLIED PHYSICS
Leading Institutions—Rating of Graduate Programs

INSTITUTION	RANK	SCORE
CALIFORNIA INSTITUTE OF TECHNOLOGY	1	4.87
HARVARD UNIVERSITY	2	4.84
PRINCETON UNIVERSITY	3	4.82
CORNELL UNIVERSITY	4	4.79
STANFORD UNIVERSITY	5	4.76
UNIVERSITY OF MICHIGAN—ANN ARBOR	6	4.74
COLUMBIA UNIVERSITY	7	4.70
YALE UNIVERSITY	8	4.66
RENSSELAER POLYTECHNIC INSTITUTE	9	4.64
CARNEGIE MELLON UNIVERSITY	10	4.60
UNIVERSITY OF COLORADO—BOULDER	11	4.57

ARCHITECTURE

Leading Institutions—Rating of Graduate Programs

INSTITUTION	RANK	SCORE
HARVARD UNIVERSITY	1	4.91
MASSACHUSETTS INSTITUTE OF TECHNOLOGY	2	4.90
PRINCETON UNIVERSITY	3	4.88
UNIVERSITY OF CALIFORNIA—BERKELEY	4	4.86
UNIVERSITY OF PENNSYLVANIA	5	4.83
CARNEGIE MELLON UNIVERSITY	6	4.80
UNIVERSITY OF MICHIGAN—ANN ARBOR	7	4.75
GEORGIA INSTITUTE OF TECHNOLOGY	8	4.74
RICE UNIVERSITY	9	4.71
COLUMBIA UNIVERSITY	10	4.66
UNIVERSITY OF TEXAS—AUSTIN	11	4.60
YALE UNIVERSITY	12	4.59
TEXAS A&M UNIVERSITY—COLLEGE STATION	13	4.54
UNIVERSITY OF CALIFORNIA—LOS ANGELES	14	4.50
UNIVERSITY OF WASHINGTON	15	4.48
OHIO STATE UNIVERSITY—COLUMBUS	16	4.47
UNIVERSITY OF ILLINOIS—URBANA-CHAMPAIGN	17	4.40
VIRGINIA POLYTECHNIC INSTITUTE AND STATE UNIVERSITY	18	4.39
UNIVERSITY OF OREGON	19	4.35
ARIZONA STATE UNIVERSITY	20	4.32
WASHINGTON UNIVERSITY	21	4.26
UNIVERSITY OF HAWAII—MANOA	22	4.25
UNIVERSITY OF FLORIDA	23	4.20
RENSSELAER POLYTECHNIC INSTITUTE	24	4.19
UNIVERSITY OF NEW MEXICO	25	4.18
UNIVERSITY OF HOUSTON	26	4.15
UNIVERSITY OF VIRGINIA	27	4.13
UNIVERSITY OF MINNESOTA—TWIN CITIES	28	4.12
UNIVERSITY OF OKLAHOMA	29	4.09

ART HISTORY
LEADING INSTITUTIONS—RATING OF GRADUATE PROGRAMS

INSTITUTION	RANK	SCORE
NEW YORK UNIVERSITY	1	4.90
HARVARD UNIVERSITY	2	4.88
YALE UNIVERSITY	3	4.85
COLUMBIA UNIVERSITY	4	4.81
PRINCETON UNIVERSITY	5	4.78
UNIVERSITY OF CALIFORNIA—BERKELEY	6	4.73
STANFORD UNIVERSITY	7	4.68
UNIVERSITY OF MICHIGAN—ANN ARBOR	8	4.63
BRYN MAWR COLLEGE	9	4.55
JOHNS HOPKINS UNIVERSITY	10	4.48
UNIVERSITY OF PENNSYLVANIA	11	4.47
NORTHWESTERN UNIVERSITY	12	4.43
UNIVERSITY OF CALIFORNIA—LOS ANGELES	13	4.41
UNIVERSITY OF CHICAGO	14	4.37
UNIVERSITY OF NORTH CAROLINA—CHAPEL HILL	15	4.35
CORNELL UNIVERSITY	16	4.31
UNIVERSITY OF PITTSBURGH	17	4.29
INDIANA UNIVERSITY—BLOOMINGTON	18	4.25
UNIVERSITY OF VIRGINIA	19	4.21
UNIVERSITY OF KANSAS	20	4.18
BOSTON UNIVERSITY	21	4.15
BROWN UNIVERSITY	22	4.13
UNIVERSITY OF MARYLAND—COLLEGE PARK	23	4.12
RUTGERS UNIVERSITY	24	4.11
UNIVERSITY OF MINNESOTA—TWIN CITIES	25	4.10
UNIVERSITY OF TEXAS—AUSTIN	26	4.09
UNIVERSITY OF CALIFORNIA—SANTA BARBARA	27	4.07
UNIVERSITY OF ILLINOIS—URBANA-CHAMPAIGN	28	4.06
UNIVERSITY OF WASHINGTON	29	4.05
OHIO STATE UNIVERSITY—COLUMBUS	30	4.03

ASTRONOMY
Leading Institutions—Rating of Graduate Programs

INSTITUTION	RANK	SCORE
CALIFORNIA INSTITUTE OF TECHNOLOGY	1	4.92
UNIVERSITY OF CALIFORNIA—BERKELEY	2	4.90
HARVARD UNIVERSITY	3	4.88
UNIVERSITY OF CHICAGO	4	4.87
UNIVERSITY OF CALIFORNIA—SANTA CRUZ	5	4.85
MASSACHUSETTS INSTITUTE OF TECHNOLOGY	6	4.82
UNIVERSITY OF ARIZONA	7	4.81
CORNELL UNIVERSITY	8	4.76
UNIVERSITY OF TEXAS—AUSTIN	9	4.72
UNIVERSITY OF HAWAII—MANOA	10	4.69
UNIVERSITY OF ILLINOIS—URBANA-CHAMPAIGN	11	4.63
UNIVERSITY OF WISCONSIN—MADISON	12	4.62
UNIVERSITY OF CALIFORNIA—LOS ANGELES	13	4.60
UNIVERSITY OF VIRGINIA	14	4.58
YALE UNIVERSITY	15	4.53
COLUMBIA UNIVERSITY	16	4.50
UNIVERSITY OF MARYLAND—COLLEGE PARK	17	4.49
PENNSYLVANIA STATE UNIVERSITY—UNIVERSITY PARK	18	4.46
OHIO STATE UNIVERSITY—COLUMBUS	19	4.37
UNIVERSITY OF MINNESOTA—TWIN CITIES	20	4.35
UNIVERSITY OF MICHIGAN—ANN ARBOR	21	4.33
STATE UNIVERSITY OF NEW YORK AT STONY BROOK	22	4.29
BOSTON UNIVERSITY	23	4.25
INDIANA UNIVERSITY—BLOOMINGTON	24	4.23
LOUISIANA STATE UNIVERSITY—BATON ROUGE	25	4.21
IOWA STATE UNIVERSITY	26	4.15
UNIVERSITY OF FLORIDA	27	4.13

BIOCHEMISTRY
LEADING INSTITUTIONS—RATING OF GRADUATE PROGRAMS

INSTITUTION	RANK	SCORE
UNIVERSITY OF CALIFORNIA—SAN FRANCISCO	1	4.94
STANFORD UNIVERSITY	2	4.92
MASSACHUSETTS INSTITUTE OF TECHNOLOGY	3	4.91
UNIVERSITY OF CALIFORNIA—BERKELEY	4	4.90
HARVARD UNIVERSITY	5	4.89
CALIFORNIA INSTITUTE OF TECHNOLOGY	6	4.87
YALE UNIVERSITY	7	4.86
UNIVERSITY OF WISCONSIN—MADISON	8	4.85
UNIVERSITY OF CALIFORNIA—SAN DIEGO	9	4.84
JOHNS HOPKINS UNIVERSITY	10	4.83
COLUMBIA UNIVERSITY	11	4.80
WASHINGTON UNIVERSITY	12	4.78
UNIVERSITY OF COLORADO—BOULDER	13	4.77
DUKE UNIVERSITY	14	4.76
UNIVERSITY OF CALIFORNIA—LOS ANGELES	15	4.75
UNIVERSITY OF PENNSYLVANIA	16	4.73
UNIVERSITY OF WASHINGTON	17	4.71
BAYLOR COLLEGE OF MEDICINE	18	4.68
BRANDEIS UNIVERSITY	19	4.66
UNIVERSITY OF TEXAS SOUTHWESTERN MEDICAL CENTER AT DALLAS SOUTHWEST	20	4.65
ROCKEFELLER UNIVERSITY	21	4.64
CORNELL UNIVERSITY	22	4.62
UNIVERSITY OF MICHIGAN MEDICAL SCHOOL	23	4.61
UNIVERSITY OF CHICAGO	24	4.60
UNIVERSITY OF MICHIGAN—ANN ARBOR	25	4.58
ALBERT EINSTEIN COLLEGE OF MEDICINE OF YESHIVA UNIVERSITY	26	4.57
UNIVERSITY OF OREGON	27	4.55
UNIVERSITY OF NORTH CAROLINA—CHAPEL HILL	28	4.53
VANDERBILT UNIVERSITY	29	4.51
UNIVERSITY OF UTAH	30	4.49

BIOMEDICAL ENGINEERING

Leading Institutions—Rating of Graduate Programs

INSTITUTION	RANK	SCORE
MASSACHUSETTS INSTITUTE OF TECHNOLOGY	1	4.90
UNIVERSITY OF CALIFORNIA—SAN DIEGO	2	4.88
DUKE UNIVERSITY	3	4.87
UNIVERSITY OF PENNSYLVANIA	4	4.85
UNIVERSITY OF WASHINGTON	5	4.83
JOHNS HOPKINS UNIVERSITY	6	4.77
UNIVERSITY OF CALIFORNIA—SAN FRANCISCO	7	4.76
UNIVERSITY OF CALIFORNIA—BERKELEY	8	4.70
RICE UNIVERSITY	9	4.69
UNIVERSITY OF MICHIGAN—ANN ARBOR	10	4.65
STANFORD UNIVERSITY	11	4.63
UNIVERSITY OF UTAH	12	4.60
CASE WESTERN RESERVE UNIVERSITY	13	4.56
UNIVERSITY OF ROCHESTER	14	4.50
NORTHWESTERN UNIVERSITY	15	4.47
VANDERBILT UNIVERSITY	16	4.36
UNIVERSITY OF MINNESOTA—TWIN CITIES	17	4.35
UNIVERSITY OF TEXAS—AUSTIN	18	4.34
UNIVERSITY OF NORTH CAROLINA—CHAPEL HILL	19	4.27
PENNSYLVANIA STATE UNIVERSITY—UNIVERSITY PARK	20	4.25
UNIVERSITY OF VIRGINIA	21	4.21
DREXEL UNIVERSITY	22	4.19
UNIVERSITY OF CALIFORNIA—DAVIS	23	4.16
OHIO STATE UNIVERSITY—COLUMBUS	24	4.14
UNIVERSITY OF IOWA	25	4.12
UNIVERSITY OF ALABAMA—BIRMINGHAM	26	4.10

BOTANY
LEADING INSTITUTIONS—RATING OF GRADUATE PROGRAMS

INSTITUTION	RANK	SCORE
UNIVERSITY OF CALIFORNIA—DAVIS	1	4.92
UNIVERSITY OF TEXAS—AUSTIN	2	4.90
UNIVERSITY OF CALIFORNIA—BERKELEY	3	4.88
UNIVERSITY OF WISCONSIN—MADISON	4	4.86
CORNELL UNIVERSITY	5	4.85
UNIVERSITY OF MICHIGAN—ANN ARBOR	6	4.84
DUKE UNIVERSITY	7	4.83
YALE UNIVERSITY	8	4.80
UNIVERSITY OF ILLINOIS—URBANA-CHAMPAIGN	9	4.76
UNIVERSITY OF CALIFORNIA—RIVERSIDE	10	4.74
MICHIGAN STATE UNIVERSITY	11	4.73
NORTH CAROLINA STATE UNIVERSITY	12	4.69
UNIVERSITY OF CALIFORNIA—LOS ANGELES	13	4.66
PENNSYLVANIA STATE UNIVERSITY—UNIVERSITY PARK	14	4.63
INDIANA UNIVERSITY—BLOOMINGTON	15	4.62
UNIVERSITY OF MINNESOTA—TWIN CITIES	16	4.61
UNIVERSITY OF NORTH CAROLINA—CHAPEL HILL	17	4.59
UNIVERSITY OF GEORGIA	18	4.57
WASHINGTON UNIVERSITY	19	4.54
PURDUE UNIVERSITY—WEST LAFAYETTE	20	4.51
OREGON STATE UNIVERSITY	21	4.49
UNIVERSITY OF WASHINGTON	22	4.46
OHIO STATE UNIVERSITY—COLUMBUS	23	4.45
UNIVERSITY OF KENTUCKY	24	4.40
IOWA STATE UNIVERSITY	25	4.38
UNIVERSITY OF MASSACHUSETTS—AMHERST	26	4.37
UNIVERSITY OF FLORIDA	27	4.35
CLAREMONT GRADUATE SCHOOL	28	4.32
UNIVERSITY OF NEBRASKA—LINCOLN	29	4.29
STATE UNIVERSITY OF NEW YORK COLLEGE OF ENVIRONMENTAL SCIENCE AND FORESTRY	30	4.27
UNIVERSITY OF OKLAHOMA	31	4.25
UNIVERSITY OF CALIFORNIA—IRVINE	32	4.21
RUTGERS UNIVERSITY	33	4.19
WASHINGTON STATE UNIVERSITY	34	4.16
UNIVERSITY OF CHICAGO	35	4.14
COLORADO STATE UNIVERSITY	36	4.13
UNIVERSITY OF HAWAII—MANOA	37	4.12
UNIVERSITY OF MARYLAND—COLLEGE PARK	38	4.11
UNIVERSITY OF MISSOURI—COLUMBIA	39	4.10
UNIVERSITY OF IOWA	40	4.09

CELL BIOLOGY

LEADING INSTITUTIONS—RATING OF GRADUATE PROGRAMS

INSTITUTION	RANK	SCORE
ROCKEFELLER UNIVERSITY	1	4.93
UNIVERSITY OF CALIFORNIA—SAN FRANCISCO	2	4.92
MASSACHUSETTS INSTITUTE OF TECHNOLOGY	3	4.91
HARVARD UNIVERSITY	4	4.90
UNIVERSITY OF CALIFORNIA—SAN DIEGO	5	4.88
CALIFORNIA INSTITUTE OF TECHNOLOGY	6	4.86
STANFORD UNIVERSITY SCHOOL OF MEDICINE	7	4.85
YALE UNIVERSITY	8	4.83
PRINCETON UNIVERSITY	9	4.82
UNIVERSITY OF WASHINGTON	10	4.80
UNIVERSITY OF CALIFORNIA—BERKELEY	11	4.78
DUKE UNIVERSITY	12	4.76
WASHINGTON UNIVERSITY	13	4.74
UNIVERSITY OF WISCONSIN—MADISON	14	4.72
UNIVERSITY OF CALIFORNIA—LOS ANGELES	15	4.69
STANFORD UNIVERSITY SCHOOL OF HUMANITIES AND SCIENCES	16	4.68
COLUMBIA UNIVERSITY	17	4.67
JOHNS HOPKINS UNIVERSITY	18	4.65
UNIVERSITY OF TEXAS SOUTHWESTERN MEDICAL CENTER AT DALLAS SOUTHWEST	19	4.63
UNIVERSITY OF PENNSYLVANIA	20	4.61
BAYLOR COLLEGE OF MEDICINE	21	4.58
UNIVERSITY OF COLORADO SCHOOL OF MEDICINE	22	4.57
NEW YORK UNIVERSITY	23	4.54
ALBERT EINSTEIN COLLEGE OF MEDICINE OF YESHIVA UNIVERSITY	24	4.52
UNIVERSITY OF ILLINOIS—URBANA-CHAMPAIGN	25	4.50
UNIVERSITY OF NORTH CAROLINA—CHAPEL HILL	26	4.49
VANDERBILT UNIVERSITY	27	4.45
UNIVERSITY OF MICHIGAN—ANN ARBOR	28	4.42
NORTHWESTERN UNIVERSITY	29	4.39
UNIVERSITY OF CALIFORNIA—DAVIS	30	4.36
CORNELL UNIVERSITY	31	4.33
INDIANA UNIVERSITY—BLOOMINGTON	32	4.29
UNIVERSITY OF MINNESOTA MEDICAL SCHOOL—MINNEAPOLIS	33	4.25
BRANDEIS UNIVERSITY	34	4.22
STATE UNIVERSITY OF NEW YORK AT STONY BROOK	35	4.20

CERAMIC SCIENCES AND ENGINEERING

LEADING INSTITUTIONS—RATING OF GRADUATE PROGRAMS

INSTITUTION	RANK	SCORE
ALFRED UNIVERSITY	1	4.91
UNIVERSITY OF ILLINOIS—URBANA-CHAMPAIGN	2	4.88
OHIO STATE UNIVERSITY—COLUMBUS	3	4.84
RUTGERS UNIVERSITY	4	4.82
PENNSYLVANIA STATE UNIVERSITY—UNIVERSITY PARK	5	4.79
GEORGIA INSTITUTE OF TECHNOLOGY	6	4.74
UNIVERSITY OF WASHINGTON	7	4.66
UNIVERSITY OF MISSOURI—ROLLA	8	4.60
IOWA STATE UNIVERSITY	9	4.53

CHEMICAL ENGINEERING
LEADING INSTITUTIONS—RATING OF GRADUATE PROGRAMS

INSTITUTION	RANK	SCORE
UNIVERSITY OF MINNESOTA—TWIN CITIES	1	4.93
MASSACHUSETTS INSTITUTE OF TECHNOLOGY	2	4.91
CALIFORNIA INSTITUTE OF TECHNOLOGY	3	4.90
UNIVERSITY OF CALIFORNIA—BERKELEY	4	4.89
STANFORD UNIVERSITY	5	4.88
UNIVERSITY OF DELAWARE	6	4.87
UNIVERSITY OF WISCONSIN—MADISON	7	4.86
UNIVERSITY OF ILLINOIS—URBANA-CHAMPAIGN	8	4.85
PRINCETON UNIVERSITY	9	4.83
UNIVERSITY OF TEXAS—AUSTIN	10	4.82
UNIVERSITY OF PENNSYLVANIA	11	4.79
CARNEGIE MELLON UNIVERSITY	12	4.77
CORNELL UNIVERSITY	13	4.76
NORTHWESTERN UNIVERSITY	14	4.75
PURDUE UNIVERSITY—WEST LAFAYETTE	15	4.74
UNIVERSITY OF MICHIGAN—ANN ARBOR	16	4.72
UNIVERSITY OF NOTRE DAME	17	4.71
UNIVERSITY OF CALIFORNIA—SANTA BARBARA	18	4.69
UNIVERSITY OF WASHINGTON	19	4.68
UNIVERSITY OF HOUSTON	20	4.65
UNIVERSITY OF MASSACHUSETTS—AMHERST	21	4.62
RICE UNIVERSITY	22	4.60
CITY UNIVERSITY OF NEW YORK GRADUATE SCHOOL	23	4.56
PENNSYLVANIA STATE UNIVERSITY—UNIVERSITY PARK	24	4.54
UNIVERSITY OF COLORADO—BOULDER	25	4.53
NORTH CAROLINA STATE UNIVERSITY	26	4.51
UNIVERSITY OF CALIFORNIA—DAVIS	27	4.49
STATE UNIVERSITY OF NEW YORK AT BUFFALO	28	4.46
LEHIGH UNIVERSITY	29	4.45
YALE UNIVERSITY	30	4.41
GEORGIA INSTITUTE OF TECHNOLOGY	31	4.40
IOWA STATE UNIVERSITY	32	4.38
UNIVERSITY OF FLORIDA	33	4.37
RENSSELAER POLYTECHNIC INSTITUTE	34	4.34
JOHNS HOPKINS UNIVERSITY	35	4.32
TEXAS A&M UNIVERSITY—COLLEGE STATION	36	4.31
UNIVERSITY OF VIRGINIA	37	4.30

CHEMISTRY
LEADING INSTITUTIONS—RATING OF GRADUATE PROGRAMS

INSTITUTION	RANK	SCORE
HARVARD UNIVERSITY	1	4.93
UNIVERSITY OF CALIFORNIA—BERKELEY	2	4.92
CALIFORNIA INSTITUTE OF TECHNOLOGY	3	4.90
MASSACHUSETTS INSTITUTE OF TECHNOLOGY	4	4.88
COLUMBIA UNIVERSITY	5	4.87
STANFORD UNIVERSITY	6	4.85
UNIVERSITY OF ILLINOIS—URBANA-CHAMPAIGN	7	4.83
UNIVERSITY OF CALIFORNIA—LOS ANGELES	8	4.82
UNIVERSITY OF CHICAGO	9	4.80
CORNELL UNIVERSITY	10	4.79
UNIVERSITY OF WISCONSIN—MADISON	11	4.78
NORTHWESTERN UNIVERSITY	12	4.76
PRINCETON UNIVERSITY	13	4.75
YALE UNIVERSITY	14	4.72
UNIVERSITY OF TEXAS—AUSTIN	15	4.70
UNIVERSITY OF NORTH CAROLINA—CHAPEL HILL	16	4.66
OHIO STATE UNIVERSITY—COLUMBUS	17	4.65
TEXAS A&M UNIVERSITY—COLLEGE STATION	18	4.64
UNIVERSITY OF CALIFORNIA—SAN DIEGO	19	4.62
INDIANA UNIVERSITY—BLOOMINGTON	20	4.60
PENNSYLVANIA STATE UNIVERSITY—UNIVERSITY PARK	21	4.58
PURDUE UNIVERSITY—WEST LAFAYETTE	22	4.55
UNIVERSITY OF MINNESOTA—TWIN CITIES	23	4.54
UNIVERSITY OF CALIFORNIA—SAN FRANCISCO	24	4.50
UNIVERSITY OF PENNSYLVANIA	25	4.48
IOWA STATE UNIVERSITY	26	4.46
JOHNS HOPKINS UNIVERSITY	27	4.45
RICE UNIVERSITY	28	4.42
UNIVERSITY OF FLORIDA	29	4.41
UNIVERSITY OF WASHINGTON	30	4.38
UNIVERSITY OF UTAH	31	4.36
UNIVERSITY OF PITTSBURGH	32	4.35
EMORY UNIVERSITY	33	4.34
UNIVERSITY OF ROCHESTER	34	4.27
UNIVERSITY OF CALIFORNIA—SANTA BARBARA	35	4.25
UNIVERSITY OF MICHIGAN—ANN ARBOR	36	4.21
UNIVERSITY OF CALIFORNIA—IRVINE	37	4.20
UNIVERSITY OF NOTRE DAME	38	4.18
MICHIGAN STATE UNIVERSITY	39	4.17
UNIVERSITY OF OREGON	40	4.16

CITY/REGIONAL PLANNING
LEADING INSTITUTIONS—RATING OF GRADUATE PROGRAMS

INSTITUTION	RANK	SCORE
MASSACHUSETTS INSTITUTE OF TECHNOLOGY	1	4.83
GEORGIA INSTITUTE OF TECHNOLOGY	2	4.81
UNIVERSITY OF SOUTHERN CALIFORNIA	3	4.80
RUTGERS UNIVERSITY	4	4.76
UNIVERSITY OF NORTH CAROLINA—CHAPEL HILL	5	4.75
UNIVERSITY OF CALIFORNIA—BERKELEY	6	4.74
VIRGINIA POLYTECHNIC INSTITUTE AND STATE UNIVERSITY	7	4.70
UNIVERSITY OF ILLINOIS—URBANA-CHAMPAIGN	8	4.68
UNIVERSITY OF CALIFORNIA—LOS ANGELES	9	4.66
PRINCETON UNIVERSITY	10	4.62
UNIVERSITY OF WISCONSIN—MADISON	11	4.60
UNIVERSITY OF MICHIGAN—ANN ARBOR	12	4.55
UNIVERSITY OF WASHINGTON	13	4.53
OHIO STATE UNIVERSITY—COLUMBUS	14	4.51
CORNELL UNIVERSITY	15	4.47
TEXAS A&M UNIVERSITY—COLLEGE STATION	16	4.44
HARVARD UNIVERSITY	17	4.42

CIVIL ENGINEERING
Leading Institutions—Rating of Graduate Programs

INSTITUTION	RANK	SCORE
UNIVERSITY OF CALIFORNIA—BERKELEY	1	4.92
MASSACHUSETTS INSTITUTE OF TECHNOLOGY	2	4.90
UNIVERSITY OF ILLINOIS—URBANA-CHAMPAIGN	3	4.89
CALIFORNIA INSTITUTE OF TECHNOLOGY	4	4.88
STANFORD UNIVERSITY	5	4.87
UNIVERSITY OF TEXAS—AUSTIN	6	4.86
CORNELL UNIVERSITY	7	4.85
NORTHWESTERN UNIVERSITY	8	4.84
PRINCETON UNIVERSITY	9	4.83
UNIVERSITY OF MICHIGAN—ANN ARBOR	10	4.82
PURDUE UNIVERSITY—WEST LAFAYETTE	11	4.81
CARNEGIE MELLON UNIVERSITY	12	4.79
UNIVERSITY OF MINNESOTA—TWIN CITIES	13	4.77
UNIVERSITY OF WASHINGTON	14	4.74
UNIVERSITY OF NORTH CAROLINA—CHAPEL HILL	15	4.73
UNIVERSITY OF CALIFORNIA—DAVIS	16	4.72
GEORGIA INSTITUTE OF TECHNOLOGY	17	4.71
LEHIGH UNIVERSITY	18	4.69
TEXAS A&M UNIVERSITY—COLLEGE STATION	19	4.68
UNIVERSITY OF CALIFORNIA—LOS ANGELES	20	4.67
UNIVERSITY OF WISCONSIN—MADISON	21	4.65
RICE UNIVERSITY	22	4.63
UNIVERSITY OF COLORADO—BOULDER	23	4.62
COLORADO STATE UNIVERSITY	24	4.60
JOHNS HOPKINS UNIVERSITY	25	4.58
DUKE UNIVERSITY	26	4.56
COLUMBIA UNIVERSITY	27	4.53
UNIVERSITY OF IOWA	28	4.51
PENNSYLVANIA STATE UNIVERSITY—UNIVERSITY PARK	29	4.49
STATE UNIVERSITY OF NEW YORK AT BUFFALO	30	4.47
UNIVERSITY OF ARIZONA	31	4.46
UNIVERSITY OF CALIFORNIA—IRVINE	32	4.43
RENSSELAER POLYTECHNIC INSTITUTE	33	4.41
UNIVERSITY OF NOTRE DAME	34	4.38
UNIVERSITY OF FLORIDA	35	4.36
UNIVERSITY OF MARYLAND—COLLEGE PARK	36	4.34
UNIVERSITY OF VIRGINIA	37	4.32
OHIO STATE UNIVERSITY—COLUMBUS	38	4.30
VIRGINIA POLYTECHNIC INSTITUTE AND STATE UNIVERSITY	39	4.29
NORTH CAROLINA STATE UNIVERSITY	40	4.26

CLASSICS
LEADING INSTITUTIONS—RATING OF GRADUATE PROGRAMS

INSTITUTION	RANK	SCORE
HARVARD UNIVERSITY	1	4.90
UNIVERSITY OF CALIFORNIA—BERKELEY	2	4.88
PRINCETON UNIVERSITY	3	4.86
YALE UNIVERSITY	4	4.84
UNIVERSITY OF MICHIGAN—ANN ARBOR	5	4.81
BROWN UNIVERSITY	6	4.77
UNIVERSITY OF CHICAGO	7	4.76
UNIVERSITY OF TEXAS—AUSTIN	8	4.71
UNIVERSITY OF CALIFORNIA—LOS ANGELES	9	4.67
COLUMBIA UNIVERSITY	10	4.64
CORNELL UNIVERSITY	11	4.63
UNIVERSITY OF PENNSYLVANIA	12	4.59
UNIVERSITY OF NORTH CAROLINA—CHAPEL HILL	13	4.56
DUKE UNIVERSITY	14	4.51
BRYN MAWR COLLEGE	15	4.45
STANFORD UNIVERSITY	16	4.41
UNIVERSITY OF ILLINOIS—URBANA-CHAMPAIGN	17	4.36
UNIVERSITY OF VIRGINIA	18	4.32
UNIVERSITY OF WISCONSIN—MADISON	19	4.28
OHIO STATE UNIVERSITY—COLUMBUS	20	4.25
UNIVERSITY OF WASHINGTON	21	4.20
UNIVERSITY OF CALIFORNIA—SANTA BARBARA	22	4.17
JOHNS HOPKINS UNIVERSITY	23	4.15
UNIVERSITY OF MINNESOTA—TWIN CITIES	24	4.14
NEW YORK UNIVERSITY	25	4.13
BOSTON UNIVERSITY	26	4.10
UNIVERSITY OF CINCINNATI	27	4.09
CATHOLIC UNIVERSITY OF AMERICA	28	4.08
FORDHAM UNIVERSITY	29	4.06

COMPARATIVE LITERATURE
LEADING INSTITUTIONS—RATING OF GRADUATE PROGRAMS

INSTITUTION	RANK	SCORE
YALE UNIVERSITY	1	4.82
DUKE UNIVERSITY	2	4.74
HARVARD UNIVERSITY	3	4.73
COLUMBIA UNIVERSITY	4	4.68
PRINCETON UNIVERSITY	5	4.64
CORNELL UNIVERSITY	6	4.59
JOHNS HOPKINS UNIVERSITY	7	4.58
UNIVERSITY OF CALIFORNIA—IRVINE	8	4.54
STANFORD UNIVERSITY	9	4.50
UNIVERSITY OF CALIFORNIA—BERKELEY	10	4.47
UNIVERSITY OF PENNSYLVANIA	11	4.41
NEW YORK UNIVERSITY	12	4.36
UNIVERSITY OF CHICAGO	13	4.32
UNIVERSITY OF WASHINGTON	14	4.28
UNIVERSITY OF MICHIGAN—ANN ARBOR	15	4.25
UNIVERSITY OF CALIFORNIA—LOS ANGELES	16	4.21
NORTHWESTERN UNIVERSITY	17	4.16
UNIVERSITY OF CALIFORNIA—SAN DIEGO	18	4.15
INDIANA UNIVERSITY—BLOOMINGTON	19	4.13
BROWN UNIVERSITY	20	4.12
UNIVERSITY OF TEXAS—AUSTIN	21	4.10
RUTGERS UNIVERSITY	22	4.09
UNIVERSITY OF SOUTHERN CALIFORNIA	23	4.08
EMORY UNIVERSITY	24	4.07
WASHINGTON UNIVERSITY	25	4.06
PENNSYLVANIA STATE UNIVERSITY—UNIVERSITY PARK	26	4.05
UNIVERSITY OF MINNESOTA—TWIN CITIES	27	4.04
UNIVERSITY OF IOWA	28	4.03
UNIVERSITY OF ILLINOIS—URBANA-CHAMPAIGN	29	4.02
UNIVERSITY OF CALIFORNIA—RIVERSIDE	30	4.01

COMPUTER SCIENCE
LEADING INSTITUTIONS—RATING OF GRADUATE PROGRAMS

INSTITUTION	RANK	SCORE
MASSACHUSETTS INSTITUTE OF TECHNOLOGY	1	4.92
STANFORD UNIVERSITY	2	4.91
CARNEGIE MELLON UNIVERSITY	3	4.90
UNIVERSITY OF CALIFORNIA—BERKELEY	4	4.88
CORNELL UNIVERSITY	5	4.86
PRINCETON UNIVERSITY	6	4.85
UNIVERSITY OF TEXAS—AUSTIN	7	4.82
UNIVERSITY OF ILLINOIS—URBANA-CHAMPAIGN	8	4.80
UNIVERSITY OF WASHINGTON	9	4.79
HARVARD UNIVERSITY	10	4.78
UNIVERSITY OF WISCONSIN—MADISON	11	4.74
CALIFORNIA INSTITUTE OF TECHNOLOGY	12	4.71
BROWN UNIVERSITY	13	4.69
UNIVERSITY OF CALIFORNIA—LOS ANGELES	14	4.67
YALE UNIVERSITY	15	4.65
UNIVERSITY OF MARYLAND—COLLEGE PARK	16	4.63
UNIVERSITY OF MASSACHUSETTS—AMHERST	17	4.59
NEW YORK UNIVERSITY	18	4.56
RICE UNIVERSITY	19	4.53
UNIVERSITY OF MICHIGAN—ANN ARBOR	20	4.50
UNIVERSITY OF SOUTHERN CALIFORNIA	21	4.46
COLUMBIA UNIVERSITY	22	4.43
UNIVERSITY OF CHICAGO	23	4.40
UNIVERSITY OF PENNSYLVANIA	24	4.39
UNIVERSITY OF CALIFORNIA—SAN DIEGO	25	4.38
PURDUE UNIVERSITY—WEST LAFAYETTE	26	4.32
RUTGERS UNIVERSITY	27	4.28
DUKE UNIVERSITY	28	4.25
UNIVERSITY OF ROCHESTER	29	4.22
UNIVERSITY OF NORTH CAROLINA—CHAPEL HILL	30	4.21
STATE UNIVERSITY OF NEW YORK AT STONY BROOK	31	4.20
UNIVERSITY OF ARIZONA	32	4.19
GEORGIA INSTITUTE OF TECHNOLOGY	33	4.16
UNIVERSITY OF CALIFORNIA—IRVINE	34	4.14
UNIVERSITY OF VIRGINIA	35	4.13
JOHNS HOPKINS UNIVERSITY	36	4.12
INDIANA UNIVERSITY—BLOOMINGTON	37	4.11
NORTHWESTERN UNIVERSITY	38	4.10
OHIO STATE UNIVERSITY—COLUMBUS	39	4.09
UNIVERSITY OF COLORADO—BOULDER	40	4.08
UNIVERSITY OF UTAH	41	4.06

DRAMA/THEATRE
LEADING INSTITUTIONS—RATING OF GRADUATE PROGRAMS

INSTITUTION	RANK	SCORE
YALE UNIVERSITY	1	4.90
UNIVERSITY OF CALIFORNIA—LOS ANGELES	2	4.89
NORTHWESTERN UNIVERSITY	3	4.88
STANFORD UNIVERSITY	4	4.87
UNIVERSITY OF IOWA	5	4.84
UNIVERSITY OF MINNESOTA—TWIN CITIES	6	4.79
INDIANA UNIVERSITY—BLOOMINGTON	7	4.76
NEW YORK UNIVERSITY	8	4.74
UNIVERSITY OF SOUTHERN CALIFORNIA	9	4.73
UNIVERSITY OF CALIFORNIA—BERKELEY	10	4.71
CARNEGIE MELLON UNIVERSITY	11	4.70
UNIVERSITY OF WISCONSIN—MADISON	12	4.69
UNIVERSITY OF WASHINGTON	13	4.68
FLORIDA STATE UNIVERSITY	14	4.66
CORNELL UNIVERSITY	15	4.62
UNIVERSITY OF ILLINOIS—URBANA-CHAMPAIGN	16	4.60
OHIO STATE UNIVERSITY—COLUMBUS	17	4.58
UNIVERSITY OF CALIFORNIA—SANTA BARBARA	18	4.55
UNIVERSITY OF TEXAS—AUSTIN	19	4.53
UNIVERSITY OF NORTH CAROLINA—CHAPEL HILL	20	4.50
UNIVERSITY OF MICHIGAN—ANN ARBOR	21	4.48
COLUMBIA UNIVERSITY	22	4.46
CASE WESTERN RESERVE UNIVERSITY	23	4.42
WAYNE STATE UNIVERSITY	24	4.38
UNIVERSITY OF OREGON	25	4.35
UNIVERSITY OF MARYLAND—COLLEGE PARK	26	4.30
TULANE UNIVERSITY	27	4.28
CATHOLIC UNIVERSITY OF AMERICA	28	4.25
MICHIGAN STATE UNIVERSITY	29	4.21
TUFTS UNIVERSITY	30	4.18
UNIVERSITY OF KANSAS	31	4.16
UNIVERSITY OF PITTSBURGH	32	4.13

ECONOMICS

LEADING INSTITUTIONS—RATING OF GRADUATE PROGRAMS

INSTITUTION	RANK	SCORE
UNIVERSITY OF CHICAGO	1	4.92
MASSACHUSETTS INSTITUTE OF TECHNOLOGY	2	4.91
HARVARD UNIVERSITY	3	4.90
PRINCETON UNIVERSITY	4	4.89
STANFORD UNIVERSITY	5	4.88
YALE UNIVERSITY	6	4.86
UNIVERSITY OF CALIFORNIA—BERKELEY	7	4.84
UNIVERSITY OF PENNSYLVANIA	8	4.82
NORTHWESTERN UNIVERSITY	9	4.81
UNIVERSITY OF MINNESOTA—TWIN CITIES	10	4.79
UNIVERSITY OF CALIFORNIA—LOS ANGELES	11	4.76
COLUMBIA UNIVERSITY	12	4.73
UNIVERSITY OF MICHIGAN—ANN ARBOR	13	4.68
UNIVERSITY OF ROCHESTER	14	4.63
UNIVERSITY OF WISCONSIN—MADISON	15	4.60
CORNELL UNIVERSITY	16	4.59
NEW YORK UNIVERSITY	17	4.55
UNIVERSITY OF CALIFORNIA—SAN DIEGO	18	4.53
UNIVERSITY OF MARYLAND—COLLEGE PARK	19	4.52
BOSTON UNIVERSITY	20	4.49
DUKE UNIVERSITY	21	4.44
BROWN UNIVERSITY	22	4.43
UNIVERSITY OF NORTH CAROLINA—CHAPEL HILL	23	4.41
UNIVERSITY OF VIRGINIA	24	4.39
MICHIGAN STATE UNIVERSITY	25	4.36
UNIVERSITY OF WASHINGTON	26	4.33
UNIVERSITY OF ILLINOIS—URBANA-CHAMPAIGN	27	4.31
WASHINGTON UNIVERSITY	28	4.29
UNIVERSITY OF IOWA	29	4.27
UNIVERSITY OF TEXAS—AUSTIN	30	4.22
JOHNS HOPKINS UNIVERSITY	31	4.21
TEXAS A&M UNIVERSITY—COLLEGE STATION	32	4.20
UNIVERSITY OF PITTSBURGH	33	4.19
OHIO STATE UNIVERSITY—COLUMBUS	34	4.17
UNIVERSITY OF ARIZONA	35	4.16
UNIVERSITY OF CALIFORNIA—DAVIS	36	4.14
STATE UNIVERSITY OF NEW YORK AT STONY BROOK	37	4.12
UNIVERSITY OF FLORIDA	38	4.11
UNIVERSITY OF SOUTHERN CALIFORNIA	39	4.09

ELECTRICAL ENGINEERING

LEADING INSTITUTIONS—RATING OF GRADUATE PROGRAMS

INSTITUTION	RANK	SCORE
STANFORD UNIVERSITY	1	4.92
MASSACHUSETTS INSTITUTE OF TECHNOLOGY	2	4.91
UNIVERSITY OF ILLINOIS—URBANA-CHAMPAIGN	3	4.90
UNIVERSITY OF CALIFORNIA—BERKELEY	4	4.88
CALIFORNIA INSTITUTE OF TECHNOLOGY	5	4.87
CORNELL UNIVERSITY	6	4.86
UNIVERSITY OF MICHIGAN—ANN ARBOR	7	4.85
PURDUE UNIVERSITY—WEST LAFAYETTE	8	4.84
PRINCETON UNIVERSITY	9	4.83
UNIVERSITY OF SOUTHERN CALIFORNIA	10	4.82
UNIVERSITY OF CALIFORNIA—LOS ANGELES	11	4.81
CARNEGIE MELLON UNIVERSITY	12	4.80
GEORGIA INSTITUTE OF TECHNOLOGY	13	4.78
UNIVERSITY OF TEXAS—AUSTIN	14	4.77
COLUMBIA UNIVERSITY	15	4.75
UNIVERSITY OF WISCONSIN—MADISON	16	4.72
UNIVERSITY OF MARYLAND—COLLEGE PARK	17	4.70
UNIVERSITY OF MINNESOTA—TWIN CITIES	18	4.68
UNIVERSITY OF CALIFORNIA—SANTA BARBARA	19	4.66
UNIVERSITY OF CALIFORNIA—SAN DIEGO	20	4.64
NORTH CAROLINA STATE UNIVERSITY	21	4.62
OHIO STATE UNIVERSITY—COLUMBUS	22	4.61
RENSSELAER POLYTECHNIC INSTITUTE	23	4.60
POLYTECHNIC UNIVERSITY	24	4.54
UNIVERSITY OF WASHINGTON	25	4.51
RICE UNIVERSITY	26	4.50
VIRGINIA POLYTECHNIC INSTITUTE AND STATE UNIVERSITY	27	4.49
PENNSYLVANIA STATE UNIVERSITY—UNIVERSITY PARK	28	4.47
UNIVERSITY OF MASSACHUSETTS—AMHERST	29	4.46
YALE UNIVERSITY	30	4.42
UNIVERSITY OF FLORIDA	31	4.40
TEXAS A&M UNIVERSITY—COLLEGE STATION	32	4.38
UNIVERSITY OF CALIFORNIA—DAVIS	33	4.34
JOHNS HOPKINS UNIVERSITY	34	4.32
BROWN UNIVERSITY	35	4.30

ENGLISH

LEADING INSTITUTIONS—RATING OF GRADUATE PROGRAMS

INSTITUTION	RANK	SCORE
YALE UNIVERSITY	1	4.93
UNIVERSITY OF CALIFORNIA—BERKELEY	2	4.92
HARVARD UNIVERSITY	3	4.91
DUKE UNIVERSITY	4	4.90
UNIVERSITY OF VIRGINIA	5	4.89
CORNELL UNIVERSITY	6	4.88
STANFORD UNIVERSITY	7	4.87
COLUMBIA UNIVERSITY	8	4.86
UNIVERSITY OF PENNSYLVANIA	9	4.83
UNIVERSITY OF CHICAGO	10	4.82
JOHNS HOPKINS UNIVERSITY	11	4.81
PRINCETON UNIVERSITY	12	4.80
UNIVERSITY OF CALIFORNIA—LOS ANGELES	13	4.78
UNIVERSITY OF CALIFORNIA—IRVINE	14	4.77
BROWN UNIVERSITY	15	4.74
UNIVERSITY OF MICHIGAN—ANN ARBOR	16	4.71
RUTGERS UNIVERSITY	17	4.70
INDIANA UNIVERSITY—BLOOMINGTON	18	4.69
NEW YORK UNIVERSITY	19	4.66
CITY UNIVERSITY OF NEW YORK GRADUATE SCHOOL	20	4.64
UNIVERSITY OF TEXAS—AUSTIN	21	4.63
UNIVERSITY OF WISCONSIN—MADISON	22	4.61
UNIVERSITY OF WASHINGTON	23	4.60
UNIVERSITY OF NORTH CAROLINA—CHAPEL HILL	24	4.59
UNIVERSITY OF PITTSBURGH	25	4.57
STATE UNIVERSITY OF NEW YORK AT BUFFALO	26	4.56
UNIVERSITY OF ILLINOIS—URBANA-CHAMPAIGN	27	4.52
NORTHWESTERN UNIVERSITY	28	4.49
UNIVERSITY OF NOTRE DAME	29	4.48
VANDERBILT UNIVERSITY	30	4.46
UNIVERSITY OF SOUTHERN CALIFORNIA	31	4.43
EMORY UNIVERSITY	32	4.41
OHIO STATE UNIVERSITY—COLUMBUS	33	4.40
UNIVERSITY OF CALIFORNIA—SANTA BARBARA	34	4.38
UNIVERSITY OF MINNESOTA—TWIN CITIES	35	4.36
UNIVERSITY OF CALIFORNIA—SAN DIEGO	36	4.35
BOSTON UNIVERSITY	37	4.32

ENTOMOLOGY
LEADING INSTITUTIONS—RATING OF GRADUATE PROGRAMS

INSTITUTION	RANK	SCORE
UNIVERSITY OF CALIFORNIA—BERKELEY	1	4.92
CORNELL UNIVERSITY	2	4.91
UNIVERSITY OF ILLINOIS—URBANA-CHAMPAIGN	3	4.90
UNIVERSITY OF CALIFORNIA—DAVIS	4	4.89
UNIVERSITY OF MINNESOTA—TWIN CITIES	5	4.88
MICHIGAN STATE UNIVERSITY	6	4.86
UNIVERSITY OF WISCONSIN—MADISON	7	4.83
PURDUE UNIVERSITY—WEST LAFAYETTE	8	4.81
UNIVERSITY OF KANSAS	9	4.80
OHIO STATE UNIVERSITY—COLUMBUS	10	4.79
IOWA STATE UNIVERSITY	11	4.76
UNIVERSITY OF CALIFORNIA—RIVERSIDE	12	4.74
OREGON STATE UNIVERSITY	13	4.72
KANSAS STATE UNIVERSITY	14	4.70
NORTH CAROLINA STATE UNIVERSITY	15	4.66
TEXAS A&M UNIVERSITY—COLLEGE STATION	16	4.63
RUTGERS UNIVERSITY	17	4.61
LOUISIANA STATE UNIVERSITY—BATON ROUGE	18	4.55
UNIVERSITY OF FLORIDA	19	4.54
PENNSYLVANIA STATE UNIVERSITY—UNIVERSITY PARK	20	4.51
UNIVERSITY OF MASSACHUSETTS—AMHERST	21	4.46
UNIVERSITY OF MISSOURI—COLUMBIA	22	4.43
UNIVERSITY OF ARIZONA	23	4.41
WASHINGTON STATE UNIVERSITY	24	4.40
UNIVERSITY OF MARYLAND—COLLEGE PARK	25	4.38
COLORADO STATE UNIVERSITY	26	4.37
AUBURN UNIVERSITY	27	4.32
UNIVERSITY OF NEBRASKA—LINCOLN	28	4.28
UNIVERSITY OF GEORGIA	29	4.22
OKLAHOMA STATE UNIVERSITY	30	4.20
VIRGINIA POLYTECHNIC INSTITUTE AND STATE UNIVERSITY	31	4.18

ENVIRONMENTAL ENGINEERING

LEADING INSTITUTIONS—RATING OF GRADUATE PROGRAMS

INSTITUTION	RANK	SCORE
CALIFORNIA INSTITUTE OF TECHNOLOGY	1	4.86
UNIVERSITY OF CINCINNATI	2	4.82
UNIVERSITY OF TEXAS—AUSTIN	3	4.81
GEORGIA INSTITUTE OF TECHNOLOGY	4	4.77
VIRGINIA POLYTECHNIC INSTITUTE AND STATE UNIVERSITY	5	4.74
UNIVERSITY OF NORTH CAROLINA—CHAPEL HILL	6	4.70
UNIVERSITY OF FLORIDA	7	4.66
UNIVERSITY OF MASSACHUSETTS—AMHERST	8	4.64
COLORADO STATE UNIVERSITY	9	4.61
CLEMSON UNIVERSITY	10	4.57

FORESTRY
LEADING INSTITUTIONS—RATING OF GRADUATE PROGRAMS

INSTITUTION	RANK	SCORE
UNIVERSITY OF WASHINGTON	1	4.92
OREGON STATE UNIVERSITY	2	4.90
UNIVERSITY OF GEORGIA	3	4.88
STATE UNIVERSITY OF NEW YORK AT SYRACUSE COLLEGE OF ENVIRONMENTAL SCIENCE AND FORESTRY	4	4.87
UNIVERSITY OF MAINE	5	4.86
UNIVERSITY OF MINNESOTA—TWIN CITIES	6	4.85
UTAH STATE UNIVERSITY	7	4.83
UNIVERSITY OF CALIFORNIA—BERKELEY	8	4.82
NORTH CAROLINA STATE UNIVERSITY	9	4.81
YALE UNIVERSITY	10	4.80
DUKE UNIVERSITY	11	4.79
UNIVERSITY OF IDAHO	12	4.75
UNIVERSITY OF MONTANA	13	4.72
UNIVERSITY OF MICHIGAN—ANN ARBOR	14	4.70
PURDUE UNIVERSITY—WEST LAFAYETTE	15	4.68
UNIVERSITY OF WISCONSIN—MADISON	16	4.65
AUBURN UNIVERSITY	17	4.64
CLEMSON UNIVERSITY	18	4.62
MISSISSIPPI STATE UNIVERSITY	19	4.58
PENNSYLVANIA STATE UNIVERSITY—UNIVERSITY PARK	20	4.55
UNIVERSITY OF MISSOURI—COLUMBIA	21	4.52
COLORADO STATE UNIVERSITY	22	4.50
MICHIGAN STATE UNIVERSITY	23	4.48
VIRGINIA POLYTECHNIC INSTITUTE AND STATE UNIVERSITY	24	4.44
TEXAS A&M UNIVERSITY—COLLEGE STATION	25	4.41
WEST VIRGINIA UNIVERSITY	26	4.40
STEPHEN F. AUSTIN STATE UNIVERSITY	27	4.37
UNIVERSITY OF MASSACHUSETTS—AMHERST	28	4.33
LOUISIANA STATE UNIVERSITY—BATON ROUGE	29	4.26
IOWA STATE UNIVERSITY	30	4.25
UNIVERSITY OF FLORIDA	31	4.24

FRENCH
Leading Institutions—Rating of Graduate Programs

INSTITUTION	RANK	SCORE
YALE UNIVERSITY	1	4.93
PRINCETON UNIVERSITY	2	4.92
COLUMBIA UNIVERSITY	3	4.91
DUKE UNIVERSITY	4	4.90
UNIVERSITY OF PENNSYLVANIA	5	4.86
STANFORD UNIVERSITY	6	4.85
UNIVERSITY OF CALIFORNIA—BERKELEY	7	4.83
CORNELL UNIVERSITY	8	4.82
UNIVERSITY OF MICHIGAN—ANN ARBOR	9	4.81
UNIVERSITY OF WISCONSIN—MADISON	10	4.80
NEW YORK UNIVERSITY	11	4.75
HARVARD UNIVERSITY	12	4.74
UNIVERSITY OF VIRGINIA	13	4.71
EMORY UNIVERSITY	14	4.68
UNIVERSITY OF CHICAGO	15	4.66
JOHNS HOPKINS UNIVERSITY	16	4.64
CITY UNIVERSITY OF NEW YORK GRADUATE SCHOOL	17	4.63
UNIVERSITY OF CALIFORNIA—IRVINE	18	4.59
UNIVERSITY OF CALIFORNIA—LOS ANGELES	19	4.56
BROWN UNIVERSITY	20	4.55
RUTGERS UNIVERSITY	21	4.52
UNIVERSITY OF TEXAS—AUSTIN	22	4.51
WASHINGTON UNIVERSITY	23	4.48
INDIANA UNIVERSITY—BLOOMINGTON	24	4.46
LOUISIANA STATE UNIVERSITY—BATON ROUGE	25	4.44
UNIVERSITY OF MINNESOTA—TWIN CITIES	26	4.40
UNIVERSITY OF IOWA	27	4.39
NORTHWESTERN UNIVERSITY	28	4.32
OHIO STATE UNIVERSITY—COLUMBUS	29	4.26
RICE UNIVERSITY	30	4.25
UNIVERSITY OF CALIFORNIA—DAVIS	31	4.20
UNIVERSITY OF ILLINOIS—URBANA-CHAMPAIGN	32	4.18

GEOGRAPHY
Leading Institutions—Rating of Graduate Programs

INSTITUTION	RANK	SCORE
UNIVERSITY OF MINNESOTA—TWIN CITIES	1	4.92
PENNSYLVANIA STATE UNIVERSITY—UNIVERSITY PARK	2	4.91
UNIVERSITY OF CALIFORNIA—BERKELEY	3	4.89
UNIVERSITY OF WISCONSIN—MADISON	4	4.87
UNIVERSITY OF CALIFORNIA—SANTA BARBARA	5	4.85
OHIO STATE UNIVERSITY—COLUMBUS	6	4.83
UNIVERSITY OF CALIFORNIA—LOS ANGELES	7	4.81
CLARK UNIVERSITY	8	4.74
UNIVERSITY OF WASHINGTON	9	4.68
UNIVERSITY OF ILLINOIS—URBANA-CHAMPAIGN	10	4.63
SYRACUSE UNIVERSITY	11	4.56
UNIVERSITY OF IOWA	12	4.51
STATE UNIVERSITY OF NEW YORK AT BUFFALO	13	4.46
LOUISIANA STATE UNIVERSITY—BATON ROUGE	14	4.38
UNIVERSITY OF TEXAS—AUSTIN	15	4.31
UNIVERSITY OF COLORADO—BOULDER	16	4.26
JOHNS HOPKINS UNIVERSITY	17	4.22
ARIZONA STATE UNIVERSITY	18	4.18
UNIVERSITY OF ARIZONA	19	4.16
UNIVERSITY OF KENTUCKY	20	4.12
RUTGERS UNIVERSITY	21	4.10
UNIVERSITY OF GEORGIA	22	4.09
UNIVERSITY OF NORTH CAROLINA—CHAPEL HILL	23	4.08
UNIVERSITY OF FLORIDA	24	4.07
INDIANA UNIVERSITY—BLOOMINGTON	25	4.06
UNIVERSITY OF MARYLAND—COLLEGE PARK	26	4.05
UNIVERSITY OF OREGON	27	4.04
UNIVERSITY OF HAWAII—MANOA	28	4.03
UNIVERSITY OF KANSAS	29	4.02
UNIVERSITY OF WISCONSIN—MILWAUKEE	30	4.01

GEOSCIENCES
Leading Institutions—Rating of Graduate Programs

INSTITUTION	RANK	SCORE
CALIFORNIA INSTITUTE OF TECHNOLOGY	1	4.91
MASSACHUSETTS INSTITUTE OF TECHNOLOGY	2	4.90
UNIVERSITY OF CALIFORNIA—BERKELEY	3	4.89
STANFORD UNIVERSITY	4	4.88
COLUMBIA UNIVERSITY	5	4.87
HARVARD UNIVERSITY	6	4.86
UNIVERSITY OF CHICAGO	7	4.85
UNIVERSITY OF CALIFORNIA—SAN DIEGO	8	4.83
UNIVERSITY OF CALIFORNIA—LOS ANGELES	9	4.80
CORNELL UNIVERSITY	10	4.79
PRINCETON UNIVERSITY	11	4.76
PENNSYLVANIA STATE UNIVERSITY—UNIVERSITY PARK	12	4.74
UNIVERSITY OF TEXAS—AUSTIN	13	4.73
UNIVERSITY OF ARIZONA	14	4.71
BROWN UNIVERSITY	15	4.69
UNIVERSITY OF MICHIGAN—ANN ARBOR	16	4.68
JOHNS HOPKINS UNIVERSITY	17	4.66
UNIVERSITY OF CALIFORNIA—SANTA BARBARA	18	4.64
NORTHWESTERN UNIVERSITY	19	4.60
UNIVERSITY OF WASHINGTON	20	4.54
UNIVERSITY OF WISCONSIN—MADISON	21	4.52
UNIVERSITY OF CALIFORNIA—SANTA CRUZ	22	4.47
RICE UNIVERSITY	23	4.46
UNIVERSITY OF ILLINOIS—URBANA-CHAMPAIGN	24	4.42
UNIVERSITY OF SOUTHERN CALIFORNIA	25	4.39
UNIVERSITY OF MINNESOTA—TWIN CITIES	26	4.38
VIRGINIA POLYTECHNIC INSTITUTE AND STATE UNIVERSITY	27	4.36
ARIZONA STATE UNIVERSITY	28	4.35
WASHINGTON UNIVERSITY	29	4.34
UNIVERSITY OF CALIFORNIA—DAVIS	30	4.31
STATE UNIVERSITY OF NEW YORK AT STONY BROOK	31	4.29
UNIVERSITY OF HAWAII—MANOA	32	4.25
TEXAS A&M UNIVERSITY—COLLEGE STATION	33	4.20
UNIVERSITY OF OREGON	34	4.18
UNIVERSITY OF COLORADO—BOULDER	35	4.16
DARTMOUTH COLLEGE	36	4.14
COLORADO SCHOOL OF MINES	37	4.12
PURDUE UNIVERSITY—WEST LAFAYETTE	38	4.10
RENSSELAER POLYTECHNIC INSTITUTE	39	4.09

GERMAN
LEADING INSTITUTIONS—RATING OF GRADUATE PROGRAMS

INSTITUTION	RANK	SCORE
UNIVERSITY OF CALIFORNIA—BERKELEY	1	4.91
PRINCETON UNIVERSITY	2	4.90
HARVARD UNIVERSITY	3	4.88
YALE UNIVERSITY	4	4.86
WASHINGTON UNIVERSITY	5	4.85
STANFORD UNIVERSITY	6	4.81
CORNELL UNIVERSITY	7	4.80
INDIANA UNIVERSITY—BLOOMINGTON	8	4.75
UNIVERSITY OF VIRGINIA	9	4.72
JOHNS HOPKINS UNIVERSITY	10	4.68
UNIVERSITY OF WISCONSIN—MADISON	11	4.67
UNIVERSITY OF WASHINGTON	12	4.66
UNIVERSITY OF TEXAS—AUSTIN	13	4.62
UNIVERSITY OF PENNSYLVANIA	14	4.60
UNIVERSITY OF CALIFORNIA—IRVINE	15	4.58
OHIO STATE UNIVERSITY—COLUMBUS	16	4.53
UNIVERSITY OF NORTH CAROLINA—CHAPEL HILL	17	4.50
UNIVERSITY OF MINNESOTA—TWIN CITIES	18	4.46
UNIVERSITY OF ILLINOIS—URBANA-CHAMPAIGN	19	4.42
UNIVERSITY OF MICHIGAN—ANN ARBOR	20	4.40
UNIVERSITY OF CALIFORNIA—LOS ANGELES	21	4.36
NEW YORK UNIVERSITY	22	4.35
UNIVERSITY OF CALIFORNIA—DAVIS	23	4.30
UNIVERSITY OF MASSACHUSETTS—AMHERST	24	4.22
PENNSYLVANIA STATE UNIVERSITY—UNIVERSITY PARK	25	4.21
UNIVERSITY OF CALIFORNIA—SANTA BARBARA	26	4.20
GEORGETOWN UNIVERSITY	27	4.18
UNIVERSITY OF PITTSBURGH	28	4.16
STATE UNIVERSITY OF NEW YORK AT BUFFALO	29	4.14
RUTGERS UNIVERSITY	30	4.12
STATE UNIVERSITY OF NEW YORK AT ALBANY	31	4.11

HISTORY
LEADING INSTITUTIONS—RATING OF GRADUATE PROGRAMS

INSTITUTION	RANK	SCORE
YALE UNIVERSITY	1	4.93
UNIVERSITY OF CALIFORNIA—BERKELEY	2	4.92
PRINCETON UNIVERSITY	3	4.91
HARVARD UNIVERSITY	4	4.90
UNIVERSITY OF MICHIGAN—ANN ARBOR	5	4.89
STANFORD UNIVERSITY	6	4.88
COLUMBIA UNIVERSITY	7	4.87
UNIVERSITY OF CHICAGO	8	4.86
JOHNS HOPKINS UNIVERSITY	9	4.85
UNIVERSITY OF WISCONSIN—MADISON	10	4.84
UNIVERSITY OF CALIFORNIA—LOS ANGELES	11	4.83
INDIANA UNIVERSITY—BLOOMINGTON	12	4.82
CORNELL UNIVERSITY	13	4.81
BROWN UNIVERSITY	14	4.79
UNIVERSITY OF PENNSYLVANIA	15	4.78
UNIVERSITY OF NORTH CAROLINA—CHAPEL HILL	16	4.76
NORTHWESTERN UNIVERSITY	17	4.74
UNIVERSITY OF ROCHESTER	18	4.72
DUKE UNIVERSITY	19	4.69
UNIVERSITY OF VIRGINIA	20	4.67
BRANDEIS UNIVERSITY	21	4.63
CITY UNIVERSITY OF NEW YORK GRADUATE SCHOOL	22	4.61
UNIVERSITY OF TEXAS—AUSTIN	23	4.58
NEW YORK UNIVERSITY	24	4.55
UNIVERSITY OF MINNESOTA—TWIN CITIES	25	4.53
UNIVERSITY OF IOWA	26	4.50
UNIVERSITY OF CALIFORNIA—SANTA BARBARA	27	4.48
RUTGERS UNIVERSITY	28	4.44
UNIVERSITY OF ILLINOIS—URBANA-CHAMPAIGN	29	4.42
UNIVERSITY OF CALIFORNIA—SAN DIEGO	30	4.40
UNIVERSITY OF WASHINGTON	31	4.38
VANDERBILT UNIVERSITY	32	4.35
UNIVERSITY OF CALIFORNIA—DAVIS	33	4.32
UNIVERSITY OF NOTRE DAME	34	4.30
UNIVERSITY OF MARYLAND—COLLEGE PARK	35	4.28
EMORY UNIVERSITY	36	4.27
RICE UNIVERSITY	37	4.26

HORTICULTURE

LEADING INSTITUTIONS—RATING OF GRADUATE PROGRAMS

INSTITUTION	RANK	SCORE
CORNELL UNIVERSITY	1	4.91
TEXAS A&M UNIVERSITY—COLLEGE STATION	2	4.89
IOWA STATE UNIVERSITY	3	4.87
PURDUE UNIVERSITY—WEST LAFAYETTE	4	4.84
UNIVERSITY OF ILLINOIS—URBANA-CHAMPAIGN	5	4.82
MICHIGAN STATE UNIVERSITY	6	4.81
UNIVERSITY OF WISCONSIN—MADISON	7	4.78
UNIVERSITY OF MINNESOTA—TWIN CITIES	8	4.76
OHIO STATE UNIVERSITY—COLUMBUS	9	4.74
KANSAS STATE UNIVERSITY	10	4.72
UNIVERSITY OF MISSOURI—COLUMBIA	11	4.71
PENNSYLVANIA STATE UNIVERSITY—UNIVERSITY PARK	12	4.70
COLORADO STATE UNIVERSITY	13	4.68
LOUISIANA STATE UNIVERSITY—BATON ROUGE	14	4.66
UNIVERSITY OF MARYLAND—COLLEGE PARK	15	4.64
UNIVERSITY OF GEORGIA	16	4.61
NORTH CAROLINA STATE UNIVERSITY	17	4.58
OREGON STATE UNIVERSITY	18	4.56
UNIVERSITY OF TENNESSEE—KNOXVILLE	19	4.55
UNIVERSITY OF NEBRASKA—LINCOLN	20	4.50
UNIVERSITY OF FLORIDA	21	4.48
AUBURN UNIVERSITY	22	4.46
WASHINGTON STATE UNIVERSITY	23	4.43
UNIVERSITY OF HAWAII—MANOA	24	4.40
VIRGINIA POLYTECHNIC INSTITUTE AND STATE UNIVERSITY	25	4.33
RUTGERS UNIVERSITY	26	4.30
UNIVERSITY OF WASHINGTON	27	4.26

INDUSTRIAL ENGINEERING
LEADING INSTITUTIONS—RATING OF GRADUATE PROGRAMS

INSTITUTION	RANK	SCORE
GEORGIA INSTITUTE OF TECHNOLOGY	1	4.91
UNIVERSITY OF CALIFORNIA—BERKELEY	2	4.90
PURDUE UNIVERSITY—WEST LAFAYETTE	3	4.88
UNIVERSITY OF MICHIGAN—ANN ARBOR	4	4.87
TEXAS A&M UNIVERSITY—COLLEGE STATION	5	4.86
NORTHWESTERN UNIVERSITY	6	4.84
STANFORD UNIVERSITY	7	4.83
PENNSYLVANIA STATE UNIVERSITY—UNIVERSITY PARK	8	4.81
UNIVERSITY OF WISCONSIN—MADISON	9	4.76
VIRGINIA POLYTECHNIC INSTITUTE AND STATE UNIVERSITY	10	4.73
NORTH CAROLINA STATE UNIVERSITY	11	4.72
OHIO STATE UNIVERSITY—COLUMBUS	12	4.69
UNIVERSITY OF ILLINOIS—URBANA-CHAMPAIGN	13	4.65
RENSSELAER POLYTECHNIC INSTITUTE	14	4.62
LEHIGH UNIVERSITY	15	4.58
OKLAHOMA STATE UNIVERSITY	16	4.54
ARIZONA STATE UNIVERSITY	17	4.51
STATE UNIVERSITY OF NEW YORK AT BUFFALO	18	4.50
UNIVERSITY OF FLORIDA	19	4.47
AUBURN UNIVERSITY	20	4.46
UNIVERSITY OF SOUTHERN CALIFORNIA	21	4.45
IOWA STATE UNIVERSITY	22	4.44
UNIVERSITY OF PITTSBURGH	23	4.43
UNIVERSITY OF IOWA	24	4.39
UNIVERSITY OF OKLAHOMA	25	4.38
UNIVERSITY OF ARKANSAS	26	4.37
UNIVERSITY OF MASSACHUSETTS—AMHERST	27	4.36
UNIVERSITY OF NEBRASKA—LINCOLN	28	4.35
KANSAS STATE UNIVERSITY	29	4.33
CLEMSON UNIVERSITY	30	4.32

INDUSTRIAL/LABOR RELATIONS

LEADING INSTITUTIONS—RATING OF GRADUATE PROGRAMS

INSTITUTION	RANK	SCORE
CORNELL UNIVERSITY	1	4.82
CASE WESTERN RESERVE UNIVERSITY	2	4.78
UNIVERSITY OF ILLINOIS—URBANA-CHAMPAIGN	3	4.74
RUTGERS UNIVERSITY	4	4.71
UNIVERSITY OF WISCONSIN—MADISON	5	4.66
UNIVERSITY OF MINNESOTA—TWIN CITIES	6	4.63
OHIO STATE UNIVERSITY—COLUMBUS	7	4.60
MICHIGAN STATE UNIVERSITY	8	4.53

INORGANIC CHEMISTRY

LEADING INSTITUTIONS—RATING OF GRADUATE PROGRAMS

INSTITUTION	RANK	SCORE
UNIVERSITY OF MINNESOTA—TWIN CITIES	1	4.90
MASSACHUSETTS INSTITUTE OF TECHNOLOGY	2	4.87
OHIO STATE UNIVERSITY—COLUMBUS	3	4.84
PURDUE UNIVERSITY—WEST LAFAYETTE	4	4.81
HARVARD UNIVERSITY	5	4.79
COLUMBIA UNIVERSITY	6	4.76
UNIVERSITY OF MICHIGAN—ANN ARBOR	7	4.73
RUTGERS UNIVERSITY	8	4.70
TEXAS A&M UNIVERSITY—COLLEGE STATION	9	4.66
UNIVERSITY OF MARYLAND—COLLEGE PARK	10	4.62
UNIVERSITY OF FLORIDA	11	4.59
UNIVERSITY OF PITTSBURGH	12	4.55
UNIVERSITY OF MISSOURI—COLUMBIA	13	4.52
YALE UNIVERSITY	14	4.49
UNIVERSITY OF NOTRE DAME	15	4.46
RENSSELAER POLYTECHNIC INSTITUTE	16	4.42

JOURNALISM

Leading Institutions—Rating of Graduate Programs

INSTITUTION	RANK	SCORE
COLUMBIA UNIVERSITY	1	4.92
NORTHWESTERN UNIVERSITY	2	4.91
UNIVERSITY OF MISSOURI—COLUMBIA	3	4.89
UNIVERSITY OF MINNESOTA—TWIN CITIES	4	4.87
UNIVERSITY OF ILLINOIS—URBANA-CHAMPAIGN	5	4.85
UNIVERSITY OF WISCONSIN—MADISON	6	4.83
UNIVERSITY OF MICHIGAN—ANN ARBOR	7	4.81
STANFORD UNIVERSITY	8	4.80
UNIVERSITY OF TEXAS—AUSTIN	9	4.77
INDIANA UNIVERSITY—BLOOMINGTON	10	4.74
UNIVERSITY OF IOWA	11	4.72
UNIVERSITY OF SOUTHERN CALIFORNIA	12	4.69
NEW YORK UNIVERSITY	13	4.65
BOSTON UNIVERSITY	14	4.60
UNIVERSITY OF MARYLAND—COLLEGE PARK	15	4.58
WAYNE STATE UNIVERSITY	16	4.53
SYRACUSE UNIVERSITY	17	4.49
MICHIGAN STATE UNIVERSITY	18	4.46
UNIVERSITY OF NORTH CAROLINA—CHAPEL HILL	19	4.43
PENNSYLVANIA STATE UNIVERSITY—UNIVERSITY PARK	20	4.42
OHIO STATE UNIVERSITY—COLUMBUS	21	4.39
OHIO UNIVERSITY	22	4.34

LANDSCAPE ARCHITECTURE
LEADING INSTITUTIONS—RATING OF GRADUATE PROGRAMS

INSTITUTION	RANK	SCORE
HARVARD UNIVERSITY	1	4.89
UNIVERSITY OF CALIFORNIA—BERKELEY	2	4.84
UNIVERSITY OF MICHIGAN—ANN ARBOR	3	4.81
UNIVERSITY OF PENNSYLVANIA	4	4.78
STATE UNIVERSITY OF NEW YORK COLLEGE OF ENVIRONMENTAL SCIENCE AND FORESTRY	5	4.75
UNIVERSITY OF ILLINOIS—URBANA-CHAMPAIGN	6	4.70
CORNELL UNIVERSITY	7	4.69
KANSAS STATE UNIVERSITY	8	4.62
UNIVERSITY OF MASSACHUSETTS—AMHERST	9	4.57
UNIVERSITY OF GEORGIA	10	4.54
UNIVERSITY OF WASHINGTON	11	4.50
NORTH CAROLINA STATE UNIVERSITY	12	4.43
OHIO STATE UNIVERSITY—COLUMBUS	13	4.42
UNIVERSITY OF COLORADO—DENVER	14	4.38
LOUISIANA STATE UNIVERSITY—BATON ROUGE	15	4.34
UNIVERSITY OF MINNESOTA—TWIN CITIES	16	4.30
UNIVERSITY OF VIRGINIA	17	4.29

LIBRARY SCIENCE
Leading Institutions—Rating of Graduate Programs

INSTITUTION	RANK	SCORE
UNIVERSITY OF MICHIGAN—ANN ARBOR	1	4.91
UNIVERSITY OF ILLINOIS—URBANA-CHAMPAIGN	2	4.90
INDIANA UNIVERSITY—BLOOMINGTON	3	4.86
UNIVERSITY OF WISCONSIN—MADISON	4	4.84
UNIVERSITY OF CALIFORNIA—LOS ANGELES	5	4.82
RUTGERS UNIVERSITY	6	4.80
UNIVERSITY OF PITTSBURGH	7	4.77
UNIVERSITY OF NORTH CAROLINA—CHAPEL HILL	8	4.74
SIMMONS COLLEGE	9	4.71
UNIVERSITY OF TEXAS—AUSTIN	10	4.66
UNIVERSITY OF WASHINGTON	11	4.62
UNIVERSITY OF MARYLAND—COLLEGE PARK	12	4.58
FLORIDA STATE UNIVERSITY	13	4.55
SYRACUSE UNIVERSITY	14	4.51
DREXEL UNIVERSITY	15	4.47
PRATT INSTITUTE	16	4.44
STATE UNIVERSITY OF NEW YORK AT ALBANY	17	4.41
WAYNE STATE UNIVERSITY	18	4.38
CATHOLIC UNIVERSITY OF AMERICA	19	4.36
LOUISIANA STATE UNIVERSITY—BATON ROUGE	20	4.35

LINGUISTICS

LEADING INSTITUTIONS—RATING OF GRADUATE PROGRAMS

INSTITUTION	RANK	SCORE
MASSACHUSETTS INSTITUTE OF TECHNOLOGY	1	4.90
STANFORD UNIVERSITY	2	4.89
UNIVERSITY OF CALIFORNIA—LOS ANGELES	3	4.86
UNIVERSITY OF CHICAGO	4	4.84
UNIVERSITY OF CALIFORNIA—BERKELEY	5	4.83
UNIVERSITY OF MASSACHUSETTS—AMHERST	6	4.79
UNIVERSITY OF CALIFORNIA—SAN DIEGO	7	4.78
UNIVERSITY OF PENNSYLVANIA	8	4.75
OHIO STATE UNIVERSITY—COLUMBUS	9	4.74
CORNELL UNIVERSITY	10	4.72
UNIVERSITY OF CALIFORNIA—SANTA CRUZ	11	4.67
UNIVERSITY OF TEXAS—AUSTIN	12	4.65
UNIVERSITY OF SOUTHERN CALIFORNIA	13	4.62
UNIVERSITY OF ARIZONA	14	4.61
UNIVERSITY OF CONNECTICUT	15	4.55
CITY UNIVERSITY OF NEW YORK GRADUATE SCHOOL	16	4.50
UNIVERSITY OF WASHINGTON	17	4.47
UNIVERSITY OF ILLINOIS—URBANA-CHAMPAIGN	18	4.46
BROWN UNIVERSITY	19	4.42
GEORGETOWN UNIVERSITY	20	4.37
HARVARD UNIVERSITY	21	4.33
STATE UNIVERSITY OF NEW YORK AT BUFFALO	22	4.29
UNIVERSITY OF PITTSBURGH	23	4.26
UNIVERSITY OF WISCONSIN—MADISON	24	4.23
UNIVERSITY OF HAWAII—MANOA	25	4.20
STATE UNIVERSITY OF NEW YORK AT STONY BROOK	26	4.19
UNIVERSITY OF OREGON	27	4.18
INDIANA UNIVERSITY—BLOOMINGTON	28	4.17
BOSTON UNIVERSITY	29	4.12
YALE UNIVERSITY	30	4.10
UNIVERSITY OF MICHIGAN—ANN ARBOR	31	4.09

MATERIALS SCIENCE
LEADING INSTITUTIONS—RATING OF GRADUATE PROGRAMS

INSTITUTION	RANK	SCORE
MASSACHUSETTS INSTITUTE OF TECHNOLOGY	1	4.93
NORTHWESTERN UNIVERSITY	2	4.92
CORNELL UNIVERSITY	3	4.91
STANFORD UNIVERSITY	4	4.90
UNIVERSITY OF CALIFORNIA—BERKELEY	5	4.89
UNIVERSITY OF ILLINOIS—URBANA-CHAMPAIGN	6	4.88
UNIVERSITY OF MASSACHUSETTS—AMHERST	7	4.87
CARNEGIE MELLON UNIVERSITY	8	4.86
CALIFORNIA INSTITUTE OF TECHNOLOGY	9	4.83
PENNSYLVANIA STATE UNIVERSITY—UNIVERSITY PARK	10	4.82
UNIVERSITY OF CALIFORNIA—SANTA BARBARA	11	4.79
UNIVERSITY OF PENNSYLVANIA	12	4.78
RENSSELAER POLYTECHNIC INSTITUTE	13	4.76
UNIVERSITY OF WISCONSIN—MADISON	14	4.73
UNIVERSITY OF FLORIDA	15	4.72
UNIVERSITY OF MICHIGAN—ANN ARBOR	16	4.71
UNIVERSITY OF MINNESOTA—TWIN CITIES	17	4.70
CASE WESTERN RESERVE UNIVERSITY	18	4.65
UNIVERSITY OF TEXAS—AUSTIN	19	4.63
OHIO STATE UNIVERSITY—COLUMBUS	20	4.60
UNIVERSITY OF VIRGINIA	21	4.58
LEHIGH UNIVERSITY	22	4.55
NORTH CAROLINA STATE UNIVERSITY	23	4.53
RUTGERS UNIVERSITY	24	4.50
UNIVERSITY OF CALIFORNIA—LOS ANGELES	25	4.46
ARIZONA STATE UNIVERSITY	26	4.44
COLUMBIA UNIVERSITY	27	4.42
UNIVERSITY OF ARIZONA	28	4.39
BROWN UNIVERSITY	29	4.36
PURDUE UNIVERSITY—WEST LAFAYETTE	30	4.31
JOHNS HOPKINS UNIVERSITY	31	4.26
VANDERBILT UNIVERSITY	32	4.22
UNIVERSITY OF UTAH	33	4.21
UNIVERSITY OF ROCHESTER	34	4.20
UNIVERSITY OF AKRON	35	4.16
DREXEL UNIVERSITY	36	4.12

MATHEMATICS
LEADING INSTITUTIONS—RATING OF GRADUATE PROGRAMS

INSTITUTION	RANK	SCORE
PRINCETON UNIVERSITY	1	4.94
UNIVERSITY OF CALIFORNIA—BERKELEY	2	4.93
HARVARD UNIVERSITY	3	4.92
MASSACHUSETTS INSTITUTE OF TECHNOLOGY	4	4.91
UNIVERSITY OF CHICAGO	5	4.90
STANFORD UNIVERSITY	6	4.89
NEW YORK UNIVERSITY	7	4.88
YALE UNIVERSITY	8	4.87
UNIVERSITY OF WISCONSIN—MADISON	9	4.86
COLUMBIA UNIVERSITY	10	4.85
UNIVERSITY OF MICHIGAN—ANN ARBOR	11	4.84
BROWN UNIVERSITY	12	4.83
CORNELL UNIVERSITY	13	4.82
UNIVERSITY OF CALIFORNIA—LOS ANGELES	14	4.81
UNIVERSITY OF ILLINOIS—URBANA-CHAMPAIGN	15	4.80
CALIFORNIA INSTITUTE OF TECHNOLOGY	16	4.79
UNIVERSITY OF MINNESOTA—TWIN CITIES	17	4.78
UNIVERSITY OF CALIFORNIA—SAN DIEGO	18	4.77
UNIVERSITY OF PENNSYLVANIA	19	4.72
UNIVERSITY OF TEXAS—AUSTIN	20	4.70
PURDUE UNIVERSITY—WEST LAFAYETTE	21	4.68
RUTGERS UNIVERSITY	22	4.66
UNIVERSITY OF WASHINGTON	23	4.64
STATE UNIVERSITY OF NEW YORK AT STONY BROOK	24	4.63
UNIVERSITY OF MARYLAND—COLLEGE PARK	25	4.59
NORTHWESTERN UNIVERSITY	26	4.58
RICE UNIVERSITY	27	4.52
JOHNS HOPKINS UNIVERSITY	28	4.48
CITY UNIVERSITY OF NEW YORK GRADUATE SCHOOL	29	4.45
OHIO STATE UNIVERSITY—COLUMBUS	30	4.43
PENNSYLVANIA STATE UNIVERSITY—UNIVERSITY PARK	31	4.40
BRANDEIS UNIVERSITY	32	4.39
UNIVERSITY OF VIRGINIA	33	4.34
UNIVERSITY OF NOTRE DAME	34	4.31
DUKE UNIVERSITY	35	4.28
UNIVERSITY OF NORTH CAROLINA—CHAPEL HILL	36	4.24
UNIVERSITY OF UTAH	37	4.23
UNIVERSITY OF ILLINOIS—CHICAGO	38	4.20
GEORGIA INSTITUTE OF TECHNOLOGY	39	4.18
RENSSELAER POLYTECHNIC INSTITUTE	40	4.16

WASHINGTON UNIVERSITY	41	4.13
CARNEGIE MELLON UNIVERSITY	42	4.11
INDIANA UNIVERSITY—BLOOMINGTON	43	4.09
UNIVERSITY OF SOUTHERN CALIFORNIA	44	4.07
MICHIGAN STATE UNIVERSITY	45	4.06
UNIVERSITY OF OREGON	46	4.03
DARTMOUTH COLLEGE	47	4.01

MECHANICAL ENGINEERING

LEADING INSTITUTIONS—RATING OF GRADUATE PROGRAMS

INSTITUTION	RANK	SCORE
MASSACHUSETTS INSTITUTE OF TECHNOLOGY	1	4.93
STANFORD UNIVERSITY	2	4.92
UNIVERSITY OF CALIFORNIA—BERKELEY	3	4.91
CALIFORNIA INSTITUTE OF TECHNOLOGY	4	4.90
UNIVERSITY OF MICHIGAN—ANN ARBOR	5	4.89
PRINCETON UNIVERSITY	6	4.88
CORNELL UNIVERSITY	7	4.86
UNIVERSITY OF MINNESOTA—TWIN CITIES	8	4.84
UNIVERSITY OF ILLINOIS—URBANA-CHAMPAIGN	9	4.83
PURDUE UNIVERSITY—WEST LAFAYETTE	10	4.82
UNIVERSITY OF CALIFORNIA—SAN DIEGO	11	4.80
BROWN UNIVERSITY	12	4.77
NORTHWESTERN UNIVERSITY	13	4.75
RENSSELAER POLYTECHNIC INSTITUTE	14	4.73
UNIVERSITY OF TEXAS—AUSTIN	15	4.72
UNIVERSITY OF CALIFORNIA—LOS ANGELES	16	4.70
GEORGIA INSTITUTE OF TECHNOLOGY	17	4.67
PENNSYLVANIA STATE UNIVERSITY—UNIVERSITY PARK	18	4.63
CARNEGIE MELLON UNIVERSITY	19	4.61
CASE WESTERN RESERVE UNIVERSITY	20	4.58
UNIVERSITY OF WISCONSIN—MADISON	21	4.55
UNIVERSITY OF PENNSYLVANIA	22	4.52
LEHIGH UNIVERSITY	23	4.49
NORTH CAROLINA STATE UNIVERSITY	24	4.47
OHIO STATE UNIVERSITY—COLUMBUS	25	4.46
UNIVERSITY OF CALIFORNIA—DAVIS	26	4.43
RICE UNIVERSITY	27	4.41
TEXAS A&M UNIVERSITY—COLLEGE STATION	28	4.40
COLUMBIA UNIVERSITY	29	4.38
VIRGINIA POLYTECHNIC INSTITUTE AND STATE UNIVERSITY	30	4.37
RUTGERS UNIVERSITY	31	4.35
UNIVERSITY OF MARYLAND—COLLEGE PARK	32	4.34
UNIVERSITY OF WASHINGTON	33	4.33
UNIVERSITY OF NOTRE DAME	34	4.32
UNIVERSITY OF ARIZONA	35	4.30
UNIVERSITY OF CALIFORNIA—IRVINE	36	4.29

MICROBIOLOGY
LEADING INSTITUTIONS—RATING OF GRADUATE PROGRAMS

INSTITUTION	RANK	SCORE
MASSACHUSETTS INSTITUTE OF TECHNOLOGY	1	4.93
ROCKEFELLER UNIVERSITY	2	4.92
UNIVERSITY OF CALIFORNIA—SAN DIEGO	3	4.91
JOHNS HOPKINS UNIVERSITY	4	4.90
DUKE UNIVERSITY	5	4.89
UNIVERSITY OF WASHINGTON	6	4.88
UNIVERSITY OF CALIFORNIA—LOS ANGELES	7	4.87
UNIVERSITY OF CHICAGO	8	4.86
UNIVERSITY OF ILLINOIS—URBANA-CHAMPAIGN	9	4.85
UNIVERSITY OF PENNSYLVANIA	10	4.84
HARVARD UNIVERSITY	11	4.83
UNIVERSITY OF CALIFORNIA—DAVIS	12	4.82
UNIVERSITY OF WISCONSIN—MADISON	13	4.81
UNIVERSITY OF MICHIGAN—ANN ARBOR	14	4.80
STANFORD UNIVERSITY	15	4.79
COLUMBIA UNIVERSITY	16	4.77
UNIVERSITY OF CALIFORNIA—SAN FRANCISCO	17	4.76
YALE UNIVERSITY	18	4.75
NEW YORK UNIVERSITY	19	4.73
UNIVERSITY OF CALIFORNIA—BERKELEY	20	4.72
UNIVERSITY OF ALABAMA—BIRMINGHAM	21	4.71
UNIVERSITY OF MINNESOTA—TWIN CITIES	22	4.69
RUTGERS UNIVERSITY	23	4.68
PURDUE UNIVERSITY—WEST LAFAYETTE	24	4.67
CORNELL UNIVERSITY MEDICAL COLLEGE	25	4.66
CORNELL UNIVERSITY	26	4.64
MICHIGAN STATE UNIVERSITY	27	4.62
UNIVERSITY OF NORTH CAROLINA—CHAPEL HILL	28	4.60
ALBERT EINSTEIN COLLEGE OF MEDICINE OF YESHIVA UNIVERSITY	29	4.59
UNIVERSITY OF TEXAS—AUSTIN	30	4.57
UNIVERSITY OF CALIFORNIA—IRVINE	31	4.54
VANDERBILT UNIVERSITY	32	4.52
UNIVERSITY OF ROCHESTER	33	4.50
UNIVERSITY OF FLORIDA	34	4.49
UNIVERSITY OF VIRGINIA	35	4.46
UNIVERSITY OF OREGON	36	4.45
TUFTS UNIVERSITY	37	4.42
VIRGINIA POLYTECHNIC INSTITUTE AND STATE UNIVERSITY	38	4.40
INDIANA UNIVERSITY—BLOOMINGTON	39	4.38
UNIVERSITY OF IOWA	40	4.34

MOLECULAR GENETICS

LEADING INSTITUTIONS—RATING OF GRADUATE PROGRAMS

INSTITUTION	RANK	SCORE
UNIVERSITY OF CALIFORNIA—SAN FRANCISCO	1	4.92
HARVARD UNIVERSITY	2	4.91
MASSACHUSETTS INSTITUTE OF TECHNOLOGY	3	4.90
STANFORD UNIVERSITY	4	4.88
UNIVERSITY OF CALIFORNIA—SAN DIEGO	5	4.86
CALIFORNIA INSTITUTE OF TECHNOLOGY	6	4.83
YALE UNIVERSITY	7	4.81
JOHNS HOPKINS UNIVERSITY	8	4.79
UNIVERSITY OF WISCONSIN—MADISON	9	4.76
UNIVERSITY OF CHICAGO	10	4.73
UNIVERSITY OF CALIFORNIA—BERKELEY	11	4.70
COLUMBIA UNIVERSITY	12	4.68
DUKE UNIVERSITY	13	4.66
BAYLOR COLLEGE OF MEDICINE	14	4.65
WASHINGTON UNIVERSITY	15	4.64
UNIVERSITY OF PENNSYLVANIA	16	4.60
UNIVERSITY OF TEXAS SOUTHWESTERN MEDICAL CENTER AT DALLAS SOUTHWEST	17	4.57
UNIVERSITY OF WASHINGTON	18	4.54
UNIVERSITY OF UTAH	19	4.52
UNIVERSITY OF MICHIGAN—ANN ARBOR	20	4.48
CORNELL UNIVERSITY	21	4.45
ALBERT EINSTEIN COLLEGE OF MEDICINE OF YESHIVA UNIVERSITY	22	4.42
UNIVERSITY OF ROCHESTER	23	4.39
STATE UNIVERSITY OF NEW YORK AT STONY BROOK	24	4.38
UNIVERSITY OF NORTH CAROLINA—CHAPEL HILL	25	4.37
UNIVERSITY OF TEXAS HEALTH SCIENCE CENTER AT HOUSTON	26	4.35
RUTGERS UNIVERSITY	27	4.32
EMORY UNIVERSITY	28	4.30
INDIANA UNIVERSITY—BLOOMINGTON	29	4.27
UNIVERSITY OF TEXAS—AUSTIN	30	4.24
UNIVERSITY OF ILLINOIS—URBANA-CHAMPAIGN	31	4.23
VANDERBILT UNIVERSITY	32	4.20
BRANDEIS UNIVERSITY	33	4.18
NORTH CAROLINA STATE UNIVERSITY	34	4.15
UNIVERSITY OF ARIZONA	35	4.13
PENNSYLVANIA STATE UNIVERSITY—UNIVERSITY PARK	36	4.10

MUSIC
LEADING INSTITUTIONS—RATING OF GRADUATE PROGRAMS

INSTITUTION	RANK	SCORE
HARVARD UNIVERSITY	1	4.91
UNIVERSITY OF CHICAGO	2	4.90
UNIVERSITY OF CALIFORNIA—BERKELEY	3	4.88
PRINCETON UNIVERSITY	4	4.86
YALE UNIVERSITY	5	4.85
CORNELL UNIVERSITY	6	4.81
UNIVERSITY OF ILLINOIS—URBANA-CHAMPAIGN	7	4.80
COLUMBIA UNIVERSITY	8	4.79
UNIVERSITY OF MICHIGAN—ANN ARBOR	9	4.77
CITY UNIVERSITY OF NEW YORK GRADUATE SCHOOL	10	4.76
UNIVERSITY OF PENNSYLVANIA	11	4.74
NEW YORK UNIVERSITY	12	4.73
STANFORD UNIVERSITY	13	4.72
UNIVERSITY OF ROCHESTER	14	4.70
UNIVERSITY OF NORTH CAROLINA—CHAPEL HILL	15	4.68
INDIANA UNIVERSITY—BLOOMINGTON	16	4.67
UNIVERSITY OF CALIFORNIA—LOS ANGELES	17	4.64
BRANDEIS UNIVERSITY	18	4.62
DUKE UNIVERSITY	19	4.60
UNIVERSITY OF TEXAS—AUSTIN	20	4.57
UNIVERSITY OF SOUTHERN CALIFORNIA	21	4.56
RUTGERS UNIVERSITY	22	4.54
NORTHWESTERN UNIVERSITY	23	4.53
OHIO STATE UNIVERSITY—COLUMBUS	24	4.51
UNIVERSITY OF NORTH TEXAS	25	4.50
STATE UNIVERSITY OF NEW YORK AT STONY BROOK	26	4.47
UNIVERSITY OF WASHINGTON	27	4.46
UNIVERSITY OF MARYLAND—COLLEGE PARK	28	4.43
UNIVERSITY OF CALIFORNIA—SANTA BARBARA	29	4.42
FLORIDA STATE UNIVERSITY	30	4.40
UNIVERSITY OF IOWA	31	4.36
UNIVERSITY OF MINNESOTA—TWIN CITIES	32	4.33
UNIVERSITY OF WISCONSIN—MADISON	33	4.32
WASHINGTON UNIVERSITY	34	4.26
UNIVERSITY OF CALIFORNIA—SAN DIEGO	35	4.23
UNIVERSITY OF CINCINNATI	36	4.22

NEAR AND MIDDLE EASTERN STUDIES

Leading Institutions—Rating of Graduate Programs

INSTITUTION	RANK	SCORE
HARVARD UNIVERSITY	1	4.82
COLUMBIA UNIVERSITY	2	4.78
JOHNS HOPKINS UNIVERSITY	3	4.76
PRINCETON UNIVERSITY	4	4.73
UNIVERSITY OF CALIFORNIA—BERKELEY	5	4.70
UNIVERSITY OF CHICAGO	6	4.66
CORNELL UNIVERSITY	7	4.65
UNIVERSITY OF MICHIGAN—ANN ARBOR	8	4.62
UNIVERSITY OF PENNSYLVANIA	9	4.58
UNIVERSITY OF CALIFORNIA—LOS ANGELES	10	4.53
NEW YORK UNIVERSITY	11	4.49
BRANDEIS UNIVERSITY	12	4.45
GEORGETOWN UNIVERSITY	13	4.43

NEUROSCIENCES

LEADING INSTITUTIONS—RATING OF GRADUATE PROGRAMS

INSTITUTION	RANK	SCORE
YALE UNIVERSITY	1	4.93
HARVARD UNIVERSITY	2	4.92
UNIVERSITY OF CALIFORNIA—SAN FRANCISCO	3	4.91
UNIVERSITY OF CALIFORNIA—SAN DIEGO	4	4.90
COLUMBIA UNIVERSITY	5	4.87
JOHNS HOPKINS UNIVERSITY	6	4.86
STANFORD UNIVERSITY	7	4.83
UNIVERSITY OF CALIFORNIA—BERKELEY	8	4.81
CALIFORNIA INSTITUTE OF TECHNOLOGY	9	4.78
UNIVERSITY OF PENNSYLVANIA	10	4.75
WASHINGTON UNIVERSITY	11	4.73
ROCKEFELLER UNIVERSITY	12	4.72
DUKE UNIVERSITY	13	4.68
UNIVERSITY OF WASHINGTON	14	4.67
CASE WESTERN RESERVE UNIVERSITY	15	4.64
UNIVERSITY OF CALIFORNIA—LOS ANGELES	16	4.62
MASSACHUSETTS INSTITUTE OF TECHNOLOGY	17	4.61
UNIVERSITY OF MICHIGAN—ANN ARBOR	18	4.57
UNIVERSITY OF CHICAGO	19	4.53
BAYLOR COLLEGE OF MEDICINE	20	4.51
UNIVERSITY OF CALIFORNIA—IRVINE	21	4.48
CORNELL UNIVERSITY	22	4.45
NORTHWESTERN UNIVERSITY	23	4.40
UNIVERSITY OF WISCONSIN—MADISON	24	4.36
UNIVERSITY OF NORTH CAROLINA—CHAPEL HILL	25	4.33
VANDERBILT UNIVERSITY	26	4.31
ALBERT EINSTEIN COLLEGE OF MEDICINE OF YESHIVA UNIVERSITY	27	4.30
UNIVERSITY OF IOWA	28	4.24
STATE UNIVERSITY OF NEW YORK AT STONY BROOK	29	4.22
UNIVERSITY OF VIRGINIA	30	4.19
MAYO MEDICAL SCHOOL	31	4.17
BRANDEIS UNIVERSITY	32	4.14
EMORY UNIVERSITY	33	4.13
UNIVERSITY OF MINNESOTA—TWIN CITIES	34	4.11
UNIVERSITY OF OREGON	35	4.10

NUCLEAR ENGINEERING

LEADING INSTITUTIONS—RATING OF GRADUATE PROGRAMS

INSTITUTION	RANK	SCORE
MASSACHUSETTS INSTITUTE OF TECHNOLOGY	1	4.91
UNIVERSITY OF MICHIGAN—ANN ARBOR	2	4.90
CORNELL UNIVERSITY	3	4.88
UNIVERSITY OF CALIFORNIA—BERKELEY	4	4.86
GEORGIA INSTITUTE OF TECHNOLOGY	5	4.85
UNIVERSITY OF ILLINOIS—URBANA-CHAMPAIGN	6	4.83
RENSSELAER POLYTECHNIC INSTITUTE	7	4.81
TEXAS A&M UNIVERSITY—COLLEGE STATION	8	4.80
OHIO STATE UNIVERSITY—COLUMBUS	9	4.76
UNIVERSITY OF WISCONSIN—MADISON	10	4.72
PURDUE UNIVERSITY—WEST LAFAYETTE	11	4.71
UNIVERSITY OF VIRGINIA	12	4.67
NORTH CAROLINA STATE UNIVERSITY	13	4.66
PENNSYLVANIA STATE UNIVERSITY—UNIVERSITY PARK	14	4.63
UNIVERSITY OF FLORIDA	15	4.60
NORTHWESTERN UNIVERSITY	16	4.57
UNIVERSITY OF CINCINNATI	17	4.51
UNIVERSITY OF ARIZONA	18	4.48
UNIVERSITY OF WASHINGTON	19	4.45
UNIVERSITY OF MISSOURI—COLUMBIA	20	4.41
KANSAS STATE UNIVERSITY	21	4.34
UNIVERSITY OF MARYLAND—COLLEGE PARK	22	4.32
UNIVERSITY OF MISSOURI—ROLLA	23	4.28
COLUMBIA UNIVERSITY	24	4.24
UNIVERSITY OF OKLAHOMA	25	4.20

NUTRITION

INSTITUTION	RANK	SCORE
CORNELL UNIVERSITY	1	4.92
COLUMBIA UNIVERSITY	2	4.91
EMORY UNIVERSITY	3	4.89
TUFTS UNIVERSITY	4	4.88
JOHNS HOPKINS UNIVERSITY	5	4.87
UNIVERSITY OF CHICAGO	6	4.86
PURDUE UNIVERSITY—WEST LAFAYETTE	7	4.83
IOWA STATE UNIVERSITY	8	4.81
HARVARD UNIVERSITY	9	4.78
PENNSYLVANIA STATE UNIVERSITY—UNIVERSITY PARK	10	4.77
UNIVERSITY OF ALABAMA—BIRMINGHAM	11	4.76
UNIVERSITY OF CALIFORNIA—DAVIS	12	4.74
UNIVERSITY OF ILLINOIS—URBANA-CHAMPAIGN	13	4.72
OHIO STATE UNIVERSITY—COLUMBUS	14	4.69
UNIVERSITY OF MINNESOTA—TWIN CITIES	15	4.68
MICHIGAN STATE UNIVERSITY	16	4.65
KANSAS STATE UNIVERSITY	17	4.63
UNIVERSITY OF WISCONSIN—MADISON	18	4.61
UNIVERSITY OF WASHINGTON	19	4.60
UNIVERSITY OF CALIFORNIA—BERKELEY	20	4.58
RUTGERS UNIVERSITY	21	4.57
UNIVERSITY OF MISSOURI—COLUMBIA	22	4.54
UNIVERSITY OF PITTSBURGH	23	4.52
UNIVERSITY OF TEXAS—AUSTIN	24	4.48
UNIVERSITY OF ARIZONA	25	4.45
COLORADO STATE UNIVERSITY	26	4.42
UNIVERSITY OF NORTH CAROLINA—CHAPEL HILL	27	4.39
TEXAS A&M UNIVERSITY—COLLEGE STATION	28	4.35
AUBURN UNIVERSITY	29	4.34
UNIVERSITY OF MARYLAND—COLLEGE PARK	30	4.30
CASE WESTERN RESERVE UNIVERSITY	31	4.28
UNIVERSITY OF FLORIDA	32	4.24
FLORIDA STATE UNIVERSITY	33	4.22
UNIVERSITY OF SOUTHERN CALIFORNIA	34	4.20
DREXEL UNIVERSITY	35	4.19
OREGON STATE UNIVERSITY	36	4.15
NORTH CAROLINA STATE UNIVERSITY	37	4.12
CLEMSON UNIVERSITY	38	4.10

OCCUPATIONAL THERAPY
Leading Institutions—Rating of Graduate Programs

INSTITUTION	RANK	SCORE
BOSTON UNIVERSITY	1	4.86
COLUMBIA UNIVERSITY	2	4.82
TUFTS UNIVERSITY	3	4.78
TEMPLE UNIVERSITY	4	4.73
UNIVERSITY OF NORTH CAROLINA—CHAPEL HILL	5	4.68
OHIO STATE UNIVERSITY—COLUMBUS	6	4.64
NEW YORK UNIVERSITY	7	4.61
COLORADO STATE UNIVERSITY	8	4.57
UNIVERSITY OF SOUTHERN CALIFORNIA	9	4.54
UNIVERSITY OF FLORIDA	10	4.50
WAYNE STATE UNIVERSITY	11	4.49
WASHINGTON UNIVERSITY	12	4.47
UNIVERSITY OF ALABAMA—BIRMINGHAM	13	4.43
UNIVERSITY OF KANSAS	14	4.39
MEDICAL UNIVERSITY OF SOUTH CAROLINA COLLEGE OF MEDICINE	15	4.36
TEXAS WOMAN'S UNIVERSITY	16	4.34
UNIVERSITY OF PITTSBURGH	17	4.32
UNIVERSITY OF WASHINGTON	18	4.29
UNIVERSITY OF ILLINOIS—CHICAGO	19	4.27
STATE UNIVERSITY OF NEW YORK AT BUFFALO	20	4.22

OCEANOGRAPHY

INSTITUTION	RANK	SCORE
UNIVERSITY OF CALIFORNIA—SAN DIEGO	1	4.91
MASSACHUSETTS INSTITUTE OF TECHNOLOGY	2	4.90
COLUMBIA UNIVERSITY	3	4.88
UNIVERSITY OF WASHINGTON	4	4.85
OREGON STATE UNIVERSITY	5	4.82
UNIVERSITY OF HAWAII—MANOA	6	4.81
STATE UNIVERSITY OF NEW YORK AT STONY BROOK	7	4.78
FLORIDA STATE UNIVERSITY	8	4.76
UNIVERSITY OF MARYLAND—COLLEGE PARK	9	4.73
UNIVERSITY OF MIAMI	10	4.71
TEXAS A&M UNIVERSITY—COLLEGE STATION	11	4.68
UNIVERSITY OF RHODE ISLAND	12	4.66
UNIVERSITY OF SOUTH FLORIDA	13	4.62
UNIVERSITY OF WISCONSIN—MADISON	14	4.59
UNIVERSITY OF NORTH CAROLINA—CHAPEL HILL	15	4.55
STANFORD UNIVERSITY	16	4.53
DUKE UNIVERSITY	17	4.51
UNIVERSITY OF SOUTH CAROLINA—COLUMBIA	18	4.49
UNIVERSITY OF ALASKA—FAIRBANKS	19	4.46
NORTH CAROLINA STATE UNIVERSITY	20	4.42
LOUISIANA STATE UNIVERSITY—BATON ROUGE	21	4.38
NAVAL POSTGRADUATE SCHOOL	22	4.35
FLORIDA INSTITUTE OF TECHNOLOGY	23	4.32
UNIVERSITY OF MASSACHUSETTS—AMHERST	24	4.29

ORGANIC CHEMISTRY

LEADING INSTITUTIONS—RATING OF GRADUATE PROGRAMS

INSTITUTION	RANK	SCORE
HARVARD UNIVERSITY	1	4.85
PURDUE UNIVERSITY—WEST LAFAYETTE	2	4.82
CORNELL UNIVERSITY	3	4.79
MASSACHUSETTS INSTITUTE OF TECHNOLOGY	4	4.75
UNIVERSITY OF MICHIGAN—ANN ARBOR	5	4.73
UNIVERSITY OF MARYLAND—COLLEGE PARK	6	4.70
COLUMBIA UNIVERSITY	7	4.66
RUTGERS UNIVERSITY	8	4.63
UNIVERSITY OF PITTSBURGH	9	4.58
UNIVERSITY OF MISSOURI—COLUMBIA	10	4.54
YALE UNIVERSITY	11	4.51
UNIVERSITY OF NOTRE DAME	12	4.48
RENSSELAER POLYTECHNIC INSTITUTE	13	4.44

PETROLEUM ENGINEERING
Leading Institutions—Rating of Graduate Programs

INSTITUTION	RANK	SCORE
UNIVERSITY OF TEXAS—AUSTIN	1	4.89
STANFORD UNIVERSITY	2	4.85
UNIVERSITY OF SOUTHERN CALIFORNIA	3	4.83
UNIVERSITY OF TULSA	4	4.80
TEXAS A&M UNIVERSITY—COLLEGE STATION	5	4.77
UNIVERSITY OF OKLAHOMA	6	4.74
LOUISIANA STATE UNIVERSITY—BATON ROUGE	7	4.70
UNIVERSITY OF CALIFORNIA—BERKELEY	8	4.66
UNIVERSITY OF KANSAS	9	4.64
PENNSYLVANIA STATE UNIVERSITY—UNIVERSITY PARK	10	4.59
COLORADO SCHOOL OF MINES	11	4.54
UNIVERSITY OF MISSOURI—ROLLA	12	4.45
UNIVERSITY OF HOUSTON	13	4.40
NEW MEXICO INSTITUTE OF MINING & TECHNOLOGY	14	4.37

PHARMACOLOGY

LEADING INSTITUTIONS—RATING OF GRADUATE PROGRAMS

INSTITUTION	RANK	SCORE
UNIVERSITY OF CALIFORNIA—SAN DIEGO	1	4.93
JOHNS HOPKINS UNIVERSITY	2	4.92
DUKE UNIVERSITY	3	4.91
YALE UNIVERSITY	4	4.90
VANDERBILT UNIVERSITY	5	4.89
UNIVERSITY OF WASHINGTON	6	4.86
UNIVERSITY OF PENNSYLVANIA	7	4.83
MASSACHUSETTS INSTITUTE OF TECHNOLOGY	8	4.82
UNIVERSITY OF NORTH CAROLINA—CHAPEL HILL	9	4.80
UNIVERSITY OF TEXAS SOUTHWESTERN MEDICAL CENTER AT DALLAS SOUTHWEST	10	4.78
NEW YORK UNIVERSITY	11	4.75
UNIVERSITY OF MICHIGAN—ANN ARBOR	12	4.72
UNIVERSITY OF WISCONSIN—MADISON	13	4.71
STANFORD UNIVERSITY	14	4.70
UNIVERSITY OF COLORADO—BOULDER	15	4.66
UNIVERSITY OF ROCHESTER	16	4.64
EMORY UNIVERSITY	17	4.60
COLUMBIA UNIVERSITY	18	4.58
UNIVERSITY OF IOWA	19	4.55
UNIVERSITY OF KANSAS	20	4.52
UNIVERSITY OF CHICAGO	21	4.50
UNIVERSITY OF MINNESOTA—TWIN CITIES	22	4.48
STATE UNIVERSITY OF NEW YORK AT STONY BROOK	23	4.47
UNIVERSITY OF TEXAS—AUSTIN	24	4.44
UNIVERSITY OF VIRGINIA	25	4.40
ALBERT EINSTEIN COLLEGE OF MEDICINE OF YESHIVA UNIVERSITY	26	4.37
MAYO MEDICAL SCHOOL	27	4.35
UNIVERSITY OF CALIFORNIA—DAVIS	28	4.32
MICHIGAN STATE UNIVERSITY	29	4.29
GEORGETOWN UNIVERSITY	30	4.25

PHILOSOPHY
Leading Institutions—Rating of Graduate Programs

INSTITUTION	RANK	SCORE
PRINCETON UNIVERSITY	1	4.92
UNIVERSITY OF PITTSBURGH	2	4.91
HARVARD UNIVERSITY	3	4.90
UNIVERSITY OF CALIFORNIA—BERKELEY	4	4.88
STANFORD UNIVERSITY	5	4.87
UNIVERSITY OF CALIFORNIA—LOS ANGELES	6	4.85
UNIVERSITY OF CHICAGO	7	4.84
UNIVERSITY OF MICHIGAN—ANN ARBOR	8	4.82
CORNELL UNIVERSITY	9	4.80
MASSACHUSETTS INSTITUTE OF TECHNOLOGY	10	4.78
UNIVERSITY OF NOTRE DAME	11	4.77
RUTGERS UNIVERSITY	12	4.73
BROWN UNIVERSITY	13	4.71
UNIVERSITY OF ARIZONA	14	4.68
UNIVERSITY OF NORTH CAROLINA—CHAPEL HILL	15	4.67
UNIVERSITY OF ILLINOIS—CHICAGO	16	4.63
CITY UNIVERSITY OF NEW YORK GRADUATE SCHOOL	17	4.60
UNIVERSITY OF MASSACHUSETTS—AMHERST	18	4.56
UNIVERSITY OF CALIFORNIA—SAN DIEGO	19	4.53
UNIVERSITY OF WISCONSIN—MADISON	20	4.50
UNIVERSITY OF CALIFORNIA—IRVINE	21	4.47
OHIO STATE UNIVERSITY—COLUMBUS	22	4.43
NORTHWESTERN UNIVERSITY	23	4.41
UNIVERSITY OF PENNSYLVANIA	24	4.39
UNIVERSITY OF TEXAS—AUSTIN	25	4.38
COLUMBIA UNIVERSITY	26	4.35
SYRACUSE UNIVERSITY	27	4.34
BOSTON UNIVERSITY	28	4.31
JOHNS HOPKINS UNIVERSITY	29	4.29
INDIANA UNIVERSITY—BLOOMINGTON	30	4.27
UNIVERSITY OF MINNESOTA—TWIN CITIES	31	4.25
UNIVERSITY OF ROCHESTER	32	4.24
UNIVERSITY OF ILLINOIS—URBANA-CHAMPAIGN	33	4.21
RICE UNIVERSITY	34	4.18
VANDERBILT UNIVERSITY	35	4.16
UNIVERSITY OF SOUTHERN CALIFORNIA	36	4.12
EMORY UNIVERSITY	37	4.11
UNIVERSITY OF VIRGINIA	38	4.10
DUKE UNIVERSITY	39	4.08
UNIVERSITY OF MARYLAND—COLLEGE PARK	40	4.06

PHYSICAL CHEMISTRY

LEADING INSTITUTIONS—RATING OF GRADUATE PROGRAMS

INSTITUTION	RANK	SCORE
UNIVERSITY OF MINNESOTA—TWIN CITIES	1	4.88
OHIO STATE UNIVERSITY—COLUMBUS	2	4.84
HARVARD UNIVERSITY	3	4.83
COLUMBIA UNIVERSITY	4	4.80
MASSACHUSETTS INSTITUTE OF TECHNOLOGY	5	4.77
PURDUE UNIVERSITY—WEST LAFAYETTE	6	4.74
UNIVERSITY OF MICHIGAN—ANN ARBOR	7	4.72
TEXAS A&M UNIVERSITY—COLLEGE STATION	8	4.69
RUTGERS UNIVERSITY	9	4.68
UNIVERSITY OF MARYLAND—COLLEGE PARK	10	4.65
UNIVERSITY OF MISSOURI—COLUMBIA	11	4.61
UNIVERSITY OF PITTSBURGH	12	4.59
YALE UNIVERSITY	13	4.58
UNIVERSITY OF FLORIDA	14	4.54
UNIVERSITY OF NOTRE DAME	15	4.52
RENSSELAER POLYTECHNIC INSTITUTE	16	4.50

PHYSICAL THERAPY
LEADING INSTITUTIONS—RATING OF GRADUATE PROGRAMS

INSTITUTION	RANK	SCORE
BOSTON UNIVERSITY	1	4.88
COLUMBIA UNIVERSITY	2	4.85
WASHINGTON UNIVERSITY	3	4.81
DUKE UNIVERSITY	4	4.76
UNIVERSITY OF SOUTHERN CALIFORNIA	5	4.70
EMORY UNIVERSITY	6	4.63
UNIVERSITY OF IOWA	7	4.58
UNIVERSITY OF PITTSBURGH	8	4.52
LONG ISLAND UNIVERSITY—BROOKLYN	9	4.44
UNIVERSITY OF ALABAMA—BIRMINGHAM	10	4.41
UNIVERSITY OF MIAMI	11	4.39
UNIVERSITY OF KANSAS	12	4.37
UNIVERSITY OF CALIFORNIA—SAN FRANCISCO	13	4.36
UNIVERSITY OF NORTH CAROLINA—CHAPEL HILL	14	4.32
MEDICAL UNIVERSITY OF SOUTH CAROLINA COLLEGE OF MEDICINE	15	4.31
UNIVERSITY OF TEXAS MEDICAL BRANCH AT GALVESTON SCHOOL OF MEDICINE	16	4.30
TEXAS WOMAN'S UNIVERSITY	17	4.25
TEMPLE UNIVERSITY	18	4.23
ST. LOUIS UNIVERSITY	19	4.22
BAYLOR UNIVERSITY	20	4.20

PHYSICS
LEADING INSTITUTIONS—RATING OF GRADUATE PROGRAMS

INSTITUTION	RANK	SCORE
HARVARD UNIVERSITY	1	4.93
CALIFORNIA INSTITUTE OF TECHNOLOGY	2	4.92
CORNELL UNIVERSITY	3	4.91
PRINCETON UNIVERSITY	4	4.90
MASSACHUSETTS INSTITUTE OF TECHNOLOGY	5	4.88
UNIVERSITY OF CALIFORNIA—BERKELEY	6	4.86
STANFORD UNIVERSITY	7	4.84
UNIVERSITY OF CHICAGO	8	4.83
UNIVERSITY OF ILLINOIS—URBANA-CHAMPAIGN	9	4.82
COLUMBIA UNIVERSITY	10	4.81
YALE UNIVERSITY	11	4.80
UNIVERSITY OF CALIFORNIA—SANTA BARBARA	12	4.77
UNIVERSITY OF PENNSYLVANIA	13	4.76
UNIVERSITY OF MICHIGAN—ANN ARBOR	14	4.75
UNIVERSITY OF CALIFORNIA—LOS ANGELES	15	4.73
UNIVERSITY OF TEXAS—AUSTIN	16	4.71
UNIVERSITY OF WASHINGTON	17	4.70
UNIVERSITY OF CALIFORNIA—SAN DIEGO	18	4.68
UNIVERSITY OF MARYLAND—COLLEGE PARK	19	4.66
ROCKEFELLER UNIVERSITY	20	4.65
STATE UNIVERSITY OF NEW YORK AT STONY BROOK	21	4.63
UNIVERSITY OF WISCONSIN—MADISON	22	4.61
RUTGERS UNIVERSITY	23	4.58
UNIVERSITY OF MINNESOTA—TWIN CITIES	24	4.55
UNIVERSITY OF ROCHESTER	25	4.53
BROWN UNIVERSITY	26	4.52
JOHNS HOPKINS UNIVERSITY	27	4.50
OHIO STATE UNIVERSITY—COLUMBUS	28	4.48
CARNEGIE MELLON UNIVERSITY	29	4.46
PURDUE UNIVERSITY—WEST LAFAYETTE	30	4.45
MICHIGAN STATE UNIVERSITY	31	4.44
UNIVERSITY OF CALIFORNIA—IRVINE	32	4.42
UNIVERSITY OF COLORADO—BOULDER	33	4.39
INDIANA UNIVERSITY—BLOOMINGTON	34	4.36
NORTHWESTERN UNIVERSITY	35	4.34
CITY UNIVERSITY OF NEW YORK GRADUATE SCHOOL	36	4.30
BOSTON UNIVERSITY	37	4.29
UNIVERSITY OF FLORIDA	38	4.25
DUKE UNIVERSITY	39	4.23
UNIVERSITY OF PITTSBURGH	40	4.21
RICE UNIVERSITY	41	4.20

PHYSIOLOGY
LEADING INSTITUTIONS—RATING OF GRADUATE PROGRAMS

INSTITUTION	RANK	SCORE
YALE UNIVERSITY	1	4.91
UNIVERSITY OF CALIFORNIA—SAN FRANCISCO	2	4.90
UNIVERSITY OF CALIFORNIA—SAN DIEGO	3	4.89
BAYLOR COLLEGE OF MEDICINE	4	4.87
UNIVERSITY OF PENNSYLVANIA	5	4.85
UNIVERSITY OF CALIFORNIA—LOS ANGELES	6	4.81
STANFORD UNIVERSITY	7	4.78
UNIVERSITY OF WASHINGTON	8	4.74
UNIVERSITY OF VIRGINIA	9	4.71
COLUMBIA UNIVERSITY	10	4.67
UNIVERSITY OF CHICAGO	11	4.63
CALIFORNIA INSTITUTE OF TECHNOLOGY	12	4.59
NEW YORK UNIVERSITY	13	4.58
UNIVERSITY OF IOWA	14	4.57
UNIVERSITY OF MICHIGAN—ANN ARBOR	15	4.56
VANDERBILT UNIVERSITY	16	4.53
ALBERT EINSTEIN COLLEGE OF MEDICINE OF YESHIVA UNIVERSITY	17	4.49
JOHNS HOPKINS UNIVERSITY	18	4.44
UNIVERSITY OF ILLINOIS—URBANA-CHAMPAIGN	19	4.42
MAYO MEDICAL SCHOOL	20	4.39
UNIVERSITY OF ALABAMA—BIRMINGHAM	21	4.37
EMORY UNIVERSITY	22	4.35
UNIVERSITY OF ARIZONA	23	4.30
UNIVERSITY OF WISCONSIN—MADISON	24	4.29
UNIVERSITY OF TEXAS HEALTH SCIENCE CENTER AT HOUSTON	25	4.26
NORTHWESTERN UNIVERSITY	26	4.22
DUKE UNIVERSITY	27	4.18
UNIVERSITY OF CALIFORNIA—DAVIS	28	4.16
DARTMOUTH COLLEGE	29	4.12
CORNELL UNIVERSITY	30	4.10

PLANT PATHOLOGY
Leading Institutions—Rating of Graduate Programs

INSTITUTION	RANK	SCORE
CORNELL UNIVERSITY	1	4.87
PURDUE UNIVERSITY—WEST LAFAYETTE	2	4.85
IOWA STATE UNIVERSITY	3	4.82
MICHIGAN STATE UNIVERSITY	4	4.80
OHIO STATE UNIVERSITY—COLUMBUS	5	4.76
UNIVERSITY OF CALIFORNIA—DAVIS	6	4.75
UNIVERSITY OF MINNESOTA—TWIN CITIES	7	4.74
UNIVERSITY OF WISCONSIN—MADISON	8	4.71
UNIVERSITY OF CALIFORNIA—BERKELEY	9	4.69
TEXAS A&M UNIVERSITY—COLLEGE STATION	10	4.65
PENNSYLVANIA STATE UNIVERSITY—UNIVERSITY PARK	11	4.64
KANSAS STATE UNIVERSITY	12	4.62
UNIVERSITY OF ILLINOIS—URBANA-CHAMPAIGN	13	4.61
UNIVERSITY OF MISSOURI—COLUMBIA	14	4.59
UNIVERSITY OF GEORGIA	15	4.55
COLORADO STATE UNIVERSITY	16	4.53
UNIVERSITY OF ARIZONA	17	4.50
UNIVERSITY OF FLORIDA	18	4.47
UNIVERSITY OF CALIFORNIA—RIVERSIDE	19	4.46
UNIVERSITY OF HAWAII—MANOA	20	4.43
NORTH CAROLINA STATE UNIVERSITY	21	4.41
LOUISIANA STATE UNIVERSITY—BATON ROUGE	22	4.39
AUBURN UNIVERSITY	23	4.37
RUTGERS UNIVERSITY	24	4.35
OREGON STATE UNIVERSITY	25	4.32
VIRGINIA POLYTECHNIC INSTITUTE AND STATE UNIVERSITY	26	4.28
UNIVERSITY OF KENTUCKY	27	4.24
MISSISSIPPI STATE UNIVERSITY	28	4.22
UNIVERSITY OF MASSACHUSETTS—AMHERST	29	4.21
WASHINGTON STATE UNIVERSITY	30	4.20

POLITICAL SCIENCE
LEADING INSTITUTIONS—RATING OF GRADUATE PROGRAMS

INSTITUTION	RANK	SCORE
YALE UNIVERSITY	1	4.92
UNIVERSITY OF MICHIGAN—ANN ARBOR	2	4.91
UNIVERSITY OF CALIFORNIA—BERKELEY	3	4.90
HARVARD UNIVERSITY	4	4.88
UNIVERSITY OF CHICAGO	5	4.86
PRINCETON UNIVERSITY	6	4.85
STANFORD UNIVERSITY	7	4.84
UNIVERSITY OF WISCONSIN—MADISON	8	4.82
UNIVERSITY OF CALIFORNIA—LOS ANGELES	9	4.80
CORNELL UNIVERSITY	10	4.78
MASSACHUSETTS INSTITUTE OF TECHNOLOGY	11	4.77
COLUMBIA UNIVERSITY	12	4.74
UNIVERSITY OF ROCHESTER	13	4.72
UNIVERSITY OF MINNESOTA—TWIN CITIES	14	4.67
DUKE UNIVERSITY	15	4.66
UNIVERSITY OF NORTH CAROLINA—CHAPEL HILL	16	4.65
UNIVERSITY OF TEXAS—AUSTIN	17	4.63
JOHNS HOPKINS UNIVERSITY	18	4.61
OHIO STATE UNIVERSITY—COLUMBUS	19	4.58
UNIVERSITY OF NOTRE DAME	20	4.57
INDIANA UNIVERSITY—BLOOMINGTON	21	4.53
UNIVERSITY OF ILLINOIS—URBANA-CHAMPAIGN	22	4.51
UNIVERSITY OF CALIFORNIA—SAN DIEGO	23	4.46
UNIVERSITY OF VIRGINIA	24	4.42
UNIVERSITY OF PENNSYLVANIA	25	4.37
NORTHWESTERN UNIVERSITY	26	4.34
UNIVERSITY OF PITTSBURGH	27	4.31
UNIVERSITY OF WASHINGTON	28	4.26
MICHIGAN STATE UNIVERSITY	29	4.24
UNIVERSITY OF IOWA	30	4.21
WASHINGTON UNIVERSITY	31	4.16
EMORY UNIVERSITY	32	4.14
RUTGERS UNIVERSITY	33	4.12
GEORGETOWN UNIVERSITY	34	4.10

PSYCHOLOGY

Leading Institutions—Rating of Graduate Programs

INSTITUTION	RANK	SCORE
STANFORD UNIVERSITY	1	4.72
YALE UNIVERSITY	2	4.70
UNIVERSITY OF PENNSYLVANIA	3	4.69
UNIVERSITY OF MICHIGAN—ANN ARBOR	4	4.68
UNIVERSITY OF MINNESOTA—TWIN CITIES	5	4.66
HARVARD UNIVERSITY	6	4.65
UNIVERSITY OF CALIFORNIA—BERKELEY	7	4.63
UNIVERSITY OF ILLINOIS—URBANA-CHAMPAIGN	8	4.60
UNIVERSITY OF CALIFORNIA—LOS ANGELES	9	4.58
UNIVERSITY OF CHICAGO	10	4.55
UNIVERSITY OF CALIFORNIA—SAN DIEGO	11	4.53
CARNEGIE MELLON UNIVERSITY	12	4.52
INDIANA UNIVERSITY—BLOOMINGTON	13	4.48
COLUMBIA UNIVERSITY	14	4.47
PRINCETON UNIVERSITY	15	4.45
UNIVERSITY OF WISCONSIN—MADISON	16	4.43
UNIVERSITY OF OREGON	17	4.42
UNIVERSITY OF VIRGINIA	18	4.41
UNIVERSITY OF TEXAS—AUSTIN	19	4.40
UNIVERSITY OF WASHINGTON	20	4.39
CORNELL UNIVERSITY	21	4.38
UNIVERSITY OF COLORADO—BOULDER	22	4.36
BROWN UNIVERSITY	23	4.35
UNIVERSITY OF NORTH CAROLINA—CHAPEL HILL	24	4.33
NORTHWESTERN UNIVERSITY	25	4.30
JOHNS HOPKINS UNIVERSITY	26	4.29
OHIO STATE UNIVERSITY—COLUMBUS	27	4.28
PURDUE UNIVERSITY—WEST LAFAYETTE	28	4.27
DUKE UNIVERSITY	29	4.26
UNIVERSITY OF ROCHESTER	30	4.25
STATE UNIVERSITY OF NEW YORK AT STONY BROOK	31	4.23
RUTGERS UNIVERSITY	32	4.19
UNIVERSITY OF IOWA	33	4.18
PENNSYLVANIA STATE UNIVERSITY—UNIVERSITY PARK	34	4.17
VANDERBILT UNIVERSITY	35	4.15
NEW YORK UNIVERSITY	36	4.14
UNIVERSITY OF SOUTHERN CALIFORNIA	37	4.13
UNIVERSITY OF CALIFORNIA—IRVINE	38	4.12
UNIVERSITY OF MASSACHUSETTS—AMHERST	39	4.11
UNIVERSITY OF FLORIDA	40	4.09

PSYCHOLOGY—CHILD DEVELOPMENT
Leading Institutions—Rating of Graduate Programs

INSTITUTION	RANK	SCORE
STANFORD UNIVERSITY	1	4.43
YALE UNIVERSITY	2	4.40
UNIVERSITY OF ILLINOIS—URBANA-CHAMPAIGN	3	4.36
UNIVERSITY OF MINNESOTA—TWIN CITIES	4	4.32
UNIVERSITY OF CALIFORNIA—BERKELEY	5	4.30
CARNEGIE MELLON UNIVERSITY	6	4.27
CORNELL UNIVERSITY	7	4.26
UNIVERSITY OF WISCONSIN—MADISON	8	4.25
UNIVERSITY OF TEXAS—AUSTIN	9	4.20
UNIVERSITY OF VIRGINIA	10	4.18
UNIVERSITY OF NORTH CAROLINA—CHAPEL HILL	11	4.15
DUKE UNIVERSITY	12	4.13
UNIVERSITY OF IOWA	13	4.12
UNIVERSITY OF FLORIDA	14	4.10

PSYCHOLOGY—CLINICAL

LEADING INSTITUTIONS—RATING OF GRADUATE PROGRAMS

INSTITUTION	RANK	SCORE
YALE UNIVERSITY	1	4.67
UNIVERSITY OF PENNSYLVANIA	2	4.65
UNIVERSITY OF MICHIGAN—ANN ARBOR	3	4.61
UNIVERSITY OF MINNESOTA—TWIN CITIES	4	4.58
UNIVERSITY OF CALIFORNIA—BERKELEY	5	4.57
UNIVERSITY OF CALIFORNIA—LOS ANGELES	6	4.53
INDIANA UNIVERSITY—BLOOMINGTON	7	4.50
UNIVERSITY OF OREGON	8	4.49
UNIVERSITY OF COLORADO—BOULDER	9	4.48
UNIVERSITY OF WASHINGTON	10	4.45
UNIVERSITY OF TEXAS—AUSTIN	11	4.43
UNIVERSITY OF NORTH CAROLINA—CHAPEL HILL	12	4.41
NORTHWESTERN UNIVERSITY	13	4.40
NEW YORK UNIVERSITY	14	4.38
PENNSYLVANIA STATE UNIVERSITY—UNIVERSITY PARK	15	4.37
DUKE UNIVERSITY	16	4.36
RUTGERS UNIVERSITY	17	4.26
UNIVERSITY OF IOWA	18	4.25
OHIO STATE UNIVERSITY—COLUMBUS	19	4.22
WASHINGTON UNIVERSITY	20	4.20
PURDUE UNIVERSITY—WEST LAFAYETTE	21	4.18
STATE UNIVERSITY OF NEW YORK AT STONY BROOK	22	4.15
UNIVERSITY OF SOUTHERN CALIFORNIA	23	4.11
VANDERBILT UNIVERSITY	24	4.05

PSYCHOLOGY—COGNITIVE
Leading Institutions—Rating of Graduate Programs

INSTITUTION	RANK	SCORE
STANFORD UNIVERSITY	1	4.58
UNIVERSITY OF MICHIGAN—ANN ARBOR	2	4.56
YALE UNIVERSITY	3	4.54
UNIVERSITY OF CALIFORNIA—LOS ANGELES	4	4.53
UNIVERSITY OF MINNESOTA—TWIN CITIES	5	4.52
UNIVERSITY OF PENNSYLVANIA	6	4.50
UNIVERSITY OF CALIFORNIA—BERKELEY	7	4.49
CARNEGIE MELLON UNIVERSITY	8	4.46
CORNELL UNIVERSITY	9	4.43
UNIVERSITY OF WISCONSIN—MADISON	10	4.40
COLUMBIA UNIVERSITY	11	4.39
UNIVERSITY OF TEXAS—AUSTIN	12	4.36
INDIANA UNIVERSITY—BLOOMINGTON	13	4.35
UNIVERSITY OF VIRGINIA	14	4.34
OHIO STATE UNIVERSITY—COLUMBUS	15	4.33
UNIVERSITY OF OREGON	16	4.32
UNIVERSITY OF COLORADO—BOULDER	17	4.31
NORTHWESTERN UNIVERSITY	18	4.30
UNIVERSITY OF NORTH CAROLINA—CHAPEL HILL	19	4.28
UNIVERSITY OF MASSACHUSETTS—AMHERST	20	4.26
DUKE UNIVERSITY	21	4.25
RUTGERS UNIVERSITY	22	4.23
UNIVERSITY OF ROCHESTER	23	4.20
JOHNS HOPKINS UNIVERSITY	24	4.18
PURDUE UNIVERSITY—WEST LAFAYETTE	25	4.17
UNIVERSITY OF IOWA	26	4.15
STATE UNIVERSITY OF NEW YORK AT BUFFALO	27	4.14
VANDERBILT UNIVERSITY	28	4.12
STATE UNIVERSITY OF NEW YORK AT STONY BROOK	29	4.10
UNIVERSITY OF FLORIDA	30	4.08
UNIVERSITY OF SOUTHERN CALIFORNIA	31	4.05

PSYCHOLOGY—DEVELOPMENTAL

LEADING INSTITUTIONS—RATING OF GRADUATE PROGRAMS

INSTITUTION	RANK	SCORE
STANFORD UNIVERSITY	1	4.61
UNIVERSITY OF MICHIGAN—ANN ARBOR	2	4.60
YALE UNIVERSITY	3	4.57
UNIVERSITY OF ILLINOIS—URBANA-CHAMPAIGN	4	4.53
UNIVERSITY OF CALIFORNIA—LOS ANGELES	5	4.52
UNIVERSITY OF PENNSYLVANIA	6	4.48
UNIVERSITY OF MINNESOTA—TWIN CITIES	7	4.46
CARNEGIE MELLON UNIVERSITY	8	4.43
UNIVERSITY OF CALIFORNIA—BERKELEY	9	4.42
CORNELL UNIVERSITY	10	4.41
UNIVERSITY OF TEXAS—AUSTIN	11	4.38
UNIVERSITY OF WASHINGTON	12	4.36
INDIANA UNIVERSITY—BLOOMINGTON	13	4.35
UNIVERSITY OF VIRGINIA	14	4.32
OHIO STATE UNIVERSITY—COLUMBUS	15	4.30
UNIVERSITY OF NORTH CAROLINA—CHAPEL HILL	16	4.26
UNIVERSITY OF OREGON	17	4.25
UNIVERSITY OF CALIFORNIA—IRVINE	18	4.23
RUTGERS UNIVERSITY	19	4.22
PURDUE UNIVERSITY—WEST LAFAYETTE	20	4.21
PENNSYLVANIA STATE UNIVERSITY—UNIVERSITY PARK	21	4.19
UNIVERSITY OF ROCHESTER	22	4.16
DUKE UNIVERSITY	23	4.14
UNIVERSITY OF IOWA	24	4.13
UNIVERSITY OF MASSACHUSETTS—AMHERST	25	4.11
UNIVERSITY OF SOUTHERN CALIFORNIA	26	4.09

PSYCHOLOGY—EXPERIMENTAL (GENERAL)

Leading Institutions—Rating of Graduate Programs

INSTITUTION	RANK	SCORE
YALE UNIVERSITY	1	4.55
UNIVERSITY OF MINNESOTA—TWIN CITIES	2	4.53
UNIVERSITY OF WASHINGTON	3	4.51
CORNELL UNIVERSITY	4	4.49
COLUMBIA UNIVERSITY	5	4.48
UNIVERSITY OF PENNSYLVANIA	6	4.46
OHIO STATE UNIVERSITY—COLUMBUS	7	4.43
UNIVERSITY OF COLORADO—BOULDER	8	4.42
UNIVERSITY OF NORTH CAROLINA—CHAPEL HILL	9	4.39
PENNSYLVANIA STATE UNIVERSITY—UNIVERSITY PARK	10	4.37
NEW YORK UNIVERSITY	11	4.34
DUKE UNIVERSITY	12	4.33
JOHNS HOPKINS UNIVERSITY	13	4.29
BROWN UNIVERSITY	14	4.28
UNIVERSITY OF IOWA	15	4.25
STATE UNIVERSITY OF NEW YORK AT STONY BROOK	16	4.20

PSYCHOLOGY—INDUSTRIAL/ORGANIZATIONAL

Leading Institutions—Rating of Graduate Programs

INSTITUTION	RANK	SCORE
UNIVERSITY OF MICHIGAN—ANN ARBOR	1	4.61
UNIVERSITY OF MINNESOTA—TWIN CITIES	2	4.60
OHIO STATE UNIVERSITY—COLUMBUS	3	4.58
PURDUE UNIVERSITY—WEST LAFAYETTE	4	4.55
NEW YORK UNIVERSITY	5	4.52
PENNSYLVANIA STATE UNIVERSITY—UNIVERSITY PARK	6	4.50
CITY UNIVERSITY OF NEW YORK GRADUATE SCHOOL	7	4.46
MICHIGAN STATE UNIVERSITY	8	4.43
NORTH CAROLINA STATE UNIVERSITY	9	4.41
UNIVERSITY OF HOUSTON	10	4.38
STATE UNIVERSITY OF NEW YORK AT BUFFALO	11	4.35
GEORGIA INSTITUTE OF TECHNOLOGY	12	4.32
ILLINOIS INSTITUTE OF TECHNOLOGY	13	4.29
UNIVERSITY OF CINCINNATI	14	4.26
GEORGE WASHINGTON UNIVERSITY	15	4.21
TEXAS A&M UNIVERSITY—COLLEGE STATION	16	4.19
WAYNE STATE UNIVERSITY	17	4.16

PSYCHOLOGY—PERSONALITY
Leading Institutions—Rating of Graduate Programs

INSTITUTION	RANK	SCORE
STANFORD UNIVERSITY	1	4.49
UNIVERSITY OF MICHIGAN—ANN ARBOR	2	4.46
YALE UNIVERSITY	3	4.42
UNIVERSITY OF MINNESOTA—TWIN CITIES	4	4.39
UNIVERSITY OF CALIFORNIA—BERKELEY	5	4.38
UNIVERSITY OF WASHINGTON	6	4.37
CORNELL UNIVERSITY	7	4.33
UNIVERSITY OF WISCONSIN—MADISON	8	4.30
COLUMBIA UNIVERSITY	9	4.28
UNIVERSITY OF TEXAS—AUSTIN	10	4.26
UNIVERSITY OF OREGON	11	4.25
NORTHWESTERN UNIVERSITY	12	4.21
DUKE UNIVERSITY	13	4.19
JOHNS HOPKINS UNIVERSITY	14	4.18
NEW YORK UNIVERSITY	15	4.17
PURDUE UNIVERSITY—WEST LAFAYETTE	16	4.16
UNIVERSITY OF MASSACHUSETTS—AMHERST	17	4.15
STATE UNIVERSITY OF NEW YORK AT STONY BROOK	18	4.14

PSYCHOLOGY—SENSATION AND PERCEPTION

LEADING INSTITUTIONS—RATING OF GRADUATE PROGRAMS

INSTITUTION	RANK	SCORE
STANFORD UNIVERSITY	1	4.53
UNIVERSITY OF MICHIGAN—ANN ARBOR	2	4.52
DUKE UNIVERSITY	3	4.48
UNIVERSITY OF PENNSYLVANIA	4	4.46
UNIVERSITY OF MINNESOTA—TWIN CITIES	5	4.45
OHIO STATE UNIVERSITY—COLUMBUS	6	4.42
UNIVERSITY OF WISCONSIN—MADISON	7	4.39
UNIVERSITY OF WASHINGTON	8	4.38
UNIVERSITY OF TEXAS—AUSTIN	9	4.37
COLUMBIA UNIVERSITY	10	4.36
PURDUE UNIVERSITY—WEST LAFAYETTE	11	4.32
JOHNS HOPKINS UNIVERSITY	12	4.29
UNIVERSITY OF VIRGINIA	13	4.27
UNIVERSITY OF ROCHESTER	14	4.23
STATE UNIVERSITY OF NEW YORK AT BUFFALO	15	4.22
UNIVERSITY OF FLORIDA	16	4.21
CASE WESTERN RESERVE UNIVERSITY	17	4.20
UNIVERSITY OF ILLINOIS—CHICAGO	18	4.16
UNIVERSITY OF CALIFORNIA—SANTA BARBARA	19	4.14
STATE UNIVERSITY OF NEW YORK AT STONY BROOK	20	4.13
UNIVERSITY OF CALIFORNIA—DAVIS	21	4.12
TULANE UNIVERSITY	22	4.11
INDIANA UNIVERSITY—BLOOMINGTON	23	4.10
LOYOLA UNIVERSITY OF CHICAGO	24	4.06

PSYCHOLOGY—SOCIAL

Leading Institutions—Rating of Graduate Programs

INSTITUTION	RANK	SCORE
STANFORD UNIVERSITY	1	4.68
UNIVERSITY OF MICHIGAN—ANN ARBOR	2	4.66
YALE UNIVERSITY	3	4.65
HARVARD UNIVERSITY	4	4.63
UNIVERSITY OF CALIFORNIA—LOS ANGELES	5	4.60
UNIVERSITY OF PENNSYLVANIA	6	4.59
CARNEGIE MELLON UNIVERSITY	7	4.58
UNIVERSITY OF CALIFORNIA—BERKELEY	8	4.56
UNIVERSITY OF MINNESOTA—TWIN CITIES	9	4.54
CORNELL UNIVERSITY	10	4.52
UNIVERSITY OF WISCONSIN—MADISON	11	4.48
COLUMBIA UNIVERSITY	12	4.46
UNIVERSITY OF TEXAS—AUSTIN	13	4.43
UNIVERSITY OF WASHINGTON	14	4.42
INDIANA UNIVERSITY—BLOOMINGTON	15	4.40
UNIVERSITY OF VIRGINIA	16	4.39
UNIVERSITY OF OREGON	17	4.36
OHIO STATE UNIVERSITY—COLUMBUS	18	4.33
NORTHWESTERN UNIVERSITY	19	4.32
UNIVERSITY OF COLORADO—BOULDER	20	4.31
UNIVERSITY OF NORTH CAROLINA—CHAPEL HILL	21	4.30
PURDUE UNIVERSITY—WEST LAFAYETTE	22	4.26
JOHNS HOPKINS UNIVERSITY	23	4.25
DUKE UNIVERSITY	24	4.22
NEW YORK UNIVERSITY	25	4.21
UNIVERSITY OF IOWA	26	4.20
PENNSYLVANIA STATE UNIVERSITY—UNIVERSITY PARK	27	4.18
UNIVERSITY OF ROCHESTER	28	4.17
RUTGERS UNIVERSITY	29	4.14
UNIVERSITY OF SOUTHERN CALIFORNIA	30	4.12
STATE UNIVERSITY OF NEW YORK AT STONY BROOK	31	4.11
UNIVERSITY OF FLORIDA	32	4.09

PUBLIC ADMINISTRATION

LEADING INSTITUTIONS—RATING OF GRADUATE PROGRAMS

INSTITUTION	RANK	SCORE
SYRACUSE UNIVERSITY	1	4.91
HARVARD UNIVERSITY	2	4.89
INDIANA UNIVERSITY—BLOOMINGTON	3	4.86
UNIVERSITY OF SOUTHERN CALIFORNIA	4	4.83
UNIVERSITY OF CALIFORNIA—BERKELEY	5	4.82
UNIVERSITY OF TEXAS—AUSTIN	6	4.79
PRINCETON UNIVERSITY	7	4.76
UNIVERSITY OF PITTSBURGH	8	4.71
UNIVERSITY OF MICHIGAN—ANN ARBOR	9	4.69
UNIVERSITY OF GEORGIA	10	4.66
CARNEGIE MELLON UNIVERSITY	11	4.64
UNIVERSITY OF MINNESOTA—TWIN CITIES	12	4.60
OHIO STATE UNIVERSITY—COLUMBUS	13	4.54
AMERICAN UNIVERSITY	14	4.50
UNIVERSITY OF NORTH CAROLINA—CHAPEL HILL	15	4.45
STATE UNIVERSITY OF NEW YORK AT ALBANY	16	4.41
GEORGE WASHINGTON UNIVERSITY	17	4.34
FLORIDA STATE UNIVERSITY	18	4.28
UNIVERSITY OF KANSAS	19	4.22

RADIO/TV/FILM

Leading Institutions—Rating of Graduate Programs

INSTITUTION	RANK	SCORE
UNIVERSITY OF SOUTHERN CALIFORNIA	1	4.88
UNIVERSITY OF CALIFORNIA—LOS ANGELES	2	4.86
NEW YORK UNIVERSITY	3	4.85
NORTHWESTERN UNIVERSITY	4	4.82
INDIANA UNIVERSITY—BLOOMINGTON	5	4.78
FLORIDA STATE UNIVERSITY	6	4.76
COLUMBIA UNIVERSITY	7	4.74
UNIVERSITY OF TEXAS—AUSTIN	8	4.70
UNIVERSITY OF NORTH CAROLINA—CHAPEL HILL	9	4.66
TEMPLE UNIVERSITY	10	4.63

RUSSIAN
Leading Institutions—Rating of Graduate Programs

INSTITUTION	RANK	SCORE
HARVARD UNIVERSITY	1	4.87
COLUMBIA UNIVERSITY	2	4.85
CORNELL UNIVERSITY	3	4.81
UNIVERSITY OF PENNSYLVANIA	4	4.77
UNIVERSITY OF WASHINGTON	5	4.72
UNIVERSITY OF ILLINOIS—URBANA-CHAMPAIGN	6	4.69
UNIVERSITY OF NORTH CAROLINA—CHAPEL HILL	7	4.66
BROWN UNIVERSITY	8	4.59
MICHIGAN STATE UNIVERSITY	9	4.54
OHIO STATE UNIVERSITY—COLUMBUS	10	4.49

SLAVIC LANGUAGES
LEADING INSTITUTIONS—RATING OF GRADUATE PROGRAMS

INSTITUTION	RANK	SCORE
HARVARD UNIVERSITY	1	4.89
COLUMBIA UNIVERSITY	2	4.86
INDIANA UNIVERSITY—BLOOMINGTON	3	4.83
CORNELL UNIVERSITY	4	4.79
UNIVERSITY OF WISCONSIN—MADISON	5	4.76
UNIVERSITY OF WASHINGTON	6	4.75
UNIVERSITY OF ILLINOIS—URBANA-CHAMPAIGN	7	4.70
UNIVERSITY OF MICHIGAN—ANN ARBOR	8	4.68
UNIVERSITY OF CALIFORNIA—BERKELEY	9	4.65
STANFORD UNIVERSITY	10	4.60
OHIO STATE UNIVERSITY—COLUMBUS	11	4.58
UNIVERSITY OF CHICAGO	12	4.54
UNIVERSITY OF NORTH CAROLINA—CHAPEL HILL	13	4.52
UNIVERSITY OF CALIFORNIA—LOS ANGELES	14	4.47
BROWN UNIVERSITY	15	4.45
YALE UNIVERSITY	16	4.40

SOCIAL WELFARE/SOCIAL WORK

LEADING INSTITUTIONS—RATING OF GRADUATE PROGRAMS

INSTITUTION	RANK	SCORE
UNIVERSITY OF CHICAGO	1	4.69
COLUMBIA UNIVERSITY	2	4.68
UNIVERSITY OF MICHIGAN—ANN ARBOR	3	4.64
UNIVERSITY OF WISCONSIN—MADISON	4	4.62
UNIVERSITY OF PENNSYLVANIA	5	4.58
CASE WESTERN RESERVE UNIVERSITY	6	4.55
BRANDEIS UNIVERSITY	7	4.52
UNIVERSITY OF PITTSBURGH	8	4.49
WASHINGTON UNIVERSITY	9	4.44
UNIVERSITY OF MINNESOTA—TWIN CITIES	10	4.42
OHIO STATE UNIVERSITY—COLUMBUS	11	4.40
UNIVERSITY OF CALIFORNIA—BERKELEY	12	4.38
YESHIVA UNIVERSITY	13	4.36
RUTGERS UNIVERSITY	14	4.34
UNIVERSITY OF SOUTHERN CALIFORNIA	15	4.31
CATHOLIC UNIVERSITY OF AMERICA	16	4.30
MICHIGAN STATE UNIVERSITY	17	4.28
ST. LOUIS UNIVERSITY	18	4.25
UNIVERSITY OF TEXAS—AUSTIN	19	4.24
TULANE UNIVERSITY	20	4.22
UNIVERSITY OF UTAH	21	4.20
UNIVERSITY OF DENVER	22	4.19
UNIVERSITY OF CALIFORNIA—LOS ANGELES	23	4.18
FLORIDA STATE UNIVERSITY	24	4.17
CITY UNIVERSITY OF NEW YORK—HUNTER COLLEGE	25	4.16
UNIVERSITY OF ILLINOIS—CHICAGO	26	4.15
UNIVERSITY OF MARYLAND—BALTIMORE COUNTY	27	4.14
SMITH COLLEGE	28	4.13
UNIVERSITY OF WASHINGTON	29	4.12
HOWARD UNIVERSITY	30	4.11
BRYN MAWR COLLEGE	31	4.10

SOCIOLOGY

LEADING INSTITUTIONS—RATING OF GRADUATE PROGRAMS

INSTITUTION	RANK	SCORE
UNIVERSITY OF WISCONSIN—MADISON	1	4.87
UNIVERSITY OF MICHIGAN—ANN ARBOR	2	4.85
UNIVERSITY OF CHICAGO	3	4.82
HARVARD UNIVERSITY	4	4.79
UNIVERSITY OF NORTH CAROLINA—CHAPEL HILL	5	4.76
UNIVERSITY OF PENNSYLVANIA	6	4.73
STANFORD UNIVERSITY	7	4.71
UNIVERSITY OF WASHINGTON	8	4.66
UNIVERSITY OF CALIFORNIA—LOS ANGELES	9	4.64
NORTHWESTERN UNIVERSITY	10	4.62
INDIANA UNIVERSITY—BLOOMINGTON	11	4.60
UNIVERSITY OF TEXAS—AUSTIN	12	4.58
UNIVERSITY OF ARIZONA	13	4.55
PRINCETON UNIVERSITY	14	4.52
COLUMBIA UNIVERSITY	15	4.51
JOHNS HOPKINS UNIVERSITY	16	4.50
YALE UNIVERSITY	17	4.48
DUKE UNIVERSITY	18	4.46
PENNSYLVANIA STATE UNIVERSITY—UNIVERSITY PARK	19	4.43
UNIVERSITY OF MINNESOTA—TWIN CITIES	20	4.42
UNIVERSITY OF CALIFORNIA—SAN DIEGO	21	4.38
STATE UNIVERSITY OF NEW YORK AT STONY BROOK	22	4.35
UNIVERSITY OF CALIFORNIA—BERKELEY	23	4.32
OHIO STATE UNIVERSITY—COLUMBUS	24	4.27
UNIVERSITY OF CALIFORNIA—SANTA BARBARA	25	4.26
VANDERBILT UNIVERSITY	26	4.22
UNIVERSITY OF ILLINOIS—URBANA-CHAMPAIGN	27	4.20
STATE UNIVERSITY OF NEW YORK AT ALBANY	28	4.16
RUTGERS UNIVERSITY	29	4.12
WASHINGTON STATE UNIVERSITY	30	4.10
UNIVERSITY OF MARYLAND—COLLEGE PARK	31	4.08
NEW YORK UNIVERSITY	32	4.06

SPANISH

<small>Leading Institutions—Rating of Graduate Programs</small>

INSTITUTION	RANK	SCORE
DUKE UNIVERSITY	1	4.87
COLUMBIA UNIVERSITY	2	4.85
PRINCETON UNIVERSITY	3	4.81
BROWN UNIVERSITY	4	4.76
UNIVERSITY OF PENNSYLVANIA	5	4.73
CORNELL UNIVERSITY	6	4.70
UNIVERSITY OF WISCONSIN—MADISON	7	4.66
UNIVERSITY OF VIRGINIA	8	4.63
HARVARD UNIVERSITY	9	4.61
UNIVERSITY OF CALIFORNIA—BERKELEY	10	4.58
UNIVERSITY OF TEXAS—AUSTIN	11	4.55
UNIVERSITY OF MICHIGAN—ANN ARBOR	12	4.53
STANFORD UNIVERSITY	13	4.51
UNIVERSITY OF CALIFORNIA—LOS ANGELES	14	4.49
INDIANA UNIVERSITY—BLOOMINGTON	15	4.46
UNIVERSITY OF CALIFORNIA—IRVINE	16	4.42
UNIVERSITY OF CALIFORNIA—SAN DIEGO	17	4.41
CITY UNIVERSITY OF NEW YORK GRADUATE SCHOOL	18	4.38
UNIVERSITY OF CALIFORNIA—DAVIS	19	4.36
UNIVERSITY OF KANSAS	20	4.35
UNIVERSITY OF ILLINOIS—URBANA-CHAMPAIGN	21	4.32
NEW YORK UNIVERSITY	22	4.30
PENNSYLVANIA STATE UNIVERSITY—UNIVERSITY PARK	23	4.27
UNIVERSITY OF CALIFORNIA—SANTA BARBARA	24	4.24
UNIVERSITY OF PITTSBURGH	25	4.20
UNIVERSITY OF MINNESOTA—TWIN CITIES	26	4.18
WASHINGTON UNIVERSITY	27	4.14
UNIVERSITY OF NORTH CAROLINA—CHAPEL HILL	28	4.12
GEORGETOWN UNIVERSITY	29	4.08
UNIVERSITY OF KENTUCKY	30	4.05

SPEECH PATHOLOGY/AUDIOLOGY
LEADING INSTITUTIONS—RATING OF GRADUATE PROGRAMS

INSTITUTION	RANK	SCORE
NORTHWESTERN UNIVERSITY	1	4.80
UNIVERSITY OF IOWA	2	4.79
UNIVERSITY OF MINNESOTA—TWIN CITIES	3	4.78
OHIO STATE UNIVERSITY—COLUMBUS	4	4.73
PENNSYLVANIA STATE UNIVERSITY—UNIVERSITY PARK	5	4.70
PURDUE UNIVERSITY—WEST LAFAYETTE	6	4.66
INDIANA UNIVERSITY—BLOOMINGTON	7	4.65
UNIVERSITY OF WASHINGTON	8	4.64
UNIVERSITY OF WISCONSIN—MADISON	9	4.60
WAYNE STATE UNIVERSITY	10	4.58
UNIVERSITY OF ILLINOIS—URBANA-CHAMPAIGN	11	4.55
MICHIGAN STATE UNIVERSITY	12	4.52
CASE WESTERN RESERVE UNIVERSITY	13	4.49
UNIVERSITY OF TEXAS—AUSTIN	14	4.46
UNIVERSITY OF UTAH	15	4.45
STATE UNIVERSITY OF NEW YORK AT BUFFALO	16	4.42
NEW YORK UNIVERSITY	17	4.39
UNIVERSITY OF COLORADO—BOULDER	18	4.38
UNIVERSITY OF PITTSBURGH	19	4.35
TEMPLE UNIVERSITY	20	4.30
BOSTON UNIVERSITY	21	4.28

STATISTICS
LEADING INSTITUTIONS—RATING OF GRADUATE PROGRAMS

INSTITUTION	RANK	SCORE
STANFORD UNIVERSITY	1	4.93
UNIVERSITY OF CALIFORNIA—BERKELEY	2	4.92
UNIVERSITY OF CHICAGO	3	4.91
CORNELL UNIVERSITY	4	4.89
HARVARD UNIVERSITY	5	4.86
UNIVERSITY OF WASHINGTON	6	4.83
PURDUE UNIVERSITY—WEST LAFAYETTE	7	4.80
UNIVERSITY OF WISCONSIN—MADISON	8	4.78
UNIVERSITY OF CALIFORNIA—LOS ANGELES	9	4.75
UNIVERSITY OF MINNESOTA—TWIN CITIES	10	4.73
UNIVERSITY OF NORTH CAROLINA—CHAPEL HILL	11	4.72
TEXAS A&M UNIVERSITY—COLLEGE STATION	12	4.71
CARNEGIE MELLON UNIVERSITY	13	4.68
IOWA STATE UNIVERSITY	14	4.66
PENNSYLVANIA STATE UNIVERSITY—UNIVERSITY PARK	15	4.64
RUTGERS UNIVERSITY	16	4.62
YALE UNIVERSITY	17	4.58
JOHNS HOPKINS UNIVERSITY	18	4.55
NORTH CAROLINA STATE UNIVERSITY	19	4.52
COLUMBIA UNIVERSITY	20	4.51
UNIVERSITY OF MICHIGAN—ANN ARBOR	21	4.49
UNIVERSITY OF ILLINOIS—URBANA-CHAMPAIGN	22	4.45
UNIVERSITY OF PENNSYLVANIA	23	4.43
OHIO STATE UNIVERSITY—COLUMBUS	24	4.40
MICHIGAN STATE UNIVERSITY	25	4.38
UNIVERSITY OF IOWA	26	4.35
FLORIDA STATE UNIVERSITY	27	4.33
UNIVERSITY OF FLORIDA	28	4.27
UNIVERSITY OF PITTSBURGH	29	4.26
NORTHWESTERN UNIVERSITY	30	4.21

TOXICOLOGY
LEADING INSTITUTIONS—RATING OF GRADUATE PROGRAMS

INSTITUTION	RANK	SCORE
JOHNS HOPKINS UNIVERSITY	1	4.91
DUKE UNIVERSITY	2	4.90
VANDERBILT UNIVERSITY	3	4.89
UNIVERSITY OF NORTH CAROLINA—CHAPEL HILL	4	4.86
MASSACHUSETTS INSTITUTE OF TECHNOLOGY	5	4.85
UNIVERSITY OF WISCONSIN—MADISON	6	4.82
UNIVERSITY OF MICHIGAN—ANN ARBOR	7	4.81
NEW YORK UNIVERSITY	8	4.80
HARVARD UNIVERSITY	9	4.76
COLUMBIA UNIVERSITY	10	4.73
UNIVERSITY OF KANSAS	11	4.71
UNIVERSITY OF CALIFORNIA—DAVIS	12	4.68
MICHIGAN STATE UNIVERSITY	13	4.66
UNIVERSITY OF ALABAMA—BIRMINGHAM	14	4.64
CORNELL UNIVERSITY	15	4.61
UNIVERSITY OF ROCHESTER	16	4.58
UNIVERSITY OF WASHINGTON	17	4.55
UNIVERSITY OF TEXAS HEALTH SCIENCE CENTER AT HOUSTON	18	4.54
UNIVERSITY OF MEDICINE AND DENTISTRY OF NEW JERSEY—NEWARK	19	4.52
DARTMOUTH COLLEGE	20	4.49
NORTHWESTERN UNIVERSITY	21	4.48
CASE WESTERN RESERVE UNIVERSITY	22	4.45
IOWA STATE UNIVERSITY	23	4.43
OHIO STATE UNIVERSITY—COLUMBUS	24	4.42
UNIVERSITY OF TEXAS MEDICAL BRANCH AT GALVESTON SCHOOL OF MEDICINE	25	4.40
UNIVERSITY OF UTAH	26	4.36
UNIVERSITY OF CALIFORNIA—IRVINE	27	4.34
PURDUE UNIVERSITY—WEST LAFAYETTE	28	4.33
RUTGERS UNIVERSITY	29	4.30
OREGON STATE UNIVERSITY	30	4.29
STATE UNIVERSITY OF NEW YORK AT BUFFALO	31	4.26
UNIVERSITY OF FLORIDA	32	4.25
UNIVERSITY OF ARIZONA	33	4.21
TEXAS A&M UNIVERSITY—COLLEGE STATION	34	4.18

Part II
THE GOURMAN REPORT
LAW SCHOOLS

THE TOP 50 U.S. LAW SCHOOLS

A RATING OF U.S. LAW SCHOOLS

THE TOP 10 LAW SCHOOLS IN CANADA

A RATING OF LAW SCHOOLS IN CANADA

A RATING OF INTERNATIONAL LAW SCHOOLS

THE TOP 50 U.S. LAW SCHOOLS

Leading Institutions

INSTITUTION	RANK	SCORE
HARVARD UNIVERSITY	1	4.92
UNIVERSITY OF MICHIGAN—ANN ARBOR	2	4.91
YALE UNIVERSITY	3	4.90
UNIVERSITY OF CHICAGO	4	4.89
UNIVERSITY OF CALIFORNIA—BERKELEY	5	4.88
STANFORD UNIVERSITY	6	4.87
COLUMBIA UNIVERSITY	7	4.86
DUKE UNIVERSITY	8	4.85
UNIVERSITY OF PENNSYLVANIA	9	4.82
CORNELL UNIVERSITY	10	4.80
NEW YORK UNIVERSITY	11	4.79
UNIVERSITY OF TEXAS—AUSTIN	12	4.77
UNIVERSITY OF CALIFORNIA—LOS ANGELES	13	4.76
NORTHWESTERN UNIVERSITY	14	4.74
VANDERBILT UNIVERSITY	15	4.73
UNIVERSITY OF VIRGINIA	16	4.72
GEORGETOWN UNIVERSITY	17	4.69
UNIVERSITY OF NOTRE DAME	18	4.68
UNIVERSITY OF MINNESOTA—TWIN CITIES	19	4.63
UNIVERSITY OF CALIFORNIA—SAN FRANCISCO	20	4.61
UNIVERSITY OF IOWA	21	4.49
UNIVERSITY OF WISCONSIN—MADISON	22	4.47
BOSTON UNIVERSITY	23	4.45
FORDHAM UNIVERSITY	24	4.44
UNIVERSITY OF NORTH CAROLINA—CHAPEL HILL	25	4.43
UNIVERSITY OF WASHINGTON	26	4.41
UNIVERSITY OF SOUTHERN CALIFORNIA	27	4.39
UNIVERSITY OF CALIFORNIA—DAVIS	28	4.36
TULANE UNIVERSITY	29	4.35
INDIANA UNIVERSITY—BLOOMINGTON	30	4.33
BOSTON COLLEGE	31	4.32
GEORGE WASHINGTON UNIVERSITY	32	4.30
UNIVERSITY OF THE PACIFIC	33	4.28
OHIO STATE UNIVERSITY—COLUMBUS	34	4.26
SOUTHERN METHODIST UNIVERSITY	35	4.25
ALBANY LAW SCHOOL OF UNION UNIVERSITY	36	4.23
LOYOLA MARYMOUNT UNIVERSITY	37	4.22
UNIVERSITY OF ILLINOIS—URBANA-CHAMPAIGN	38	4.20
STATE UNIVERSITY OF NEW YORK AT BUFFALO	39	4.19
MARQUETTE UNIVERSITY	40	4.18

WASHINGTON UNIVERSITY	41	4.17
UNIVERSITY OF UTAH	42	4.16
HOFSTRA UNIVERSITY	43	4.15
ILLINOIS INSTITUTE OF TECHNOLOGY	44	3.90
CATHOLIC UNIVERSITY OF AMERICA	45	3.89
TEMPLE UNIVERSITY	46	3.88
UNIVERSITY OF GEORGIA	47	3.87
UNIVERSITY OF SAN DIEGO	48	3.86
PEPPERDINE UNIVERSITY	49	3.85
UNIVERSITY OF SAN FRANCISCO	50	3.84

A RATING OF U.S. LAW SCHOOLS

INSTITUTION (ALPHABETICAL ORDER)	RANK	SCORE
UNIVERSITY OF AKRON School of Law Akron, OH	124	2.88
UNIVERSITY OF ALABAMA School of Law Tuscaloosa, AL	101	3.23
ALBANY LAW SCHOOL OF UNION UNIVERSITY Albany, NY	36	4.23
AMERICAN UNIVERSITY Washington College of Law Washington, D.C.	54	3.80
ARIZONA STATE UNIVERSITY College of Law Tempe, AZ	95	3.29
UNIVERSITY OF ARIZONA College of Law Tucson, AZ	92	3.32
UNIVERSITY OF ARKANSAS School of Law Fayetteville, AR	127	2.85
UNIVERSITY OF ARKANSAS—LITTLE ROCK School of Law Little Rock, AR	155	2.41
UNIVERSITY OF BALTIMORE School of Law Baltimore, MD	145	2.61
BAYLOR UNIVERSITY School of Law Waco, TX	94	3.30
BOSTON COLLEGE Law School Newton, MA	31	4.32
BOSTON UNIVERSITY School of Law Boston, MA	23	4.45

Very Strong = 4.51-4.99   Strong = 4.01-4.49   Good = 3.61-3.99   Acceptable Plus = 3.01-3.59
Adequate = 2.51-2.99   Marginal = 2.01-2.49   Not Sufficient for Graduate Programs = 0.

BRIGHAM YOUNG UNIVERSITY   57   3.77
J. Reuben Clark Law School
Provo, UT

BROOKLYN LAW SCHOOL   72   3.62
Brooklyn, NY

CALIFORNIA WESTERN   125   2.87
School of Law
San Diego, CA

UNIVERSITY OF CALIFORNIA—BERKELEY   5   4.88
Boalt Hall School of Law
Berkeley, CA

UNIVERSITY OF CALIFORNIA—DAVIS   28   4.36
School of Law
Davis, CA

UNIVERSITY OF CALIFORNIA—LOS ANGELES   13   4.76
School of Law
Los Angeles, CA

UNIVERSITY OF CALIFORNIA—SAN FRANCISCO   20   4.61
Hastings College of Law
San Francisco, CA

CAMPBELL UNIVERSITY   166   2.24
Norman Adrian Wiggins School of Law
Buies Creek, NC

CAPITAL UNIVERSITY LAW SCHOOL   130   2.81
Columbus, OH

CASE WESTERN RESERVE UNIVERSITY   60   3.74
School of Law
Cleveland, OH

CATHOLIC UNIVERSITY OF AMERICA   45   3.89
Columbus School of Law
Washington, D.C.

CATHOLIC UNIVERSITY OF PUERTO RICO   164   2.28
Universidad Católica de Puerto Rico Escuela de Derecho
Ponce, PR

UNIVERSITY OF CHICAGO   4   4.89
Law School
Chicago, IL

UNIVERSITY OF CINCINNATI   97   3.27
College of Law
Cincinnati, OH

Very Strong = 4.51-4.99   Strong = 4.01-4.49   Good = 3.61-3.99   Acceptable Plus = 3.01-3.59
Adequate = 2.51-2.99   Marginal = 2.01-2.49   Not Sufficient for Graduate Programs = 0.

CITY UNIVERSITY OF NEW YORK—QUEENS COLLEGE School of Law at Queens College Flushing, NY	171	2.19
CLEVELAND STATE UNIVERSITY Cleveland-Marshall College of Law Cleveland, OH	115	3.09
UNIVERSITY OF COLORADO—BOULDER School of Law Boulder, CO	75	3.49
COLUMBIA UNIVERSITY School of Law New York, NY	7	4.86
UNIVERSITY OF CONNECTICUT School of Law Hartford, CT	87	3.37
CORNELL UNIVERSITY Law School Ithaca, NY	10	4.80
CREIGHTON UNIVERSITY School of Law Omaha, NE	114	3.10
UNIVERSITY OF DAYTON School of Law Dayton, OH	147	2.59
UNIVERSITY OF DENVER College of Law Denver, CO	53	3.81
DEPAUL UNIVERSITY College of Law Chicago, IL	78	3.46
DETROIT COLLEGE OF LAW AT MICHIGAN STATE UNIVERSITY East Lansing, MI	91	3.33
UNIVERSITY OF DETROIT School of Law Detroit, MI	79	3.45
DICKINSON SCHOOL OF LAW Carlisle, PA	98	3.26
DISTRICT OF COLUMBIA SCHOOL OF LAW Washington, D.C.	175	2.10

Very Strong = 4.51-4.99   Strong = 4.01-4.49   Good = 3.61-3.99   Acceptable Plus = 3.01-3.59
Adequate = 2.51-2.99   Marginal = 2.01-2.49   Not Sufficient for Graduate Programs = 0.

DRAKE UNIVERSITY
Law School
Des Moines, IA

117   3.07

DUKE UNIVERSITY
School of Law
Durham, NC

8   4.85

DUQUESNE UNIVERSITY
School of Law
Pittsburgh, PA

105   3.19

EMORY UNIVERSITY
School of Law
Atlanta, GA

51   3.83

FLORIDA STATE UNIVERSITY
College of Law
Tallahassee, FL

83   3.41

UNIVERSITY OF FLORIDA
College of Law
Gainesville, FL

56   3.78

FORDHAM UNIVERSITY
School of Law
New York, NY

24   4.44

FRANKLIN PIERCE LAW CENTER
Concord, NH

143   2.65

GEORGE MASON UNIVERSITY
School of Law
Arlington, VA

161   2.31

GEORGE WASHINGTON UNIVERSITY
Law School
Washington, D.C.

32   4.30

GEORGETOWN UNIVERSITY
Law Center
Washington, D.C.

17   4.69

GEORGIA STATE UNIVERSITY
College of Law
Atlanta, GA

170   2.20

UNIVERSITY OF GEORGIA
School of Law
Athens, GA

47   3.87

Very Strong = 4.51-4.99   Strong = 4.01-4.49   Good = 3.61-3.99   Acceptable Plus = 3.01-3.59
Adequate = 2.51-2.99   Marginal = 2.01-2.49   Not Sufficient for Graduate Programs = 0.

GOLDEN GATE UNIVERSITY School of Law San Francisco, CA	82	3.42
GONZAGA UNIVERSITY School of Law Spokane, WA	77	3.47
HAMLINE UNIVERSITY School of Law St. Paul, MN	131	2.80
HARVARD UNIVERSITY Law School Cambridge, MA	1	4.92
UNIVERSITY OF HAWAII—MANOA William S. Richardson School of Law Honolulu, HI	146	2.60
HOFSTRA UNIVERSITY School of Law Hempstead, NY	43	4.15
UNIVERSITY OF HOUSTON Law Center Houston, TX	66	3.68
HOWARD UNIVERSITY School of Law Washington, D.C.	126	2.86
UNIVERSITY OF IDAHO Moscow, ID	133	2.78
ILLINOIS INSTITUTE OF TECHNOLOGY Chicago-Kent College of Law Chicago, IL	44	3.90
UNIVERSITY OF ILLINOIS—URBANA-CHAMPAIGN College of Law Champaign, IL	38	4.20
INDIANA UNIVERSITY—BLOOMINGTON School of Law Bloomington, IN	30	4.33
INDIANA UNIVERSITY—INDIANAPOLIS School of Law Indianapolis, IN	110	3.14
INTER-AMERICAN UNIVERSITY OF PUERTO RICO School of Law Santurce, PR	167	2.23

Very Strong = 4.51-4.99   Strong = 4.01-4.49   Good = 3.61-3.99   Acceptable Plus = 3.01-3.59
Adequate = 2.51-2.99   Marginal = 2.01-2.49   Not Sufficient for Graduate Programs = 0.

UNIVERSITY OF IOWA   21   4.49
College of Law
Iowa City, IA

THE JOHN MARSHALL LAW SCHOOL   173   2.14
John Marshall Law School
Chicago, IL

UNIVERSITY OF KANSAS   63   3.71
School of Law
Lawrence, KS

UNIVERSITY OF KENTUCKY   99   3.25
College of Law
Lexington, KY

LEWIS AND CLARK COLLEGE   108   3.16
Northwestern School of Law
Portland, OR

LOUISIANA STATE UNIVERSITY—BATON ROUGE   86   3.38
Paul M. Hebert Law Center
Baton Rouge, LA

UNIVERSITY OF LOUISVILLE   96   3.28
School of Law
Louisville, KY

LOYOLA MARYMOUNT UNIVERSITY   37   4.22
Loyola Law School
Los Angeles, CA

LOYOLA UNIVERSITY NEW ORLEANS   152   2.49
School of Law
New Orleans, LA

LOYOLA UNIVERSITY OF CHICAGO   76   3.48
School of Law
Chicago, IL

UNIVERSITY OF MAINE   148   2.56
University of Maine School of Law
Portland, ME

MARQUETTE UNIVERSITY   40   4.18
Law School
Milwaukee, WI

UNIVERSITY OF MARYLAND—BALTIMORE COUNTY   71   3.63
School of Law
Baltimore, MD

Very Strong = 4.51-4.99   Strong = 4.01-4.49   Good = 3.61-3.99   Acceptable Plus = 3.01-3.59
Adequate = 2.51-2.99   Marginal = 2.01-2.49   Not Sufficient for Graduate Programs = 0.

THE UNIVERSITY OF MEMPHIS   141   2.68
Cecil C. Humphreys School of Law
Memphis, TN

MERCER UNIVERSITY   119   2.93
Walter F. George School of Law
Macon, GA

UNIVERSITY OF MIAMI   90   3.34
School of Law
Coral Gables, FL

UNIVERSITY OF MICHIGAN—ANN ARBOR   2   4.91
School of Law
Ann Arbor, MI

UNIVERSITY OF MINNESOTA—TWIN CITIES   19   4.63
Law School
Minneapolis, MN

MISSISSIPPI COLLEGE   168   2.22
School of Law
Jackson, MS

UNIVERSITY OF MISSISSIPPI   100   3.24
School of Law
University, MS

UNIVERSITY OF MISSOURI—COLUMBIA   62   3.72
School of Law
Columbia, MO

UNIVERSITY OF MISSOURI—KANSAS CITY   88   3.36
School of Law
Kansas City, MO

UNIVERSITY OF MONTANA   129   2.83
School of Law
Missoula, MT

UNIVERSITY OF NEBRASKA—LINCOLN   102   3.22
College of Law
Lincoln, NE

NEW ENGLAND SCHOOL OF LAW   116   3.08
Boston, MA

UNIVERSITY OF NEW MEXICO   128   2.84
School of Law
Albuquerque, NM

NEW YORK LAW SCHOOL   89   3.35
New York, NY

Very Strong = 4.51-4.99   Strong = 4.01-4.49   Good = 3.61-3.99   Acceptable Plus = 3.01-3.59
Adequate = 2.51-2.99   Marginal = 2.01-2.49   Not Sufficient for Graduate Programs = 0.

NEW YORK UNIVERSITY School of Law New York, NY	11	4.79
NORTH CAROLINA CENTRAL UNIVERSITY School of Law Durham, NC	165	2.26
UNIVERSITY OF NORTH CAROLINA—CHAPEL HILL School of Law Chapel Hill, NC	25	4.43
UNIVERSITY OF NORTH DAKOTA School of Law Grand Forks, ND	158	2.34
NORTHEASTERN UNIVERSITY School of Law Boston, MA	120	2.92
NORTHERN ILLINOIS UNIVERSITY College of Law De Kalb, IL	156	2.39
NORTHERN KENTUCKY UNIVERSITY Salmon P. Chase College of Law Highland Heights, KY	162	2.30
NORTHWESTERN UNIVERSITY School of Law Chicago, IL	14	4.74
UNIVERSITY OF NOTRE DAME Notre Dame Law School Notre Dame, IN	18	4.68
NOVA SOUTHEASTERN UNIVERSITY Shepard Broad Law Center Fort Lauderdale, FL	142	2.66
OHIO NORTHERN UNIVERSITY Claude W. Pettit College of Law Ada, OH	144	2.63
OHIO STATE UNIVERSITY—COLUMBUS College of Law Columbus, OH	34	4.26
OKLAHOMA CITY UNIVERSITY School of Law Oklahoma City, OK	135	2.76

Very Strong = 4.51-4.99 Strong = 4.01-4.49 Good = 3.61-3.99 Acceptable Plus = 3.01-3.59
Adequate = 2.51-2.99   Marginal = 2.01-2.49   Not Sufficient for Graduate Programs = 0.

UNIVERSITY OF OKLAHOMA College of Law Norman, OK	84	3.40
UNIVERSITY OF OREGON School of Law Eugene, OR	67	3.67
PACE UNIVERSITY School of Law White Plains, NY	157	2.36
UNIVERSITY OF THE PACIFIC McGeorge School of Law Sacramento, CA	33	4.28
UNIVERSITY OF PENNSYLVANIA School of Law Philadelphia, PA	9	4.82
PEPPERDINE UNIVERSITY School of Law Malibu, CA	49	3.85
UNIVERSITY OF PITTSBURGH School of Law Pittsburgh, PA	59	3.75
UNIVERSITY OF PUERTO RICO School of Law Rio Piedras, PR	160	2.32
QUINNIPIAC COLLEGE School of Law Hamden, CT	163	2.29
UNIVERSITY OF RICHMOND The T.C. Wiliams School of Law Richmond, VA	140	2.69
RUTGERS UNIVERSITY—CAMDEN School of Law at Camden Camden, NJ	65	3.69
RUTGERS UNIVERSITY—NEWARK School of Law Newark, NJ	61	3.73
ST. JOHN'S UNIVERSITY School of Law Jamaica, NY	64	3.70

Very Strong = 4.51-4.99   Strong = 4.01-4.49   Good = 3.61-3.99   Acceptable Plus = 3.01-3.59
Adequate = 2.51-2.99   Marginal = 2.01-2.49   Not Sufficient for Graduate Programs = 0.

ST. LOUIS UNIVERSITY
School of Law
St. Louis, MO

69   3.65

ST. MARY'S UNIVERSITY
School of Law
San Antonio, TX

150   2.52

SAMFORD UNIVERSITY
Cumberland School of Law
Birmingham, AL

134   2.77

UNIVERSITY OF SAN DIEGO
School of Law
San Diego, CA

48   3.86

UNIVERSITY OF SAN FRANCISCO
School of Law
San Francisco, CA

50   3.84

SANTA CLARA UNIVERSITY
School of Law
Santa Clara, CA

55   3.79

SEATTLE UNIVERSITY
School of Law
Tacoma, WA

118   2.94

SETON HALL UNIVERSITY
School of Law
Newark, NJ

81   3.43

UNIVERSITY OF SOUTH CAROLINA—COLUMBIA
School of Law
Columbia, SC

121   2.91

UNIVERSITY OF SOUTH DAKOTA
School of Law
Vermillion, SD

154   2.43

SOUTH TEXAS COLLEGE OF LAW
Houston, TX

132   2.79

UNIVERSITY OF SOUTHERN CALIFORNIA
Law School
Los Angeles, CA

27   4.39

SOUTHERN ILLINOIS UNIVERSITY—CARBONDALE
School of Law
Carbondale, IL

109   3.15

Very Strong = 4.51-4.99   Strong = 4.01-4.49   Good = 3.61-3.99   Acceptable Plus = 3.01-3.59
Adequate = 2.51-2.99   Marginal = 2.01-2.49   Not Sufficient for Graduate Programs = 0.

SOUTHERN METHODIST UNIVERSITY   35   4.25
School of Law
Dallas, TX

SOUTHERN UNIVERSITY—BATON ROUGE   172   2.18
Law Center
Baton Rouge, LA

SOUTHWESTERN UNIVERSITY   85   3.39
School of Law
Los Angeles, CA

STANFORD UNIVERSITY   6   4.87
School of Law
Stanford, CA

STATE UNIVERSITY OF NEW YORK AT BUFFALO   39   4.19
School of Law
Buffalo, NY

STETSON UNIVERSITY   138   2.72
College of Law
St. Petersburg, FL

SUFFOLK UNIVERSITY   112   3.12
School of Law
Boston, MA

SYRACUSE UNIVERSITY   58   3.76
College of Law
Syracuse, NY

TEMPLE UNIVERSITY   46   3.88
School of Law
Philadelphia, PA

UNIVERSITY of TENNESSEE—KNOXVILLE   113   3.11
College of Law
Knoxville, TN

TEXAS SOUTHERN UNIVERSITY   159   2.33
Thurgood Marshall School of Law
Houston, TX

TEXAS TECH UNIVERSITY   107   3.17
School of Law
Lubbock, TX

UNIVERSITY OF TEXAS—AUSTIN   12   4.77
School of Law
Austin, TX

Very Strong = 4.51-4.99   Strong = 4.01-4.49   Good = 3.61-3.99   Acceptable Plus = 3.01-3.59
Adequate = 2.51-2.99   Marginal = 2.01-2.49   Not Sufficient for Graduate Programs = 0.

THOMAS M. COOLEY LAW SCHOOL
Thomas M. Cooley Law School
Lansing, MI
123   2.89

UNIVERSITY OF TOLEDO
College of Law
Toledo, OH
153   2.47

TOURO COLLEGE
Jacob D. Fuchsberg Law Center
New York, NY
169   2.21

TULANE UNIVERSITY
School of Law
New Orleans, LA
29   4.35

UNIVERSITY OF TULSA
College of Law
Tulsa, OK
104   3.20

UNIVERSITY OF UTAH
College of Law
Salt Lake City, UT
42   4.16

VALPARAISO UNIVERSITY
School of Law
Valparaiso, IN
74   3.60

VANDERBILT UNIVERSITY
School of Law
Nashville, TN
15   4.73

VERMONT LAW SCHOOL
Vermont Law School
South Royalton, VT
151   2.50

VILLANOVA UNIVERSITY
School of Law
Villanova, PA
70   3.64

UNIVERSITY OF VIRGINIA
School of Law
Charlottesville, VA
16   4.72

WAKE FOREST UNIVERSITY
School of Law
Winston-Salem, NC
111   3.13

WASHBURN UNIVERSITY
School of Law
Topeka, KS
93   3.31

Very Strong = 4.51-4.99   Strong = 4.01-4.49   Good = 3.61-3.99   Acceptable Plus = 3.01-3.59
Adequate = 2.51-2.99   Marginal = 2.01-2.49   Not Sufficient for Graduate Programs = 0.

WASHINGTON AND LEE UNIVERSITY   103   3.21
School of Law
Lexington, VA

WASHINGTON UNIVERSITY   41   4.17
School of Law
St. Louis, MO

UNIVERSITY OF WASHINGTON   26   4.41
School of Law
Seattle, WA

WAYNE STATE UNIVERSITY   68   3.66
Law School
Detroit, MI

WEST VIRGINIA UNIVERSITY   106   3.18
College of Law
Morgantown, WV

WESTERN NEW ENGLAND COLLEGE   136   2.75
School of Law
Springfield, MA

WHITTIER COLLEGE   149   2.54
School of Law
Los Angeles, CA

WIDENER UNIVERSITY   139   2.71
Delaware Law School
Wilmington, DE

WIDENER UNIVERSITY—HARRISBURG   174   2.13
School of Law
Harrisburg, PA

THE COLLEGE OF WILLIAM AND MARY   80   3.44
School of Law
Williamsburg, VA

WILLIAM MITCHELL COLLEGE OF LAW   122   2.90
St. Paul, MN

WILLIAMETTE UNIVERSITY   73   3.61
College of Law
Salem, OR

UNIVERSITY OF WISCONSIN—MADISON   22   4.47
Law School
Madison, WI

Very Strong = 4.51-4.99   Strong = 4.01-4.49   Good = 3.61-3.99   Acceptable Plus = 3.01-3.59
Adequate = 2.51-2.99   Marginal = 2.01-2.49   Not Sufficient for Graduate Programs = 0.

UNIVERSITY OF WYOMING College of Law Laramie, WY	137	2.74
YALE UNIVERSITY Yale Law School New Haven, CT	3	4.90
YESHIVA UNIVERSITY Benjamin N. Cardozo School of Law New York, NY	52	3.82

Very Strong = 4.51-4.99   Strong = 4.01-4.49   Good = 3.61-3.99   Acceptable Plus = 3.01-3.59
Adequate = 2.51-2.99   Marginal = 2.01-2.49   Not Sufficient for Graduate Programs = 0.

THE TOP 10 LAW SCHOOLS IN CANADA

INSTITUTION	RANK	SCORE
UNIVERSITY OF TORONTO	1	4.70
UNIVERSITY OF BRITISH COLUMBIA	2	4.66
McGILL UNIVERSITY	3	4.64
YORK UNIVERSITY	4	4.56
UNIVERSITY OF OTTAWA	5	3.96
DALHOUSIE UNIVERSITY	6	3.60
UNIVERSITY OF MANITOBA	7	3.58
UNIVERSITY OF ALBERTA	8	3.51
QUEEN'S UNIVERSITY	9	3.40
UNIVERSITY OF VICTORIA	10	3.36

A RATING OF LAW SCHOOLS IN CANADA

Leading Institutions

INSTITUTION (ALPHABETICAL ORDER)	RANK	SCORE
UNIVERSITY OF ALBERTA Edmonton Faculty of Law Edmonton, Alberta	8	3.51
UNIVERSITY OF BRITISH COLUMBIA Faculty of Law Vancouver, British Columbia	2	4.66
UNIVERSITY OF CALGARY Faculty of Law Calgary, Alberta	12	3.18
DALHOUSIE UNIVERSITY Dalhousie Law School Halifax, Nova Scotia	6	3.60
UNIVERSITY OF MANITOBA Faculty of Law Winnipeg, Manitoba	7	3.58
McGILL UNIVERSITY Faculty of Law Montreal, Quebec	3	4.64
UNIVERSITY OF OTTAWA Faculty of Law Ottawa, Ontario	5	3.96
QUEEN'S UNIVERSITY Faculty of Law Kingston, Ontario	9	3.40
UNIVERSITY OF SASKATCHEWAN College of Law Saskatoon, Saskatchewan	14	3.10
UNIVERSITY OF TORONTO Faculty of Law Toronto, Ontario	1	4.70
UNIVERSITY OF VICTORIA Faculty of Law Victoria, British Columbia	10	3.36

Very Strong = 4.51-4.99   Strong = 4.01-4.49   Good = 3.61-3.99   Acceptable Plus = 3.01-3.59
Adequate = 2.51-2.99   Marginal = 2.01-2.49   Not Sufficient for Graduate Programs = 0.

INSTITUTION (ALPHABETICAL ORDER)	RANK	SCORE
UNIVERSITY OF WESTERN ONTARIO Faculty of Law London, Ontario	13	3.15
UNIVERSITY OF WINDSOR Faculty of Law Windsor, Ontario	11	3.20
YORK UNIVERSITY OSGOODE HALL Law School North York, Ontario	4	4.56

Very Strong = 4.51-4.99   Strong = 4.01-4.49   Good = 3.61-3.99   Acceptable Plus = 3.01-3.59
Adequate = 2.51-2.99   Marginal = 2.01-2.49   Not Sufficient for Graduate Programs = 0.

A RATING OF INTERNATIONAL LAW SCHOOLS

Leading Institutions

INSTITUTION	COUNTRY	Rank	Score
UNIVERSITY OF PARIS I/PANTHÉON-SORBONNE	France	1	4.92
UNIVERSITY OF LAW, ECONOMICS AND SOCIAL SCIENCES/PARIS II	France	1	4.92
UNIVERSITY OF PARIS X/NANTERRE	France	1	4.92
UNIVERSITY OF PARIS VAL-DE-MARNE/PARIS XII	France	1	4.92
UNIVERSITY OF PARIS-NORD/PARIS XIII	France	1	4.92
UNIVERSITY OF OXFORD	United Kingdom	2	4.91
UNIVERSITY OF CAMBRIDGE	United Kingdom	3	4.90
RUPERT CHARLES UNIVERSITY OF HEIDELBERG	Federal Republic of Germany	4	4.87
UNIVERSITY JEAN MOULIN/LYONS III	France	5	4.86
LUDWIG MAXIMILIANS-UNIVERSITY OF MUNICH	Federal Republic of Germany	6	4.83
UNIVERSITY OF MONTPELLIER I	France	7	4.82
FREE UNIVERSITY OF BRUSSELS	Belgium	8	4.81
GEORG AUGUST UNIVERSITY OF GÖTTINGEN	Federal Republic of Germany	9	4.78
FRIEDRICH ALEXANDER UNIVERSITY OF ERLANGEN-NUREMBERG	Federal Republic of Germany	10	4.77
UNIVERSITY OF AIX-MARSEILLES II	France	11	4.76
UNIVERSITY OF EDINBURGH	United Kingdom	12	4.75
UNIVERSITY OF BORDEAUX I TALENCE	France	13	4.74
RHENISH FRIEDRICH-WILHELM UNIVERSITY OF BONN	Federal Republic of Germany	14	4.73
UNIVERSITY OF LAW AND HEALTH SCIENCES/LILLE II	France	15	4.72
UNIVERSITY OF BURGUNDY DIJON	France	16	4.71
UNIVERSITY OF NANCY II	France	17	4.68
UNIVERSITY OF FRANCHE-COMTÉ BESANÇON	France	18	4.66
UNIVERSITY PIERRE MENDÈS FRANCE/GRENOBLE II	France	19	4.64

Very Strong = 4.51-4.99   Strong = 4.01-4.49   Good = 3.61-3.99   Acceptable Plus = 3.01-3.59
Adequate = 2.51-2.99   Marginal = 2.01-2.49   Not Sufficient for Graduate Programs = 0.

INSTITUTION	COUNTRY	Rank	Score
UNIVERSITY OF CLERMONT-FERRAND I	France	20	4.62
UNIVERSITY OF ROUEN-HAUTE-NORMANDIE	France	21	4.60
UNIVERSITY OF RHEIMS CHAMPAGNE-ARDENNES	France	22	4.58
UNIVERSITY OF COLOGNE	Federal Republic of Germany	23	4.57
UNIVERSITY OF RENNES I	France	24	4.55
UNIVERSITY OF VIENNA	Austria	25	4.54
CHRISTIAN ALBRECHT UNIVERSITY OF KIEL	Federal Republic of Germany	26	4.51
STOCKHOLM UNIVERSITY	Sweden	27	4.49
UNIVERSITY OF NICE	France	28	4.48
UNIVERSITY OF CAEN	France	29	4.47
UNIVERSITY OF POITIERS	France	30	4.44
UNIVERSITY OF SOCIAL SCIENCES/TOULOUSE I	France	31	4.42
UNIVERSITY OF LIMOGES	France	32	4.40
UNIVERSITY OF NANTES	France	33	4.39
UNIVERSITY OF COPENHAGEN	Denmark	34	4.38
JOHANNES GUTENBERG UNIVERSITY OF MAINZ	Federal Republic of Germany	35	4.35
UNIVERSITY OF ORLÉANS	France	36	4.34
JEAN MONNET UNIVERSITY SAINT-ETIENNE	France	37	4.33
UNIVERSITY OF TOKYO	Japan	38	4.32
ALBERT LUDWIG UNIVERSITY OF FREIBURG IM BREISGAU	Federal Republic of Germany	39	4.31
EBERHARD KARL UNIVERSITY OF TÜBINGEN	Federal Republic of Germany	40	4.30
UNIVERSITY OF INNSBRUCK	Austria	41	4.29
UNIVERSITY OF MÜNSTER	Federal Republic of Germany	42	4.27
BAYERISCHE JULIUS-MAXIMILIANS UNIVERSITY OF WÜRZBURG	Federal Republic of Germany	43	4.26

Very Strong = 4.51-4.99   Strong = 4.01-4.49   Good = 3.61-3.99   Acceptable Plus = 3.01-3.59
Adequate = 2.51-2.99   Marginal = 2.01-2.49   Not Sufficient for Graduate Programs = 0.

INSTITUTION	COUNTRY	Rank	Score
THE UNIVERSITY OF DUBLIN-TRINITY COLLEGE	Ireland	44	4.25
THE HEBREW UNIVERSITY OF JERUSALEM	Israel	45	4.23
UNIVERSITY OF MADRID	Spain	46	4.22
UNIVERSITY OF MARBURG	Federal Republic of Germany	47	4.20
UNIVERSITY OF GENEVA	Switzerland	48	4.19
UNIVERSITY OF LONDON	United Kingdom	49	4.16
UNIVERSITY OF FRIBOURG	Switzerland	50	4.15
UNIVERSITY OF ROME I 'LA SAPIENZA'	Italy	51	4.14
UNIVERSITY OF AMSTERDAM	Netherlands	52	4.12
NATIONAL AND CAPODISTRIAN UNIVERSITY OF ATHENS	Greece	53	4.05

Very Strong = 4.51-4.99   Strong = 4.01-4.49   Good = 3.61-3.99   Acceptable Plus = 3.01-3.59
Adequate = 2.51-2.99   Marginal = 2.01-2.49   Not Sufficient for Graduate Programs = 0.

Part III

THE GOURMAN REPORT
MEDICAL SCHOOLS

THE TOP 50 U.S. MEDICAL SCHOOLS
A RATING OF U.S. MEDICAL SCHOOLS
A RATING OF MEDICAL SCHOOLS IN CANADA
A RATING OF MEDICAL SCHOOLS IN JAPAN
A RATING OF INTERNATIONAL MEDICAL SCHOOLS

THE TOP 50 U.S. MEDICAL SCHOOLS

INSTITUTION	RANK	SCORE
HARVARD MEDICAL SCHOOL	1	4.93
JOHNS HOPKINS UNIVERSITY	2	4.92
UNIVERSITY OF PENNSYLVANIA	3	4.91
UNIVERSITY OF CALIFORNIA—SAN FRANCISCO	4	4.90
YALE UNIVERSITY	5	4.89
UNIVERSITY OF CHICAGO	6	4.88
COLUMBIA UNIVERSITY	7	4.86
STANFORD UNIVERSITY	8	4.85
CORNELL UNIVERSITY MEDICAL COLLEGE	9	4.84
UNIVERSITY OF MICHIGAN—ANN ARBOR	10	4.82
UNIVERSITY OF CALIFORNIA—LOS ANGELES	11	4.81
DUKE UNIVERSITY	12	4.78
WASHINGTON UNIVERSITY	13	4.76
NORTHWESTERN UNIVERSITY	14	4.73
UNIVERSITY OF MINNESOTA—TWIN CITIES	15	4.71
TULANE UNIVERSITY	16	4.70
UNIVERSITY OF ROCHESTER	17	4.68
VANDERBILT UNIVERSITY	18	4.65
NEW YORK UNIVERSITY	19	4.62
UNIVERSITY OF CALIFORNIA—SAN DIEGO	20	4.49
UNIVERSITY OF VIRGINIA	21	4.48
UNIVERSITY OF NORTH CAROLINA—CHAPEL HILL	22	4.47
TUFTS UNIVERSITY	23	4.46
UNIVERSITY OF CALIFORNIA—DAVIS	24	4.45
BOSTON UNIVERSITY	25	4.44
INDIANA UNIVERSITY—INDIANAPOLIS	26	4.43
UNIVERSITY OF WISCONSIN—MADISON	27	4.42
UNIVERSITY OF ILLINOIS—CHICAGO	28	4.41
UNIVERSITY OF IOWA	29	4.40
UNIVERSITY OF WASHINGTON	30	4.39
GEORGETOWN UNIVERSITY	31	4.38
OHIO STATE UNIVERSITY—COLUMBUS	32	4.37
STATE UNIVERSITY OF NEW YORK AT BUFFALO	33	4.36
GEORGE WASHINGTON UNIVERSITY	34	4.35
UNIVERSITY OF CALIFORNIA—IRVINE	35	4.34
BAYLOR COLLEGE OF MEDICINE	36	4.33
BOWMAN GRAY	37	4.32
EMORY UNIVERSITY	38	4.31
UNIVERSITY OF PITTSBURGH	39	4.30
LOMA LINDA UNIVERSITY	40	4.29

ALBERT EINSTEIN COLLEGE OF MEDICINE OF YESHIVA UNIVERSITY	41	4.28
UNIVERSITY OF LOUISVILLE	42	4.26
LOYOLA UNIVERSITY OF CHICAGO	43	4.25
ST. LOUIS UNIVERSITY	44	4.24
DARTMOUTH MEDICAL SCHOOL	45	4.22
UNIVERSITY OF SOUTHERN CALIFORNIA	46	4.20
UNIVERSITY OF MISSOURI—COLUMBIA	47	4.19
WAYNE STATE UNIVERSITY	48	4.18
TEMPLE UNIVERSITY	49	4.17
STATE UNIVERSITY OF NEW YORK AT STONY BROOK HEALTH SCIENCES CENTER	50	4.15

A RATING OF U.S. MEDICAL SCHOOLS

INSTITUTION (ALPHABETICAL ORDER)	RANK	SCORE
UNIVERSITY OF ALABAMA—BIRMINGHAM School of Medicine Birmingham, AL	75	3.67
ALBANY MEDICAL COLLEGE Albany, NY	60	3.82
ALBERT EINSTEIN COLLEGE OF MEDICINE OF YESHIVA UNIVERSITY Bronx, NY	41	4.28
UNIVERSITY OF ARIZONA College of Medicine Tucson, AZ	88	3.42
UNIVERSITY OF ARKANSAS FOR MEDICAL SCIENCES College of Medicine Little Rock, AR	86	3.45
BAYLOR COLLEGE OF MEDICINE Houston, TX	36	4.33
BOSTON UNIVERSITY School of Medicine Boston, MA	25	4.44
BOWMAN GRAY School of Medicine of Wake Forest University Winston-Salem, NC	37	4.32
BROWN UNIVERSITY School of Medicine Providence, RI	51	4.14
UNIVERSITY OF CALIFORNIA—DAVIS School of Medicine Davis, CA	24	4.45
UNIVERSITY OF CALIFORNIA—IRVINE College of Medicine Irvine, CA	35	4.34
UNIVERSITY OF CALIFORNIA—LOS ANGELES UCLA School of Medicine Los Angeles, CA	11	4.81
UNIVERSITY OF CALIFORNIA—SAN DIEGO School of Medicine La Jolla, CA	20	4.49

Very Strong = 4.51-4.99   Strong = 4.01-4.49   Good = 3.61-3.99   Acceptable Plus = 3.01-3.59
Adequate = 2.51-2.99   Marginal = 2.01-2.49   Not Sufficient for Graduate Programs = 0.

UNIVERSITY OF CALIFORNIA—SAN FRANCISCO   4   4.90
School of Medicine
San Francisco, CA

CASE WESTERN RESERVE UNIVERSITY   52   3.90
School of Medicine
Cleveland, OH

UNIVERSIDAD CENTRAL DEL CARIBE   124   3.03
Escuela de Medicina
Bayamon, PR

UNIVERSITY OF CHICAGO   6   4.88
Pritzker School of Medicine
Chicago, IL

UNIVERSITY OF CINCINNATI   72   3.70
College of Medicine
Cincinnati, OH

UNIVERSITY OF COLORADO—DENVER   57   3.85
School of Medicine
Denver, CO

COLUMBIA UNIVERSITY   7   4.86
College of Physicians and Surgeons
New York, NY

UNIVERSITY OF CONNECTICUT—FARMINGTON   54   3.88
School of Medicine
Farmington, CT

CORNELL UNIVERSITY MEDICAL COLLEGE   9   4.84
New York, NY

CREIGHTON UNIVERSITY   56   3.86
School of Medicine
Omaha, NE

DARTMOUTH MEDICAL SCHOOL   45   4.22
Hanover, NH

DUKE UNIVERSITY   12   4.78
School of Medicine
Durham, NC

EAST CAROLINA UNIVERSITY   113   3.14
School of Medicine
Greenville, NC

EAST TENNESSEE STATE UNIVERSITY   116   3.11
James H. Quillen College of Medicine
Johnson City, TN

Very Strong = 4.51-4.99   Strong = 4.01-4.49   Good = 3.61-3.99   Acceptable Plus = 3.01-3.59
Adequate = 2.51-2.99   Marginal = 2.01-2.49   Not Sufficient for Graduate Programs = 0.

EASTERN VIRGINIA MEDICAL SCHOOL 115 3.12
Norfolk, VA

EMORY UNIVERSITY 38 4.31
School of Medicine
Atlanta, GA

UNIVERSITY OF FLORIDA 62 3.80
College of Medicine
Gainesville, FL

GEORGE WASHINGTON UNIVERSITY 34 4.35
School of Medicine and Health Sciences
Washington, D.C.

GEORGETOWN UNIVERSITY 31 4.38
School of Medicine
Washington, D.C.

HARVARD MEDICAL SCHOOL 1 4.93
Boston, MA

UNIVERSITY OF HAWAII—MANOA 103 3.25
John A. Burns School of Medicine
Honolulu, HI

UNIVERSITY OF HEALTH SCIENCES 97 3.31
Chicago Medical School
North Chicago, IL

HOWARD UNIVERSITY 98 3.30
College of Medicine
Washington, D.C.

UNIVERSITY OF ILLINOIS—CHICAGO 28 4.41
College of Medicine
Chicago, IL

INDIANA UNIVERSITY—INDIANAPOLIS 26 4.43
School of Medicine
Indianapolis, IN

UNIVERSITY OF IOWA 29 4.40
College of Medicine
Iowa City, IA

JEFFERSON MEDICAL COLLEGE OF THOMAS JEFFERSON UNIVERSITY 82 3.49
Philadelphia, PA

JOHNS HOPKINS UNIVERSITY 2 4.92
School of Medicine
Baltimore, MD

Very Strong = 4.51-4.99   Strong = 4.01-4.49   Good = 3.61-3.99   Acceptable Plus = 3.01-3.59
Adequate = 2.51-2.99   Marginal = 2.01-2.49   Not Sufficient for Graduate Programs = 0.

UNIVERSITY OF KANSAS—KANSAS CITY School of Medicine Kansas City, KS	55	3.87
UNIVERSITY OF KENTUCKY College of Medicine Lexington, KY	77	3.65
LOMA LINDA UNIVERSITY School of Medicine Loma Linda, CA	40	4.29
LOUISIANA STATE UNIVERSITY—NEW ORLEANS School of Medicine in New Orleans New Orleans, LA	74	3.68
LOUISIANA STATE UNIVERSITY—SHREVEPORT School of Medicine in Shreveport Shreveport, LA	79	3.63
UNIVERSITY OF LOUISVILLE School of Medicine Louisville, KY	42	4.26
LOYOLA UNIVERSITY OF CHICAGO Stritch School of Medicine Maywood, IL	43	4.25
MARSHALL UNIVERSITY School of Medicine Huntington, WV	114	3.13
UNIVERSITY OF MARYLAND—BALTIMORE School of Medicine Baltimore, MD	63	3.79
UNIVERSITY OF MASSACHUSETTS—WORCESTER Medical School Worcester, MA	104	3.24
MAYO MEDICAL SCHOOL Rochester, MN	58	3.84
MEDICAL COLLEGE OF GEORGIA School of Medicine Augusta, GA	95	3.33
MEDICAL COLLEGE OF OHIO Toledo, OH	96	3.32
MEDICAL COLLEGE OF WISCONSIN Milwaukee, WI	105	3.23
MEDICAL UNIVERSITY OF SOUTH CAROLINA College of Medicine Charleston, SC	90	3.40

Very Strong = 4.51-4.99   Strong = 4.01-4.49   Good = 3.61-3.99   Acceptable Plus = 3.01-3.59
Adequate = 2.51-2.99   Marginal = 2.01-2.49   Not Sufficient for Graduate Programs = 0.

UNIVERSITY OF MEDICINE AND DENTISTRY OF NEW JERSEY—NEWARK
New Jersey Medical School
Newark, NJ

87   3.43

UNIVERSITY OF MEDICINE AND DENTISTRY OF NEW JERSEY—PISCATAWAY
Robert Wood Johnson Medical School
Piscataway, NJ

102   3.26

MEHARRY MEDICAL COLLEGE
School of Medicine
Nashville, TN

92   3.37

MERCER UNIVERSITY
School of Medicine
Macon, GA

122   3.05

UNIVERSITY OF MIAMI
School of Medicine
Miami, FL

64   3.78

MICHIGAN STATE UNIVERSITY
College of Human Medicine
East Lansing, MI

65   3.77

UNIVERSITY OF MICHIGAN—ANN ARBOR
Medical School
Ann Arbor, MI

10   4.82

UNIVERSITY OF MINNESOTA—TWIN CITIES
Medical School—Minneapolis
Minneapolis, MN

15   4.71

UNIVERSITY OF MISSISSIPPI—JACKSON
School of Medicine
Jackson, MS

91   3.39

UNIVERSITY OF MISSOURI—COLUMBIA
School of Medicine
Columbia, MO

47   4.19

UNIVERSITY OF MISSOURI—KANSAS CITY
School of Medicine
Kansas City, MO

67   3.75

MOREHOUSE SCHOOL OF MEDICINE
Atlanta, GA

121   3.06

MOUNT SINAI
School of Medicine of City University of New York
New York, NY

53   3.89

Very Strong = 4.51-4.99   Strong = 4.01-4.49   Good = 3.61-3.99   Acceptable Plus = 3.01-3.59
Adequate = 2.51-2.99   Marginal = 2.01-2.49   Not Sufficient for Graduate Programs = 0.

UNIVERSITY OF NEBRASKA—OMAHA College of Medicine Omaha, NE	76	3.66
UNIVERSITY OF NEVADA—RENO School of Medicine Reno, NV	108	3.20
UNIVERSITY OF NEW MEXICO School of Medicine Albuquerque, NM	99	3.29
NEW YORK MEDICAL COLLEGE Valhalla, NY	81	3.50
NEW YORK UNIVERSITY School of Medicine New York, NY	19	4.62
UNIVERSITY OF NORTH CAROLINA—CHAPEL HILL School of Medicine Chapel Hill, NC	22	4.47
UNIVERSITY OF NORTH DAKOTA School of Medicine Grand Forks, ND	110	3.17
NORTHEASTERN OHIO UNIVERSITIES College of Medicine Rootstown, OH	112	3.15
NORTHWESTERN UNIVERSITY Medical School Chicago, IL	14	4.73
OHIO STATE UNIVERSITY—COLUMBUS College of Medicine Columbus, OH	32	4.37
UNIVERSITY OF OKLAHOMA—OKLAHOMA CITY College of Medicine Oklahoma City, OK	83	3.48
OREGON HEALTH SCIENCES UNIVERSITY School of Medicine Portland, OR	59	3.83
PENNSYLVANIA STATE UNIVERSITY—HERSHEY College of Medicine Hershey, PA	70	3.72
UNIVERSITY OF PENNSYLVANIA School of Medicine Philadelphia, PA	3	4.91

Very Strong = 4.51-4.99   Strong = 4.01-4.49   Good = 3.61-3.99   Acceptable Plus = 3.01-3.59
Adequate = 2.51-2.99   Marginal = 2.01-2.49   Not Sufficient for Graduate Programs = 0.

UNIVERSITY OF PITTSBURGH School of Medicine Pittsburgh, PA	39	4.30
PONCE SCHOOL OF MEDICINE Ponce, PR	123	3.04
UNIVERSITY OF PUERTO RICO—MEDICAL SCIENCES CAMPUS School of Medicine San Juan, PR	106	3.22
UNIVERSITY OF ROCHESTER School of Medicine and Dentistry Rochester, NY	17	4.68
RUSH MEDICAL COLLEGE OF RUSH UNIVERSITY Chicago, IL	93	3.36
ST. LOUIS UNIVERSITY School of Medicine St. Louis, MO	44	4.24
UNIVERSITY OF SOUTH ALABAMA College of Medicine Mobile, AL	117	3.10
UNIVERSITY OF SOUTH CAROLINA—COLUMBIA School of Medicine Columbia, SC	107	3.21
UNIVERSITY OF SOUTH DAKOTA School of Medicine Vermillion, SD	111	3.16
UNIVERSITY OF SOUTH FLORIDA College of Medicine Tampa, FL	89	3.41
UNIVERSITY OF SOUTHERN CALIFORNIA School of Medicine Los Angeles, CA	46	4.20
SOUTHERN ILLINOIS UNIVERSITY—SPRINGFIELD School of Medicine Springfield, IL	100	3.28
STANFORD UNIVERSITY School of Medicine Palo Alto, CA	8	4.85
STATE UNIVERSITY OF NEW YORK AT BUFFALO School of Medicine and Biomedical Sciences Buffalo, NY	33	4.36

Very Strong = 4.51-4.99   Strong = 4.01-4.49   Good = 3.61-3.99   Acceptable Plus = 3.01-3.59
Adequate = 2.51-2.99   Marginal = 2.01-2.49   Not Sufficient for Graduate Programs = 0.

STATE UNIVERSITY OF NEW YORK AT STONY BROOK   50   4.15
HEALTH SCIENCES CENTER
School of Medicine
Stony Brook, NY

STATE UNIVERSITY OF NEW YORK HEALTH SCIENCE CENTER   71   3.71
AT BROOKLYN
College of Medicine
Brooklyn, NY

STATE UNIVERSITY OF NEW YORK HEALTH SCIENCE CENTER   73   3.69
AT SYRACUSE
College of Medicine
Syracuse, NY

TEMPLE UNIVERSITY   49   4.17
School of Medicine
Philadelphia, PA

UNIVERSITY OF TENNESSEE—MEMPHIS   80   3.62
College of Medicine
Memphis, TN

TEXAS A&M UNIVERSITY—COLLEGE STATION   118   3.09
College of Medicine
College Station, TX

UNIVERSITY OF TEXAS HEALTH SCIENCE CENTER   69   3.73
AT SAN ANTONIO
San Antonio, TX

TEXAS TECH UNIVERSITY HEALTH SCIENCES CENTER   101   3.27
School of Medicine
Lubbock, TX

UNIVERSITY OF TEXAS—DALLAS   66   3.76
Southwestern Medical Center at Dallas Southwest
Dallas, TX

UNIVERSITY OF TEXAS—GALVESTON   68   3.74
Medical Branch at Galveston School of Medicine
Galveston, TX

UNIVERSITY OF TEXAS—HOUSTON   85   3.46
Medical School at Houston
Houston, TX

TUFTS UNIVERSITY   23   4.46
School of Medicine
Boston, MA

TULANE UNIVERSITY   16   4.70
School of Medicine
New Orleans, LA

Very Strong = 4.51-4.99   Strong = 4.01-4.49   Good = 3.61-3.99   Acceptable Plus = 3.01-3.59
Adequate = 2.51-2.99   Marginal = 2.01-2.49   Not Sufficient for Graduate Programs = 0.

LAUNIFORMED SERVICES UNIVERSITY OF THE HEALTH SCIENCES   109   3.18
F. Edward Herbert School of Medicine
Bethesda, MD

UNIVERSITY OF UTAH   61   3.81
School of Medicine
Salt Lake City, UT

STATE UNIVERSITY OF NEW YORK HEALTH SCIENCE CENTER   18   4.65
AT BROOKLYN
College of Medicine
Brooklyn, NY

UNIVERSITY OF VERMONT   78   3.64
College of Medicine
Burlington, VT

VIRGINIA COMMONWEALTH UNIVERSITY   94   3.34
Medical College of Virginia
Richmond, VA

HAHNEMANN UNIVERSITY   119   3.08
School of Medicine
Philadelphia, PA

UNIVERSITY OF VIRGINIA   21   4.48
School of Medicine
Charlottesville, VA

WASHINGTON UNIVERSITY   13   4.76
School of Medicine
St. Louis, MO

UNIVERSITY OF WASHINGTON   30   4.39
School of Medicine
Seattle, WA

WAYNE STATE UNIVERSITY   48   4.18
School of Medicine
Detroit, MI

WEST VIRGINIA UNIVERSITY   84   3.47
School of Medicine
Morgantown, WV

UNIVERSITY OF WISCONSIN—MADISON   27   4.42
Medical School
Madison, WI

WRIGHT STATE UNIVERSITY   120   3.07
School of Medicine
Dayton, OH

YALE UNIVERSITY   5   4.89
School of Medicine
New Haven, CT

Very Strong = 4.51-4.99   Strong = 4.01-4.49   Good = 3.61-3.99   Acceptable Plus = 3.01-3.59
Adequate = 2.51-2.99   Marginal = 2.01-2.49   Not Sufficient for Graduate Programs = 0.

THE TOP 10 MEDICAL SCHOOLS IN CANADA

INSTITUTION	RANK	SCORE
McGILL UNIVERSITY	1	4.91
UNIVERSITY OF TORONTO	2	4.90
UNIVERSITY OF BRITISH COLUMBIA	3	4.85
UNIVERSITY OF MONTREAL	4	4.78
McMASTER UNIVERSITY	5	4.74
QUEEN'S UNIVERSITY	6	4.68
LAVAL UNIVERSITY	7	4.62
UNIVERSITY OF MANITOBA	8	4.57
UNIVERSITY OF OTTAWA	9	4.51
UNIVERSITY OF WESTERN ONTARIO	10	4.48

A RATING OF MEDICAL SCHOOLS IN CANADA

INSTITUTIONS (ALPHABETICAL ORDER)	RANK	SCORE
UNIVERSITY OF ALBERTA Faculty of Medicine and Oral Health Sciences Edmonton, Alberta	11	4.46
UNIVERSITY OF BRITISH COLUMBIA Faculty of Medicine Vancouver, British Columbia	3	4.85
UNIVERSITY OF CALGARY Faculty of Medicine Calgary, Alberta	12	4.43
DALHOUSIE UNIVERSITY School of Medicine Halifax, Nova Scotia	14	4.33
UNIVERSITÉ LAVAL Faculty of Medicine Sainte-Foy, Quebec	7	4.62
UNIVERSITY OF MANITOBA Faculty of Medicine Winnipeg, Manitoba	8	4.57
McGILL UNIVERSITY Faculty of Medicine Montreal, Quebec	1	4.91
McMASTER UNIVERSITY School of Medicine Hamilton, Ontario	5	4.74
MEMORIAL UNIVERSITY OF NEWFOUNDLAND Faculty of Medicine St. John's, Newfoundland	13	4.37
UNIVERSITY OF MONTREAL Faculty of Medicine Montreal, Quebec	4	4.78
UNIVERSITY OF OTTAWA Faculty of Medicine Ottawa, Ontario	9	4.51
QUEEN'S UNIVERSITY Faculty of Medicine Kingston, Ontario	6	4.68

Very Strong = 4.51-4.99   Strong = 4.01-4.49   Good = 3.61-3.99   Acceptable Plus = 3.01-3.59
Adequate = 2.51-2.99   Marginal = 2.01-2.49   Not Sufficient for Graduate Programs = 0.

UNIVERSITY OF SASKATCHEWAN　　　　　　　　　16　　4.16
College of Medicine
Saskatoon, Saskatchewan

UNIVERSITY OF SHERBROOKE　　　　　　　　　　15　　4.25
Faculty of Medicine
Sherbrooke, Quebec

UNIVERSITY OF TORONTO　　　　　　　　　　　　2　　4.90
Faculty of Medicine
Toronto, Ontario

UNIVERSITY OF WESTERN ONTARIO　　　　　　　10　　4.48
Faculty of Medicine
London, Ontario

Very Strong = 4.51-4.99　　Strong = 4.01-4.49　　Good = 3.61-3.99　　Acceptable Plus = 3.01-3.59
Adequate = 2.51-2.99　　Marginal = 2.01-2.49　　Not Sufficient for Graduate Programs = 0.

A RATING OF MEDICAL SCHOOLS IN JAPAN

Leading Institutions

INSTITUTION	RANK	SCORE
NIHON UNIVERSITY	1	4.88
THE UNIVERSITY OF TOKYO	2	4.87
OSAKA UNIVERSITY	3	4.86
KYUSHO UNIVERSITY	4	4.85
HOKKAIDO UNIVERSITY	5	4.84
HIROSHIMA UNIVERSITY	6	4.83
TOKYO MEDICAL AND DENTAL UNIVERSITY	7	4.82
IWATE MEDICAL UNIVERSITY	8	4.81
KEIO UNIVERSITY	9	4.80
NAGOYA UNIVERSITY	10	4.79
SHOWA UNIVERSITY	11	4.78
TOKYO MEDICAL COLLEGE	12	4.77
FUKUI MEDICAL SCHOOL	13	4.76
CHIBA UNIVERSIT	14	4.75
KAGAWA MEDICAL SCHOOL	15	4.71
KOBE UNIVERSITY	16	4.68
KOCHI MEDICAL SCHOOL	17	4.65
NIIGATA UNIVERSITY	18	4.63
NIPPON MEDICAL SCHOO	19	4.60
SAGA MEDICAL SCHOOL	20	4.55
SHIGA UNIVERSITY OF MEDICAL SCIENCES	21	4.48
TOKAI UNIVERSITY	22	4.46
HAMAMATSU UNIVERSITY SCHOOL OF MEDICINE	23	4.45
DOKKYO UNIVERSITY SCHOOL OF MEDICINE	24	4.44
AICHI MEDICAL UNIVERSITY	25	4.42
GUNMA UNIVERSITY	26	4.40
HIROSAKI UNIVERSITY	27	4.39
JICHI MEDICAL SCHOOL	28	4.38
KANSAI MEDICAL UNIVERSITY	29	4.37
MIE UNIVERSITY	30	4.36
NARA MEDICAL UNIVERSITY	31	4.35
SHIMANE MEDICAL UNIVERISTY	32	4.31
TOYAMA MEDICAL & PHARMACEUTICAL UNIVERSITY	33	4.27
UNIVERSITY OF THE RYUKYUS	34	4.25
YAMAGATA UNIVERSITY	35	4.22
EHIME UNIVERSITY	36	4.18
AKITA UNIVERSITY	37	4.15
HYOGO COLLEGE OF MEDICINE	38	4.10

KANAZAWA MEDICAL UNIVERSITY	39	4.08
KANSAI MEDICAL UNIVERSITY	40	4.03
KINKI UNIVERSITY	41	3.98
KYOTO PREFECTURAL UNIVERSITY OF MEDICINE	42	3.95
KYOTO UNIVERSITY	43	3.92
MIYAZAKI MEDICAL COLLEGE	44	3.88
ASAHIKAWA MEDICAL COLLEGE	45	3.86
FUJITA-GAKUEN HEALTH UNIVERSITY	46	3.85
FUKUOKA UNIVERSITY	47	3.84
JIKEI UNIVERSITY SCHOOL OF MEDICINE	48	3.80
KANAZAWA UNIVERSITY	49	3.79
KITASATO UNIVERSITY	50	3.78
MEDICAL COLLEGE OF OITA	51	3.76
NAGASAKI UNIVERSITY	52	3.75
OSAKA MEDICAL COLLEGE	53	3.74
GIFU UNIVERSITY	54	3.73
TEIKYO UNIVERSITY	55	3.70
TOHO UNIVERSITY	56	3.69
TOHOKU UNIVERSITY	57	3.67
SAITAMA MEDICAL COLLEGE	58	3.65
SAPPORO MEDICAL COLLEGE	59	3.64
OKAYAMA UNIVERSITY	60	3.62
KYORIN UNIVERSITY	61	3.58
UNIVERSITY OF TOKUSHIMA	62	3.55
WAKAYAMA MEDICAL COLLEGE	63	3.54
YAMAGUICHI UNIVERSITY	64	3.50
YAMANASHI MEDICAL COLLEGE	65	3.47
FUKUSHIMA MEDICAL COLLEGE	66	3.45
JUNTENDO UNIVERSITY	67	3.43
KAGOSHIMA UNIVERSITY	68	3.40
KUMAMOTO UNIVERSITY	69	3.38
KURUME UNIVERSITY	70	3.36
SHINSHU UNIVERSITY	71	3.34
ST. MARIANNA UNIVERSITY SCHOOL OF MEDICINE	72	3.32
TOKYO WOMEN'S MEDICAL COLLEGE	73	3.29
UNIVERSITY OF TOTTORI	74	3.25
UNIVERSITY OF TSUKUBA	75	3.21
NAGOYA CITY UNIVERSITY	76	3.18
OSAKA CITY UNIVERSITY	77	3.15
UNIVERSITY OF OCCUP. & ENVIRON. HEALTH, JAPAN	78	3.12
YOKOHAMA CITY UNIVERSITY	79	3.10

A RATING OF INTERNATIONAL MEDICAL SCHOOLS

INSTITUTION	COUNTRY	Rank	Score
UNIVERSITY RENÉ DESCARTES/PARIS V	France	1	4.92
UNIVERSITY PIERRE AND MARIE CURIE/PARIS VI	France	1	4.92
UNIVERSITY OF PARIS VII	France	1	4.92
UNIVERSITY OF PARIS-SUD/PARIS XI	France	1	4.92
UNIVERSITY OF PARIS VAL-DE-MARNE/PARIS XII	France	1	4.92
UNIVERSITY OF PARIS-NORD/PARIS XIII	France	1	4.92
UNIVERSITY OF OXFORD	United Kingdom	2	4.91
UNIVERSITY OF CAMBRIDGE	United Kingdom	3	4.90
RUPERT CHARLES UNIVERSITY OF HEIDELBERG	Federal Republic of Germany	4	4.89
LUDWIG MAXIMILIANS-UNIVERSITY OF MUNICH	Federal Republic of Germany	5	4.88
UNIVERSITY CLAUDE BERNARD/LYONS I	France	6	4.87
UNIVERSITY OF VIENNA	Austria	7	4.86
UNIVERSITY OF MONTPELLIER I	France	8	4.84
UNIVERSITY OF ZÜRICH	Switzerland	9	4.82
GEORG AUGUST UNIVERSITY OF GÖTTINGEN	Federal Republic of Germany	10	4.81
UNIVERSITY OF EDINBURGH	United Kingdom	11	4.80
UNIVERSITY OF LAW AND HEALTH SCIENCES/LILLE II	France	12	4.78
FREE UNIVERSITY OF BRUSSELS	Belgium	13	4.77
UNIVERSITY OF BURGUNDY DIJON	France	14	4.73
CATHOLIC FACULTIES OF LILLE/FACULTÉ LIBRE DE MÉDICINE	France	15	4.72
UNIVERSITY OF GENEVA	Switzerland	16	4.71
KEIO UNIVERSITY	Japan	17	4.67
FRIEDRICH ALEXANDER UNIVERSITY OF ERLANGEN-NUREMBERG	Federal Republic of Germany	18	4.66
TOKYO MEDICAL COLLEGE	Japan	19	4.63
UNIVERSITY OF AIX-MARSEILLES II	France	20	4.59
UNIVERSITY OF NANCY I	France	21	4.57

Very Strong = 4.51-4.99   Strong = 4.01-4.49   Good = 3.61-3.99   Acceptable Plus = 3.01-3.59
Adequate = 2.51-2.99   Marginal = 2.01-2.49   Not Sufficient for Graduate Programs = 0.

UNIVERSITY OF NICE	France	22	4.56
UNIVERSITY OF RHEIMS CHAMPAGNE-ARDENNES	France	23	4.55
UNIVERSITY OF CLERMONT-FERRAND I	France	24	4.54
UNIVERSITY OF RENNES I	France	25	4.53
UNIVERSITY OF ROUEN-HAUTE-NORMANDIE	France	26	4.52
UNIVERSITY OF BORDEAUX II	France	27	4.46
RHENISH FRIEDRICH-WILHELM UNIVERSITY OF BONN	Federal Republic of Germany	28	4.37
BAYERISCHE JULIUS-MAXIMILIANS UNIVERSITY OF WÜRZBURG	Federal Republic of Germany	29	4.36
THE HEBREW UNIVERSITY OF JERUSALEM	Israel	30	4.33
UNIVERSITY OF LONDON:	United Kingdom	31	4.32
Charing Cross and Westminster Medical School	United Kingdom	31	4.32
King's College London	United Kingdom	31	4.32
The London Hospital Medical College	United Kingdom	31	4.32
The Middlesex Hospital Medical School	United Kingdom	31	4.32
Royal Free Hospital School of Medicine	United Kingdom	31	4.32
St. Bartholomew's Hospital Medical College	United Kingdom	31	4.32
St. George's Hospital Medical School	United Kingdom	31	4.32
St. Mary's Hospital Medical School	United Kingdom	31	4.32
United Medical and Dental Schools of Guy's and St. Thomas's Hospitals	United Kingdom	31	4.32
University College London	United Kingdom	31	4.32
ALBERT LUDWIG UNIVERSITY OF FREIBURG IM BREISGAU	Federal Republic of Germany	32	4.31
UNIVERSITY OF HAMBURG	Federal Republic of Germany	33	4.30
UNIVERSITY OF PICARDIE AMIENS	France	34	4.29
UNIVERSITY OF FRANCHE-COMTÉ BESANÇON	France	35	4.28
UNIVERSITY 'JOSEPH FOURIER'/GRENOBLE I	France	36	4.27
UNIVERSITY OF MARBURG	Federal Republic of Germany	37	4.26
EBERHARD KARL UNIVERSITY OF TÜBINGEN	Federal Republic of Germany	38	4.25

Very Strong = 4.51-4.99   Strong = 4.01-4.49   Good = 3.61-3.99   Acceptable Plus = 3.01-3.59
Adequate = 2.51-2.99   Marginal = 2.01-2.49   Not Sufficient for Graduate Programs = 0.

UNIVERSITY OF POITIERS	France	39	4.24
UNIVERSITY OF LIMOGES	France	40	4.23
JEAN MONNET UNIVERSITY SAINT-ETIENNE	France	41	4.22
JOHANNES GUTENBERG UNIVERSITY OF MAINZ	Federal Republic of Germany	42	4.21
LOUIS PASTEUR UNIVERSITY/STRASBOURG I	France	43	4.20
UNIVERSITY OF CAEN	France	44	4.19
STOCKHOLM UNIVERSITY	Sweden	45	4.18
CATHOLIC UNIVERSITY OF LOUVAIN	Belgium	46	4.17
UNIVERSITY OF AMSTERDAM	Netherlands	47	4.16
ROYAL COLLEGE OF SURGEONS IN IRELAND	Ireland	48	4.15
LEIDEN UNIVERSITY	Netherlands	49	4.13
UNIVERSITY OF TOURS	France	50	4.12
UNIVERSITY PAUL SABATIER/TOULOUSE III	France	51	4.11
JOHANN WOLFGANG GOETHE UNIVERSITY OF FRANKFURT	Federal Republic of Germany	52	4.10
UNIVERSITY OF ANGERS	France	53	4.09
UNIVERSITY OF MÜNSTER	Federal Republic of Germany	54	4.08
UNIVERSITY OF NANTES	France	55	4.06

Very Strong = 4.51-4.99   Strong = 4.01-4.49   Good = 3.61-3.99   Acceptable Plus = 3.01-3.59
Adequate = 2.51-2.99   Marginal = 2.01-2.49   Not Sufficient for Graduate Programs = 0.

Part IV
THE GOURMAN REPORT
HEALTH PROGRAMS

THE TOP 25 U.S. DENTAL SCHOOLS

A RATING OF U.S. DENTAL SCHOOLS

A RATING OF DENTAL SCHOOLS IN CANADA

A RATING OF DENTAL SCHOOLS IN JAPAN

A RATING OF U.S. NURSING SCHOOLS

A RATING OF U.S. OPTOMETRY SCHOOLS

A RATING OF U.S. PHARMACY SCHOOLS

A RATING OF PHARMACY SCHOOLS IN CANADA

A RATING OF SCHOOLS OF PHARMACEUTICAL SCIENCE IN JAPAN

A RATING OF U.S. PUBLIC HEALTH SCHOOLS

A RATING OF GRADUATE PROGRAMS IN VETERINARY
MEDICINE/SCIENCES

A RATING OF VETERINARY SCIENCE SCHOOLS IN JAPAN

THE TOP 25 U.S. DENTAL SCHOOLS

INSTITUTION	RANK	SCORE
HARVARD SCHOOL OF DENTAL MEDICINE	1	4.93
UNIVERSITY OF CALIFORNIA—SAN FRANCISCO	2	4.92
UNIVERSITY OF MICHIGAN—ANN ARBOR	3	4.91
COLUMBIA UNIVERSITY	4	4.90
UNIVERSITY OF PENNSYLVANIA	5	4.88
UNIVERSITY OF CALIFORNIA—LOS ANGELES	6	4.86
TUFTS UNIVERSITY	7	4.85
NORTHWESTERN UNIVERSITY DENTAL SCHOOL	8	4.83
UNIVERSITY OF WASHINGTON	9	4.79
OHIO STATE UNIVERSITY—COLUMBUS	10	4.77
UNIVERSITY OF MINNESOTA—TWIN CITIES	11	4.76
UNIVERSITY OF ILLINOIS—CHICAGO	12	4.72
NEW YORK UNIVERSITY	13	4.64
STATE UNIVERSITY OF NEW YORK AT BUFFALO	14	4.58
UNIVERSITY OF PITTSBURGH	15	4.55
CREIGHTON UNIVERSITY	16	4.54
UNIVERSITY OF SOUTHERN CALIFORNIA	17	4.51
MARQUETTE UNIVERSITY	18	4.48
CASE WESTERN RESERVE UNIVERSITY	19	4.45
UNIVERSITY OF INDIANA—INDIANAPOLIS	20	4.43
UNIVERSITY OF NORTH CAROLINA—CHAPEL HILL	21	4.42
TEMPLE UNIVERSITY	22	4.41
UNIVERSITY OF IOWA	23	4.38
STATE UNIVERSITY OF NEW YORK AT STONY BROOK	24	4.36
BAYLOR COLLEGE OF DENTISTRY	25	4.35

A RATING OF U.S. DENTAL SCHOOLS

INSTITUTIONS IN ALPHABETICAL ORDER	RANK	SCORE
UNIVERSITY OF ALABAMA—BIRMINGHAM School of Dentistry Birmingham, AL	35	4.25
THE BALTIMORE COLLEGE OF DENTAL SURGERY Dental School at the University of Maryland—Baltimore County Baltimore, MD	41	4.17
BAYLOR COLLEGE OF DENTISTRY Dallas, TX	25	4.35
BOSTON UNIVERSITY MEDICAL CENTER Henry M. Goldman School of Dental Medicine Boston, MA	29	4.31
UNIVERSITY OF CALIFORNIA—LOS ANGELES School of Dentistry Los Angeles, CA	6	4.86
UNIVERSITY OF CALIFORNIA—SAN FRANCISCO School of Dentistry San Francisco, CA	2	4.92
CASE WESTERN RESERVE UNIVERSITY School of Dentistry Cleveland, OH	19	4.45
UNIVERSITY OF COLORADO—DENVER School of Dentistry Denver, CO	47	4.10
COLUMBIA UNIVERSITY School of Dental and Oral Surgery New York, NY	4	4.90
UNIVERSITY OF CONNECTICUT—FARMINGTON School of Dental Medicine Farmington, CT	38	4.22
CREIGHTON UNIVERSITY School of Dentistry Omaha, NE	16	4.54
UNIVERSITY OF DETROIT MERCY School of Dentistry Detroit, MI	37	4.23

Very Strong = 4.51-4.99   Strong = 4.01-4.49   Good = 3.61-3.99   Acceptable Plus = 3.01-3.59
Adequate = 2.51-2.99   Marginal = 2.01-2.49   Not Sufficient for Graduate Programs = 0.

UNIVERSITY OF FLORIDA   49   4.08
College of Dentistry
Gainesville, FL

HARVARD SCHOOL OF DENTAL MEDICINE   1   4.93
Boston, MA

HOWARD UNIVERSITY   53   4.04
College of Dentistry
Washington, D.C.

UNIVERSITY OF ILLINOIS—CHICAGO   12   4.72
Health Sciences Center-College of Dentistry
Chicago, IL

UNIVERSITY OF INDIANA—INDIANAPOLIS   20   4.43
School of Dentistry
Indianapolis, IN

UNIVERSITY OF IOWA   23   4.38
College of Dentistry
Iowa City, IA

UNIVERSITY OF KENTUCKY   50   4.07
College of Dentistry
Lexington, KY

LOMA LINDA UNIVERSITY   31   4.29
School of Dentistry
Loma Linda, CA

LOUISIANA STATE UNIVERSITY—NEW ORLEANS   34   4.26
School of Dentistry
New Orleans, LA

UNIVERSITY OF LOUISVILLE   28   4.32
School of Dentistry
Louisville, KY

MARQUETTE UNIVERSITY   18   4.48
School of Dentistry
Milwaukee, WI

MEDICAL COLLEGE OF GEORGIA   44   4.14
School of Dentistry
Augusta, GA

MEDICAL UNIVERSITY OF SOUTH CAROLINA   39   4.21
College of Dental Medicine
Charleston, SC

Very Strong = 4.51-4.99   Strong = 4.01-4.49   Good = 3.61-3.99   Acceptable Plus = 3.01-3.59
Adequate = 2.51-2.99   Marginal = 2.01-2.49   Not Sufficient for Graduate Programs = 0.

UNIVERSITY OF MEDICINE AND DENTISTRY OF NEW JERSEY—NEWARK   46   4.11
New Jersey Dental School
Newark, NJ

MEHARRY MEDICAL COLLEGE   45   4.13
School of Dentistry
Nashville, TN

UNIVERSITY OF MICHIGAN—ANN ARBOR   3   4.91
School of Dentistry
Ann Arbor, MI

UNIVERSITY OF MINNESOTA—TWIN CITIES   11   4.76
School of Dentistry
Minneapolis, MN

UNIVERSITY OF MISSISSIPPI—JACKSON   52   4.05
School of Dentistry
Jackson, MS

UNIVERSITY OF MISSOURI—KANSAS CITY   33   4.27
School of Dentistry
Kansas City, MO

UNIVERSITY OF NEBRASKA MEDICAL CENTER   42   4.16
College of Dentistry
Lincoln, NE

NEW YORK UNIVERSITY   13   4.64
College of Dentistry-David B. Kriser Dental Center
New York, NY

UNIVERSITY OF NORTH CAROLINA—CHAPEL HILL   21   4.42
School of Dentistry
Chapel Hill, NC

NORTHWESTERN UNIVERSITY DENTAL SCHOOL   8   4.83
Chicago, IL

OHIO STATE UNIVERSITY—COLUMBUS   10   4.77
College of Dentistry
Columbus, OH

UNIVERSITY OF OKLAHOMA—OKLAHOMA CITY   48   4.09
College of Dentistry
Oklahoma City, OK

OREGON HEALTH SCIENCES UNIVERSITY   27   4.33
School of Dentistry
Portland, OR

Very Strong = 4.51-4.99   Strong = 4.01-4.49   Good = 3.61-3.99   Acceptable Plus = 3.01-3.59
Adequate = 2.51-2.99   Marginal = 2.01-2.49   Not Sufficient for Graduate Programs = 0.

UNIVERSITY OF THE PACIFIC   30   4.30
School of Dentistry
San Francisco, CA

UNIVERSITY OF PENNSYLVANIA   5   4.88
School of Dental Medicine
Philadelphia, PA

UNIVERSITY OF PITTSBURGH   15   4.55
School of Dental Medicine
Pittsburgh, PA

UNIVERSITY OF PUERTO RICO—MEDICAL SCIENCES CAMPUS   54   4.03
School of Dentistry
San Juan, PR

UNIVERSITY OF SOUTHERN CALIFORNIA   17   4.51
School of Dentistry
Los Angeles, CA

SOUTHERN ILLINOIS UNIVERSITY—ALTON   51   4.06
School of Dental Medicine
Alton, IL

STATE UNIVERSITY OF NEW YORK AT BUFFALO   14   4.58
School of Dentistry
Buffalo, NY

STATE UNIVERSITY OF NEW YORK AT STONY BROOK   24   4.36
School of Dental Medicine
Stony Brook, NY

TEMPLE UNIVERSITY   22   4.41
School of Dentistry
Philadelphia, PA

UNIVERSITY OF TENNESSEE—MEMPHIS   36   4.24
College of Dentistry
Memphis, TN

UNIVERSITY OF TEXAS HEALTH SCIENCE CENTER AT HOUSTON   26   4.34
Dental Branch
Houston, TX

UNIVERSITY OF TEXAS HEALTH SCIENCE CENTER AT SAN ANTONIO   32   4.28
Dental School
San Antonio, TX

Very Strong = 4.51-4.99   Strong = 4.01-4.49   Good = 3.61-3.99   Acceptable Plus = 3.01-3.59
Adequate = 2.51-2.99   Marginal = 2.01-2.49   Not Sufficient for Graduate Programs = 0.

TUFTS UNIVERSITY School of Dental Medicine Boston, MA	7	4.85
VIRGINIA COMMONWEALTH UNIVERSITY Medical College of Virginia School of Dentistry Richmond, VA	43	4.15
UNIVERSITY OF WASHINGTON School of Dentistry Seattle, WA	9	4.79
WEST VIRGINIA UNIVERSITY School of Dentistry Morgantown, WV	40	4.18

Very Strong = 4.51-4.99   Strong = 4.01-4.49   Good = 3.61-3.99   Acceptable Plus = 3.01-3.59
Adequate = 2.51-2.99   Marginal = 2.01-2.49   Not Sufficient for Graduate Programs = 0.

THE TOP 10 DENTAL SCHOOLS IN CANADA

INSTITUTION	RANK	SCORE
McGILL UNIVERSITY	1	4.91
UNIVERSITY OF TORONTO	2	4.88
UNIVERSITY OF BRITISH COLUMBIA	3	4.86
UNIVERSITÉ DE MONTREAL	4	4.78
UNIVERSITÉ LAVAL	5	4.71
UNIVERSITY OF MANITOBA	6	4.68
UNIVERSITY OF WESTERN ONTARIO	7	4.59
UNIVERSITY OF ALBERTA	8	4.52
DALHOUSIE UNIVERSITY	9	4.47
UNIVERSITY OF SASKATCHEWAN	10	4.37

A RATING OF DENTAL SCHOOLS IN CANADA

INSTITUTIONS IN ALPHABETICAL ORDER	RANK	SCORE
UNIVERSITY OF ALBERTA Faculty of Medicine and Oral Health Sciences Edmonton, Alberta	8	4.52
UNIVERSITY OF BRITISH COLUMBIA Faculty of Dentistry Vancouver, British Columbia	3	4.86
DALHOUSIE UNIVERSITY Faculty of Dentistry Halifax, Nova Scotia	9	4.47
UNIVERSITÉ LAVAL Faculté de Médecine Dentaire Sainte-Foy, Quebec	5	4.71
UNIVERSITY OF MANITOBA Faculty of Dentistry Winnipeg, Manitoba	6	4.68
McGILL UNIVERSITY Faculty of Dentistry Montreal, Quebec	1	4.91
UNIVERSITÉ DE MONTRÉAL Faculté de Médecine Dentaire Montréal, Quebec	4	4.78
UNIVERSITY OF SASKATCHEWAN College of Dentistry Saskatoon, Saskatchewan	10	4.37
UNIVERSITY OF TORONTO Faculty of Dentistry Toronto, Ontario	2	4.88
UNIVERSITY OF WESTERN ONTARIO Faculty of Dentistry London, Ontario	7	4.59

Very Strong = 4.51-4.99   Strong = 4.01-4.49   Good = 3.61-3.99   Acceptable Plus = 3.01-3.59
Adequate = 2.51-2.99   Marginal = 2.01-2.49   Not Sufficient for Graduate Programs = 0.

A RATING OF DENTAL SCHOOLS IN JAPAN

Leading Institutions

INSTITUTION	RANK	SCORE
NIHON UNIVERSITY	1	4.80
OSAKA UNIVERSITY	2	4.79
KYUSHU DENTAL COLLEGE	3	4.76
KYUSHU UNIVERSITY	4	4.73
HOKKAIDO	5	4.72
HIROSHIMA UNIVERSITY	6	4.70
TOKYO MEDICAL AND DENTAL UNIVERSITY	7	4.66
TOKYO DENTAL COLLEGE	8	4.61
NIPPON DENTAL UNIVERSITY	9	4.58
AICHI GAKUIN UNIVERSITY	10	4.52
IWATE MEDICAL UNIVERSITY	11	4.49
NIIGATA UNIVERSITY	12	4.47
KANAGAWA DENTAL COLLEGE	13	4.43
SHOWA UNIVERSITY	14	4.40
TOHOKU DENTAL UNIVERSITY	15	4.38
TOHOKU UNIVERSITY	16	4.37
HIGASHI NIPPON GAKUEN UNIVERSITY	17	4.34
OKAYAMA UNIVERSITY	18	4.31
TSURUMI UNIVERSITY	19	4.29
ASAHI UNIVERSITY	20	4.24
KAGASHIMA UNIVERSITY	21	4.18
NAGASAKI UNIVERSITY	22	4.10
OSAKA DENTAL UNIVERSITY	23	3.97
FUKUOKA DENTAL COLLEGE	24	3.94
MEIKAI UNIVERSITY	25	3.90
MATSUMOTO DENTAL COLLEGE	26	3.81

THE TOP 25 GRADUATE PROGRAMS IN NURSING

INSTITUTION	RANK	SCORE
UNIVERSITY OF CALIFORNIA—SAN FRANCISCO	1	4.93
CASE WESTERN RESERVE UNIVERSITY	2	4.92
UNIVERSITY OF MICHIGAN—ANN ARBOR	3	4.91
NEW YORK UNIVERSITY	4	4.90
UNIVERSITY OF WASHINGTON	5	4.89
UNIVERSITY OF PENNSYLVANIA	6	4.88
UNIVERSITY OF ILLINOIS—CHICAGO	7	4.87
UNIVERSITY OF PITTSBURGH	8	4.86
WAYNE STATE UNIVERSITY	9	4.85
CATHOLIC UNIVERSITY OF AMERICA	10	4.84
YALE UNIVERSITY	11	4.83
COLUMBIA UNIVERSITY	12	4.82
UNIVERSITY OF MINNESOTA—TWIN CITIES	13	4.81
INDIANA UNIVERSITY—PURDUE UNIVERSITY—INDIANAPOLIS	14	4.80
UNIVERSITY OF TEXAS—AUSTIN	15	4.79
OHIO STATE UNIVERSITY—COLUMBUS	16	4.78
UNIVERSITY OF WISCONSIN—MADISON	17	4.77
UNIVERSITY OF COLORADO HEALTH SCIENCES CENTER	18	4.76
UNIVERSITY OF CALIFORNIA—LOS ANGELES	19	4.75
VANDERBILT UNIVERSITY	20	4.74
UNIVERSITY OF UTAH	21	4.73
STATE UNIVERSITY OF NEW YORK AT BUFFALO	22	4.72
CITY UNIVERSITY OF NEW YORK—HUNTER COLLEGE	23	4.70
COLUMBIA UNIVERSITY—TEACHERS COLLEGE	24	4.68
UNIVERSITY OF NORTH CAROLINA—CHAPEL HILL	25	4.67

A RATING OF GRADUATE PROGRAMS IN NURSING

NSTITUTIONS IN ALPHABETICAL ORDER	RANK	SCORE
ADELPHI UNIVERSITY School of Nursing Garden City, NY	53	4.00
UNIVERSITY OF ALABAMA—BIRMINGHAM School of Nursing Birmingham, AL	35	4.44
ARIZONA STATE UNIVERSITY College of Nursing Tempe, AZ	55	3.86
UNIVERSITY OF ARIZONA College of Nursing Tucson, AZ	33	4.46
UNIVERSITY OF ARKANSAS FOR MEDICAL SCIENCES College of Nursing Little Rock, AR	57	3.83
BOSTON COLLEGE School of Nursing Chestnut Hill, MA	51	4.08
BRIGHAM YOUNG UNIVERSITY College of Nursing Provo, UT	68	3.67
CALIFORNIA STATE UNIVERSITY—FRESNO Department of Nursing Fresno, CA	72	3.61
CALIFORNIA STATE UNIVERSITY—LOS ANGELES Department of Nursing Los Angeles, CA	69	3.65
UNIVERSITY OF CALIFORNIA—LOS ANGELES School of Nursing Los Angeles, CA	19	4.75
UNIVERSITY OF CALIFORNIA—SAN FRANCISCO School of Nursing San Francisco, CA	1	4.93
CASE WESTERN RESERVE UNIVERSITY Frances Payne Bolton School of Nursing Cleveland, OH	2	4.92

Very Strong = 4.51-4.99   Strong = 4.01-4.49   Good = 3.61-3.99   Acceptable Plus = 3.01-3.59
Adequate = 2.51-2.99   Marginal = 2.01-2.49   Not Sufficient for Graduate Programs = 0.

CATHOLIC UNIVERSITY OF AMERICA School of Nursing Washington, D.C.	10	4.84
UNIVERSITY OF CINCINNATI College of Nursing and Health Cincinnati, OH	45	4.21
CITY UNIVERSITY OF NEW YORK—HUNTER COLLEGE Hunter-Bellevue School of Nursing New York, NY	23	4.70
UNIVERSITY OF COLORADO HEALTH SCIENCES CENTER School of Nursing Denver, CO	18	4.76
COLUMBIA UNIVERSITY School of Nursing New York, NY	12	4.82
COLUMBIA UNIVERSITY—TEACHERS COLLEGE Department of Nursing Education New York, NY	24	4.68
UNIVERSITY OF CONNECTICUT School of Nursing Storrs, CT	49	4.13
UNIVERSITY OF DELAWARE College of Nursing Newark, DE	66	3.70
DEPAUL UNIVERSITY Department of Nursing Chicago, IL	65	3.71
EMORY UNIVERSITY Nell Hodgson Woodruff School of Nursing Atlanta, GA	34	4.45
UNIVERSITY OF FLORIDA College of Nursing Gainesville, FL	41	4.28
UNIVERSITY OF ILLINOIS—CHICAGO College of Nursing Chicago, IL	7	4.87
INDIANA UNIVERSITY—PURDUE UNIVERSITY—INDIANAPOLIS School of Nursing Indianapolis, IN	14	4.80

Very Strong = 4.51-4.99   Strong = 4.01-4.49   Good = 3.61-3.99   Acceptable Plus = 3.01-3.59
Adequate = 2.51-2.99   Marginal = 2.01-2.49   Not Sufficient for Graduate Programs = 0.

UNIVERSITY OF IOWA   32   4.47
College of Nursing
Iowa City, IA

UNIVERSITY OF KANSAS—KANSAS CITY   38   4.34
School of Nursing
Kansas City, KS

UNIVERSITY OF KENTUCKY   50   4.10
College of Nursing
Lexington, KY

LOMA LINDA UNIVERSITY   44   4.22
Department of Graduate Nursing
Loma Linda, CA

LOUISIANA STATE UNIVERSITY MEDICAL CENTER   43   4.24
School of Nursing
New Orleans, LA

LOYOLA UNIVERSITY OF CHICAGO   37   4.37
Marcella Niehoff School of Nursing
Chicago, IL

MARQUETTE UNIVERSITY   46   4.20
College of Nursing
Milwaukee, WI

UNIVERSITY OF MARYLAND—BALTIMORE   28   4.62
School of Nursing
Baltimore, MD

MEDICAL COLLEGE OF GEORGIA   39   4.32
Graduate Programs in Nursing
Augusta, GA

UNIVERSITY OF MICHIGAN—ANN ARBOR   3   4.91
School of Nursing
Ann Arbor, MI

UNIVERSITY OF MINNESOTA—TWIN CITIES   13   4.81
School of Nursing
Minneapolis, MN

UNIVERSITY OF MISSOURI—COLUMBIA   56   3.85
School of Nursing
Columbia, MO

UNIVERSITY OF NEBRASKA MEDICAL CENTER   58   3.81
Graduate Program in Nursing
Omaha, NE

Very Strong = 4.51-4.99   Strong = 4.01-4.49   Good = 3.61-3.99   Acceptable Plus = 3.01-3.59
Adequate = 2.51-2.99   Marginal = 2.01-2.49   Not Sufficient for Graduate Programs = 0.

NEW YORK UNIVERSITY   4   4.90
School of Education, Division of Nursing
New York, NY

UNIVERSITY OF NORTH CAROLINA—CHAPEL HILL   25   4.67
School of Nursing
Chapel Hill, NC

UNIVERSITY OF NORTH CAROLINA—CHAPEL HILL   26   4.66
School of Public Health
Chapel Hill, NC

NORTHERN ILLINOIS UNIVERSITY   60   3.77
School of Nursing
De Kalb, IL

OHIO STATE UNIVERSITY—COLUMBUS   16   4.78
College of Nursing
Columbus, OH

UNIVERSITY OF OKLAHOMA HEALTH SCIENCES CENTER   59   3.79
College of Nursing
Oklahoma City, OK

OREGON HEALTH SCIENCES UNIVERSITY   27   4.63
School of Nursing
Portland, OR

PENNSYLVANIA STATE UNIVERSITY—UNIVERSITY PARK   48   4.15
Department of Nursing
University Park, PA

UNIVERSITY OF PENNSYLVANIA   6   4.88
School of Nursing
Philadelphia, PA

UNIVERSITY OF PITTSBURGH   8   4.86
School of Nursing
Pittsburgh, PA

UNIVERSITY OF PUERTO RICO—MEDICAL SCIENCES CAMPUS   73   3.60
School of Nursing
San Juan, PR

UNIVERSITY OF ROCHESTER   29   4.61
School of Nursing
Rochester, NY

RUSH UNIVERSITY   30   4.60
College of Nursing
Chicago, IL

Very Strong = 4.51-4.99   Strong = 4.01-4.49   Good = 3.61-3.99   Acceptable Plus = 3.01-3.59
Adequate = 2.51-2.99   Marginal = 2.01-2.49   Not Sufficient for Graduate Programs = 0.

RUTGERS UNIVERSITY—NEWARK   61   3.76
College of Nursing
Newark, NJ

SAGE GRADUATE SCHOOL   70   3.64
Department of Nursing
Troy, NY

ST. LOUIS UNIVERSITY   36   4.42
School of Nursing
St. Louis, MO

UNIVERSITY OF SOUTH CAROLINA—COLUMBIA   62   3.75
College of Nursing
Columbia, SC

UNIVERSITY OF SOUTHERN MISSISSIPPI   71   3.63
School of Nursing
Hattiesburg, MS

STATE UNIVERSITY OF NEW YORK AT BINGHAMTON   63   3.73
School of Nursing
Binghamton, NY

STATE UNIVERSITY OF NEW YORK AT BUFFALO   22   4.72
School of Nursing
Buffalo, NY

SYRACUSE UNIVERSITY   42   4.26
College of Nursing
Syracuse, NY

UNIVERSITY OF TENNESSEE—MEMPHIS   40   4.30
College of Nursing
Memphis, TN

UNIVERSITY OF TEXAS HEALTH SCIENCE CENTER AT HOUSTON   64   3.72
School of Nursing
Houston, TX

UNIVERSITY OF TEXAS HEALTH SCIENCE CENTER AT SAN ANTONIO   31   4.49
School of Nursing
San Antonio, TX

TEXAS WOMAN'S UNIVERSITY   54   3.88
College of Nursing
Denton, TX

UNIVERSITY OF TEXAS—AUSTIN   15   4.79
School of Nursing
Austin, TX

Very Strong = 4.51-4.99   Strong = 4.01-4.49   Good = 3.61-3.99   Acceptable Plus = 3.01-3.59
Adequate = 2.51-2.99   Marginal = 2.01-2.49   Not Sufficient for Graduate Programs = 0.

UNIVERSITY OF UTAH
College of Nursing
Salt Lake City, UT
21   4.73

VANDERBILT UNIVERSITY
Graduate School and School of Nursing
Nashville, TN
20   4.74

VIRGINIA COMMONWEALTH UNIVERSITY
School of Nursing
Richmond, VA
52   4.03

UNIVERSITY OF VIRGINIA
School of Nursing
Charlottesville, VA
47   4.17

UNIVERSITY OF WASHINGTON
School of Nursing
Seattle, WA
5   4.89

WAYNE STATE UNIVERSITY
College of Nursing
Detroit, MI
9   4.85

UNIVERSITY OF WISCONSIN—MADISON
School of Nursing
Madison, WI
17   4.77

UNIVERSITY OF WISCONSIN—MILWAUKEE
School of Nursing
Milwaukee, WI
67   3.68

YALE UNIVERSITY
School of Nursing
New Haven, CT
11   4.83

Very Strong = 4.51-4.99   Strong = 4.01-4.49   Good = 3.61-3.99   Acceptable Plus = 3.01-3.59
Adequate = 2.51-2.99   Marginal = 2.01-2.49   Not Sufficient for Graduate Programs = 0.

THE TOP 10 GRADUATE PROGRAMS IN OPTOMETRY

INSTITUTION	RANK	SCORE
UNIVERSITY OF CALIFORNIA—BERKELEY	1	4.93
OHIO STATE UNIVERSITY—COLUMBUS	2	4.92
INDIANA UNIVERSITY—BLOOMINGTON	3	4.90
SOUTHERN CALIFORNIA COLLEGE OF OPTOMETRY	4	4.88
UNIVERSITY OF HOUSTON	5	4.84
UNIVERSITY OF ALABAMA—BIRMINGHAM	6	4.83
STATE UNIVERSITY OF NEW YORK COLLEGE OF OPTOMETRY	7	4.75
UNIVERSITY OF MISSOURI—ST. LOUIS	8	4.74
PENNSYLVANIA COLLEGE OF OPTOMETRY	9	4.72
FERRIS STATE UNIVERSITY	10	4.66

A RATING OF GRADUATE PROGRAMS IN OPTOMETRY

INSTITUTIONS IN ALPHABETICAL ORDER	RANK	SCORE
UNIVERSITY OF ALABAMA—BIRMINGHAM School of Optometry Birmingham, AL	6	4.83
UNIVERSITY OF CALIFORNIA—BERKELEY School of Optometry Berkeley, CA	1	4.93
FERRIS STATE UNIVERSITY College of Optometry Big Rapids, MI	10	4.66
UNIVERSITY OF HOUSTON College of Optometry Houston, TX	5	4.84
ILLINOIS COLLEGE OF OPTOMETRY Chicago, IL	13	4.53
INDIANA UNIVERSITY—BLOOMINGTON School of Optometry Bloomington, IN	3	4.90
INTER AMERICAN UNIVERSITY OF PUERTO RICO—METROPOLITAN CAMPUS School of Optometry San Juan, PR	16	4.14
UNIVERSITY OF MISSOURI—ST. LOUIS School of Optometry St. Louis, MO	8	4.74
NEW ENGLAND COLLEGE OF OPTOMETRY Boston, MA	11	4.60
NORTHEASTERN STATE UNIVERSITY College of Optometry Tahlequah, OK	15	4.33
NOVA SOUTHEASTERN UNIVERSITY College of Optometry Fort Lauderdale, FL	17	4.12
OHIO STATE UNIVERSITY—COLUMBUS College of Optometry Columbus, OH	2	4.92
PACIFIC UNIVERSITY College of Optometry Forest Grove, OR	12	4.59

Very Strong = 4.51-4.99   Strong = 4.01-4.49   Good = 3.61-3.99   Acceptable Plus = 3.01-3.59
Adequate = 2.51-2.99   Marginal = 2.01-2.49   Not Sufficient for Graduate Programs = 0.

PENNSYLVANIA COLLEGE OF OPTOMETRY   9   4.72
Philadelphia, PA

SOUTHERN CALIFORNIA COLLEGE OF OPTOMETRY   4   4.88
Fullerton, CA

SOUTHERN COLLEGE OF OPTOMETRY   14   4.37
Memphis, TN

STATE UNIVERSITY OF NEW YORK COLLEGE OF OPTOMETRY   7   4.75
New York, NY

Very Strong = 4.51-4.99   Strong = 4.01-4.49   Good = 3.61-3.99   Acceptable Plus = 3.01-3.59
Adequate = 2.51-2.99   Marginal = 2.01-2.49   Not Sufficient for Graduate Programs = 0.

THE TOP 25 U.S. PHARMACY SCHOOLS

INSTITUTION	RANK	SCORE
UNIVERSITY OF CALIFORNIA—SAN FRANCISCO	1	4.93
UNIVERSITY OF NORTH CAROLINA—CHAPEL HILL	2	4.92
UNIVERSITY OF WASHINGTON	3	4.91
UNIVERSITY OF WISCONSIN—MADISON	4	4.90
UNIVERSITY OF COLORADO HEALTH SCIENCES CENTER	5	4.88
UNIVERSITY OF IOWA	6	4.86
UNIVERSITY OF MINNESOTA—TWIN CITIES	7	4.85
UNIVERSITY OF MICHIGAN—ANN ARBOR	8	4.83
UNIVERSITY OF TEXAS—AUSTIN	9	4.81
UNIVERSITY OF SOUTHERN CALIFORNIA	10	4.79
UNIVERSITY OF KENTUCKY	11	4.78
MEDICAL UNIVERSITY OF SOUTH CAROLINA	12	4.77
UNIVERSITY OF PITTSBURGH	13	4.76
UNIVERSITY OF UTAH	14	4.75
UNIVERSITY OF CINCINNATI	15	4.73
OREGON STATE UNIVERSITY	16	4.71
WEST VIRGINIA UNIVERSITY	17	4.69
UNIVERSITY OF FLORIDA	18	4.67
OHIO STATE UNIVERSITY—COLUMBUS	19	4.66
UNIVERSITY OF TENNESSEE—MEMPHIS	20	4.65
UNIVERSITY OF ILLINOIS—CHICAGO	21	4.64
WASHINGTON STATE UNIVERSITY	22	4.63
UNIVERSITY OF MARYLAND—BALTIMORE	23	4.60
TEMPLE UNIVERSITY	24	4.58
UNIVERSITY OF CONNECTICUT	25	4.56

A RATING OF U.S. PHARMACY SCHOOLS

NSTITUTIONS IN ALPHABETICAL ORDER	RANK	SCORE
ALBANY COLLEGE OF PHARMACY OF UNION UNIVERSITY Albany, NY	27	4.53
UNIVERSITY OF ARIZONA College of Pharmacy Tucson, AZ	40	4.34
UNIVERSITY OF ARKANSAS FOR MEDICAL SCIENCES College of Pharmacy Little Rock, AR	45	4.27
AUBURN UNIVERSITY School of Pharmacy and Graduate School Auburn University, AL	53	4.19
BUTLER UNIVERSITY College of Pharmacy Indianapolis, IN	38	4.36
UNIVERSITY OF CALIFORNIA—SAN FRANCISCO Department of Pharmaceutical Chemistry San Francisco, CA	1	4.93
UNIVERSITY OF CINCINNATI College of Pharmacy Cincinnati, OH	15	4.73
UNIVERSITY OF COLORADO HEALTH SCIENCES CENTER School of Pharmacy Denver, CO	5	4.88
UNIVERSITY OF CONNECTICUT School of Pharmacy Storrs, CT	25	4.56
CREIGHTON UNIVERSITY School of Pharmacy and Allied Health Professions Omaha, NE	37	4.37
DUQUESNE UNIVERSITY School of Pharmacy Pittsburgh, PA	48	4.24

Very Strong = 4.51-4.99   Strong = 4.01-4.49   Good = 3.61-3.99   Acceptable Plus = 3.01-3.59
Adequate = 2.51-2.99   Marginal = 2.01-2.49   Not Sufficient for Graduate Programs = 0.

FERRIS STATE UNIVERSITY
College of Pharmacy
Big Rapids, MI
56   4.14

FLORIDA A&M UNIVERSITY
College of Pharmacy and Pharmaceutical Sciences
Tallahassee, FL
57   4.13

UNIVERSITY OF FLORIDA
College of Pharmacy and Graduate School
Gainesville, FL
18   4.67

UNIVERSITY OF GEORGIA
College of Pharmacy and Graduate School
Athens, GA
44   4.30

UNIVERSITY OF HOUSTON
College of Pharmacy
Houston, TX
34   4.42

IDAHO STATE UNIVERSITY
College of Pharmacy
Pocatello, ID
59   4.10

UNIVERSITY OF ILLINOIS—CHICAGO
College of Pharmacy
Chicago, IL
21   4.64

UNIVERSITY OF IOWA
College of Pharmacy and Graduate College
Iowa City, IA
6   4.86

UNIVERSITY OF KANSAS
School of Pharmacy
Lawrence, KS
28   4.52

UNIVERSITY OF KENTUCKY
College of Pharmacy and Graduate School
Lexington, KY
11   4.78

LONG ISLAND UNIVERSITY—BROOKLYN CAMPUS
Arnold and Marie Schwartz College of Pharmacy and Health Sciences
Brooklyn, NY
51   4.21

UNIVERSITY OF MARYLAND—BALTIMORE
School of Pharmacy and Graduate School
Baltimore, MD
23   4.60

MASSACHUSETTS COLLEGE OF PHARMACY AND ALLIED HEALTH SCIENCES
Boston, MA
46   4.26

Very Strong = 4.51-4.99   Strong = 4.01-4.49   Good = 3.61-3.99   Acceptable Plus = 3.01-3.59
Adequate = 2.51-2.99   Marginal = 2.01-2.49   Not Sufficient for Graduate Programs = 0.

MEDICAL UNIVERSITY OF SOUTH CAROLINA 12 4.77
Department of Pharmaceutical Sciences
Charleston, SC

UNIVERSITY OF MICHIGAN—ANN ARBOR 8 4.83
College of Pharmacy
Ann Arbor, MI

UNIVERSITY OF MINNESOTA—TWIN CITIES 7 4.85
College of Pharmacy and Graduate School
Minneapolis, MN

UNIVERSITY OF MISSISSIPPI 32 4.46
School of Pharmacy
University, MS

UNIVERSITY OF MISSOURI—KANSAS CITY 49 4.23
School of Pharmacy
Kansas City, MO

UNIVERSITY OF NEBRASKA—OMAHA 42 4.32
College of Pharmacy
Omaha, NE

UNIVERSITY OF NEW MEXICO 47 4.25
College of Pharmacy
Albuquerque, NM

UNIVERSITY OF NORTH CAROLINA—CHAPEL HILL 2 4.92
School of Pharmacy and Graduate School
Chapel Hill, NC

NORTH DAKOTA STATE UNIVERSITY 54 4.17
College of Pharmacy
Fargo, ND

NOVA SOUTHEASTERN UNIVERSITY 55 4.15
College of Pharmacy
Fort Lauderdale, FL

OHIO STATE UNIVERSITY—COLUMBUS 19 4.66
College of Pharmacy and Graduate School
Columbus, OH

UNIVERSITY OF OKLAHOMA HEALTH SCIENCES CENTER 31 4.48
College of Pharmacy
Oklahoma City, OK

OREGON STATE UNIVERSITY 16 4.71
College of Pharmacy
Corvallis, OR

Very Strong = 4.51-4.99   Strong = 4.01-4.49   Good = 3.61-3.99   Acceptable Plus = 3.01-3.59
Adequate = 2.51-2.99   Marginal = 2.01-2.49   Not Sufficient for Graduate Programs = 0.

UNIVERSITY OF THE PACIFIC
School of Pharmacy
Stockton, CA

50 4.22

PHILADELPHIA COLLEGE OF PHARMACY AND SCIENCE
Philadelphia, PA

35 4.40

UNIVERSITY OF PITTSBURGH
School of Pharmacy
Pittsburgh, PA

13 4.76

UNIVERSITY OF PUERTO RICO—MEDICAL SCIENCES CAMPUS
College of Pharmacy
San Juan, PR

36 4.38

PURDUE UNIVERSITY—WEST LAFAYETTE
School of Pharmacy and Pharmacal Sciences and Graduate School
West Lafayette, IN

30 4.49

UNIVERSITY OF RHODE ISLAND
College of Pharmacy
Kingston, RI

43 4.31

RUTGERS UNIVERSITY—NEW BRUNSWICK
Program in Pharmaceutical Science
New Brunswick, NJ

39 4.35

ST. JOHN'S UNIVERSITY
College of Pharmacy and Allied Health Professions
Jamaica, NY

33 4.44

ST. LOUIS COLLEGE OF PHARMACY
St. Louis, MO

58 4.12

UNIVERSITY OF SOUTH CAROLINA—COLUMBIA
College of Pharmacy and Graduate School
Columbia, SC

41 4.33

UNIVERSITY OF SOUTHERN CALIFORNIA
School of Pharmacy
Los Angeles, CA

10 4.79

STATE UNIVERSITY OF NEW YORK AT BUFFALO
School of Pharmacy
Buffalo, NY

29 4.50

TEMPLE UNIVERSITY
School of Pharmacy
Philadelphia, PA

24 4.58

UNIVERSITY OF TENNESSEE—MEMPHIS
College of Graduate Health Sciences and Pharmacy
Memphis, TN

20 4.65

Very Strong = 4.51-4.99   Strong = 4.01-4.49   Good = 3.61-3.99   Acceptable Plus = 3.01-3.59
Adequate = 2.51-2.99   Marginal = 2.01-2.49   Not Sufficient for Graduate Programs = 0.

UNIVERSITY OF TEXAS—AUSTIN
College of Pharmacy
Austin, TX

9   4.81

UNIVERSITY OF UTAH
College of Pharmacy and Graduate School
Salt Lake City, UT

14   4.75

VIRGINIA COMMONWEALTH UNIVERSITY
School of Pharmacy Graduate Programs
Richmond, VA

52   4.20

WASHINGTON STATE UNIVERSITY
College of Pharmacy
Pullman, WA

22   4.63

UNIVERSITY OF WASHINGTON
School of Pharmacy and Graduate School
Seattle, WA

3   4.91

WAYNE STATE UNIVERSITY
Faculty of Pharmacy
Detroit, MI

26   4.55

WEST VIRGINIA UNIVERSITY
School of Pharmacy
Morgantown, WV

17   4.69

UNIVERSITY OF WISCONSIN—MADISON
School of Pharmacy
Madison, WI

4   4.90

THE TOP 8 PHARMACY SCHOOLS IN CANADA

INSTITUTION	RANK	SCORE
UNIVERSITY OF TORONTO	1	4.84
UNIVERSITY OF BRITISH COLUMBIA	2	4.81
UNIVERSITÉ DE MONTRÉAL	3	4.73
UNIVERSITÉ LAVAL	4	4.68
UNIVERSITY OF MANITOBA	5	4.60
UNIVERSITY OF ALBERTA	6	4.51
DALHOUSIE UNIVERSITY	7	4.45
UNIVERSITY OF SASKATCHEWAN	8	4.37

A RATING OF PHARMACY SCHOOLS IN CANADA

INSTITUTIONS IN ALPHABETICAL ORDER	RANK	SCORE
UNIVERSITY OF ALBERTA Faculty of Pharmacy and Pharmaceutical Sciences Edmonton, Alberta	6	4.51
UNIVERSITY OF BRITISH COLUMBIA Faculty of Pharmaceutical Sciences Vancouver, British Columbia	2	4.81
DALHOUSIE UNIVERSITY College of Pharmacy Halifax, Nova Scotia	7	4.45
UNIVERSITÉ LAVAL School of Pharmacy Sainte-Foy, Quebec	4	4.68
UNIVERSITY OF MANITOBA Faculty of Pharmacy Winnipeg, Manitoba	5	4.60
UNIVERSITÉ DE MONTRÉAL Faculty of Pharmacy Montréal, Quebec	3	4.73
UNIVERSITY OF SASKATCHEWAN College of Pharmacy and Nutrition Saskatoon, Saskatchewan	8	4.37
UNIVERSITY OF TORONTO Department of Pharmacy Toronto, Ontario	1	4.84

Very Strong = 4.51-4.99   Strong = 4.01-4.49   Good = 3.61-3.99   Acceptable Plus = 3.01-3.59
Adequate = 2.51-2.99   Marginal = 2.01-2.49   Not Sufficient for Graduate Programs = 0.

A RATING OF SCHOOLS OF PHARMACEUTICAL SCIENCE IN JAPAN

Leading Institutions

INSTITUTION	RANK	SCORE
THE UNIVERSITY OF TOYKO	1	4.79
HOKKAIDO UNIVERSITY	2	4.76
HIROSHIMA UNIVERSITY	3	4.74
CHIBA UNIVERSITY	4	4.73
OSAKA UNIVERSITY	5	4.71
KYOTO UNIVERSITY	6	4.68
TOHOKU UNIVERSITY	7	4.66
MEIJO UNIVERSITY	8	4.63
UNIVERSITY OF TOKUSHIMA	9	4.62
TOYAMA MEDICAL & PHARMACEUTICAL UNIVERSITY	10	4.58
KANAZAWA UNIVERSITY	11	4.55
KOKURIKU UNIVERSITY	12	4.53
TEIKYO UNIVERSITY	13	4.48
TOHO UNIVERSITY	14	4.46
KYOTO PHARMECEUTICAL	15	4.43
TOKYO COLLEGE OF PHARMACY	16	4.42
HOSHI UNIVERSITY	17	4.39
TOHOKU COLLEGE OF PHARMACY	18	4.38
NAGASAKI UNIVERSITY	19	4.36
KYUSHU UNIVERSITY	20	4.34
MIEIJ COLLEGE OF PHARMACY	21	4.30
NAGOYA CITY UNIVERSITY	22	4.28
OSAKA UNIVERSITY OF PHARMACEUTICAL SCEINCES	23	4.25
KUMAMOTO UNIVERSITY	24	4.19
GIFU PHARMACEUTICAL UNIVERSITY	25	4.15
SCIENCE UNIVERSITY OF TOKYO	26	4.13
KINKI UNIVERSITY	27	4.12
JOSAI UNIVERSITY	28	4.09
FUKUOKA UNIVERSITY	29	4.06
HIGASHI NIPPON GAKUEN UNIVERSITY	30	4.04
KITASATO UNIVERSITY	31	3.91
OKAYAMA UNIVERSITY	32	3.86
TOKUSHIMA BUNRI UNIVERSITY	33	3.84
HOKKAIDO INSTITUTE OF PHARMACEUTICAL SCIENCES	34	3.80
KOBE-GAKUIN UNIVERSITY	35	3.75
SHOWA UNIVERSITY	36	3.72
KYORITSU COLLEGE OF PHARMACY	37	3.68
FUKUYAMA UNIVERSITY	38	3.64
SHIZUOKA PREFECTURAL UNIVERSITY	39	3.62

SHOWA COLLEGE OF PHARMACEUTICAL SCIENCES	40	3.61
KOBE WOMENíS COLLEGE OF PHARMACY	41	3.58
NIGATA COLLEGE OF PHARMACY	42	3.54
MUKOGAWA WOMENíS UNIVERSITY	43	3.50
DAIICHI COLLEGE OF PHARMACEUTICAL SCIENCES	44	3.45
SETSUNAN UNIVERSITY	45	3.40

THE TOP 10 GRADUATE PROGRAMS IN PUBLIC HEALTH

INSTITUTION	RANK	SCORE
JOHNS HOPKINS UNIVERSITY	1	4.95
UNIVERSITY OF CALIFORNIA—BERKELEY	2	4.94
HARVARD UNIVERSITY	3	4.92
UNIVERSITY OF MICHIGAN—ANN ARBOR	4	4.91
UNIVERSITY OF CALIFORNIA—LOS ANGELES	5	4.90
YALE UNIVERSITY	6	4.89
UNIVERSITY OF MINNESOTA—TWIN CITIES	7	4.86
UNIVERSITY OF NORTH CAROLINA—CHAPEL HILL	8	4.84
COLUMBIA UNIVERSITY	9	4.82
TULANE UNIVERSITY	10	4.80

A RATING OF GRADUATE PROGRAMS IN PUBLIC HEALTH

INSTITUTIONS IN ALPHABETICAL ORDER	RANK	SCORE
UNIVERSITY OF ALABAMA—BIRMINGHAM School of Public Health Birmingham, AL	15	4.68
BOSTON UNIVERSITY School of Public Health Boston, MA	19	4.58
UNIVERSITY OF CALIFORNIA—BERKELEY School of Public Health Berkeley, CA	2	4.94
UNIVERSITY OF CALIFORNIA—LOS ANGELES Graduate Programs in Environmental Health Sciences Los Angeles, CA	5	4.90
COLUMBIA UNIVERSITY School of Public Health New York, NY	9	4.82
EMORY UNIVERSITY Rollins School of Public Health Atlanta, GA	12	4.74
HARVARD UNIVERSITY School of Public Health Boston, MA	3	4.92
UNIVERSITY OF HAWAII—MANOA School of Public Health Honolulu, HI	21	4.48
UNIVERSITY OF ILLINOIS—CHICAGO School of Public Health Chicago, IL	25	4.31
JOHNS HOPKINS UNIVERSITY School of Hygiene and Public Health Baltimore, MD	1	4.95
LOMA LINDA UNIVERSITY School of Public Health Loma Linda, CA	17	4.63
UNIVERSITY OF MASSACHUSETTS—AMHERST School of Public Health and Health Sciences Amherst, MA	18	4.60

Very Strong = 4.51-4.99   Strong = 4.01-4.49   Good = 3.61-3.99   Acceptable Plus = 3.01-3.59
Adequate = 2.51-2.99   Marginal = 2.01-2.49   Not Sufficient for Graduate Programs = 0.

UNIVERSITY OF MICHIGAN—ANN ARBOR   4   4.91
School of Public Health
Ann Arbor, MI

UNIVERSITY OF MINNESOTA—TWIN CITIES   7   4.86
School of Public Health
Minneapolis, MN

UNIVERSITY OF NORTH CAROLINA—CHAPEL HILL   8   4.84
School of Public Health
Chapel Hill, NC

UNIVERSITY OF OKLAHOMA HEALTH SCIENCES CENTER   16   4.66
College of Public Health
Oklahoma City, OK

UNIVERSITY OF PITTSBURGH   13   4.72
Graduate School of Public Health
Pittsburgh, PA

UNIVERSITY OF PUERTO RICO—MEDICAL SCIENCES CAMPUS   20   4.52
Graduate School of Public Health
San Juan, PR

ST. LOUIS UNIVERSITY   23   4.40
School of Public Health
St. Louis, MO

UNIVERSITY OF SOUTH CAROLINA—COLUMBIA   22   4.45
School of Public Health
Columbia, SC

UNIVERSITY OF SOUTH FLORIDA   24   4.35
College of Public Health
Tampa, FL

STATE UNIVERSITY OF NEW YORK AT ALBANY   26   4.28
School of Public Health
Albany, NY

UNIVERSITY OF TEXAS HEALTH SCIENCE CENTER AT HOUSTON   14   4.71
School of Public Health
Houston, TX

TULANE UNIVERSITY   10   4.80
School of Public Health and Tropical Medicine
New Orleans, LA

UNIVERSITY OF WASHINGTON   11   4.76
School of Public Health and Community Medicine
Seattle, WA

YALE UNIVERSITY   6   4.89
Department of Epidemiology and Public Health
New Haven, CT

Very Strong = 4.51-4.99   Strong = 4.01-4.49   Good = 3.61-3.99   Acceptable Plus = 3.01-3.59
Adequate = 2.51-2.99   Marginal = 2.01-2.49   Not Sufficient for Graduate Programs = 0.

THE TOP 10 GRADUATE PROGRAMS IN VETERINARY MEDICINE/SCIENCES

INSTITUTION	RANK	SCORE
UNIVERSITY OF CALIFORNIA—DAVIS	1	4.92
CORNELL UNIVERSITY	2	4.90
UNIVERSITY OF PENNSYLVANIA	3	4.85
OHIO STATE UNIVERSITY—COLUMBUS	4	4.80
COLORADO STATE UNIVERSITY	5	4.79
MICHIGAN STATE UNIVERSITY	6	4.77
IOWA STATE UNIVERSITY OF SCIENCE AND TECHNOLOGY	7	4.73
UNIVERSITY OF MINNESOTA—TWIN CITIES	8	4.68
PURDUE UNIVERSITY—WEST LAFAYETTE	9	4.66
UNIVERSITY OF MISSOURI—COLUMBIA	10	4.64

A RATING OF GRADUATE PROGRAMS IN VETERINARY MEDICINE/SCIENCES

INSTITUTIONS IN ALPHABETICAL ORDER	RANK	SCORE
AUBURN UNIVERSITY College of Veterinary Medicine Auburn University, AL	20	4.27
UNIVERSITY OF CALIFORNIA—DAVIS School of Veterinary Medicine Davis, CA	1	4.92
COLORADO STATE UNIVERSITY College of Veterinary Medicine and Biomedical Sciences Fort Collins, CO	5	4.79
CORNELL UNIVERSITY Professional School of Veterinary Medicine Ithaca, NY	2	4.90
UNIVERSITY OF FLORIDA College of Veterinary Medicine Gainesville, FL	21	4.20
UNIVERSITY OF GEORGIA College of Veterinary Medicine Athens, GA	16	4.46
UNIVERSITY OF ILLINOIS—URBANA-CHAMPAIGN College of Veterinary Medicine Champaign, IL	13	4.57
IOWA STATE UNIVERSITY OF SCIENCE AND TECHNOLOGY College of Veterinary Medicine Ames, IA	7	4.73
KANSAS STATE UNIVERSITY College of Veterinary Medicine Manhattan, KS	15	4.52
LOUISIANA STATE UNIVERSITY—BATON ROUGE School of Veterinary Medicine Baton Rouge, LA	17	4.42
MICHIGAN STATE UNIVERSITY College of Veterinary Medicine East Lansing, MI	6	4.77
UNIVERSITY OF MINNESOTA—TWIN CITIES College of Veterinary Medicine Minneapolis, MN	8	4.68

Very Strong = 4.51-4.99   Strong = 4.01-4.49   Good = 3.61-3.99   Acceptable Plus = 3.01-3.59
Adequate = 2.51-2.99   Marginal = 2.01-2.49   Not Sufficient for Graduate Programs = 0.

MISSISSIPPI STATE UNIVERSITY   24   4.08
College of Veterinary Medicine
Mississippi State, MS

UNIVERSITY OF MISSOURI—COLUMBIA   10   4.64
School of Veterinary Medicine
Columbia, MO

NORTH CAROLINA STATE UNIVERSITY   18   4.37
College of Veterinary Medicine
Raleigh, NC

OHIO STATE UNIVERSITY—COLUMBUS   4   4.80
College of Veterinary Medicine
Columbus, OH

OKLAHOMA STATE UNIVERSITY   25   4.04
College of Veterinary Medicine
Stillwater, OK

OREGON STATE UNIVERSITY   22   4.17
College of Veterinary Medicine
Corvallis, OR

UNIVERSITY OF PENNSYLVANIA   3   4.85
School of Veterinary Medicine
Philadelphia, PA

PURDUE UNIVERSITY—WEST LAFAYETTE   9   4.66
School of Veterinary Medicine
West Lafayette, IN

UNIVERSITY OF TENNESSEE—KNOXVILLE   26   4.01
College of Veterinary Medicine
Knoxville, TN

TEXAS A&M UNIVERSITY—COLLEGE STATION   11   4.62
College of Veterinary Medicine
College Station, TX

TUFTS UNIVERSITY   14   4.54
School of Veterinary Medicine
Medford, MA

VIRGINIA POLYTECHNIC INSTITUTE AND STATE UNIVERSITY   19   4.30
Virginia-Maryland Regional College of Veterinary Medicine
Blacksburg, VA

WASHINGTON STATE UNIVERSITY   23   4.11
College of Veterinary Medicine
Pullman, WA

UNIVERSITY OF WISCONSIN—MADISON   12   4.59
School of Veterinary Medicine
Madison, WI

Very Strong = 4.51-4.99   Strong = 4.01-4.49   Good = 3.61-3.99   Acceptable Plus = 3.01-3.59
Adequate = 2.51-2.99   Marginal = 2.01-2.49   Not Sufficient for Graduate Programs = 0.

A RATING OF VETERINARY SCIENCES SCHOOLS IN JAPAN

LEADING INSTITUTIONS

INSTITUTION	RANK	SCORE
NIHON UNIVERSITY	1	4.71
THE UNIVERSITY OF TOKYO	2	4.68
HOKKAIDO UNIVERSITY	3	4.62
NIPPON VETERINATY & ZOOTECHNICAL COLLEGE	4	4.58
AZABU UNIVERSITY	5	4.53
KITASATO UNIVERSITY	6	4.46
OBIHIRO UNIVERSITY OF AGRICULTURE & VETERINARY MEDICINE	7	4.42
RAKUNO GAKUEN UNIVERSITY	8	4.31
TOKYO UNIVERSITY OF AGRICULTURE & TECHNOLOGY	9	4.22
UNIVERSITY OF OSAKA PREFECTURE	10	4.16
IWATE UNIVERSITY	11	3.81
YAMAGUCHI UNIVERSITY	12	3.77
GIFU UNIVERSITY	13	3.62
MIYAZAKI UNIVERSITY	14	3.50
UNIVERSITY OF TOTTORI	15	3.43
KAGOSHIMA UNIVERSITY	16	3.29

Part V
THE GOURMAN REPORT
ENGINEERING PROGRAMS

THE TOP 50 GRADUATE SCHOOLS IN ENGINEERING

A RATING OF GRADUATE SCHOOLS IN ENGINEERING

THE TOP 50 GRADUATE SCHOOLS IN ENGINEERING

(ALL MAJORS EVALUATED)

INSTITUTION	RANK	SCORE
MASSACHUSETTS INSTITUTE OF TECHNOLOGY	1	4.93
UNIVERSITY OF CALIFORNIA—BERKELEY	2	4.91
UNIVERSITY OF ILLINOIS—URBANA-CHAMPAIGN	3	4.90
STANFORD UNIVERSITY	4	4.89
CALIFORNIA INSTITUTE OF TECHNOLOGY	5	4.88
CORNELL UNIVERSITY	6	4.86
GEORGIA INSTITUTE OF TECHNOLOGY	7	4.84
PURDUE UNIVERSITY—WEST LAFAYETTE	8	4.83
UNIVERSITY OF TEXAS—AUSTIN	9	4.80
UNIVERSITY OF MICHIGAN—ANN ARBOR	10	4.79
UNIVERSITY OF PENNSYLVANIA	11	4.77
UNIVERSITY OF MINNESOTA—TWIN CITIES	12	4.75
UNIVERSITY OF WISCONSIN—MADISON	13	4.73
CARNEGIE MELLON UNIVERSITY	14	4.71
OHIO STATE UNIVERSITY—COLUMBUS	15	4.69
PRINCETON UNIVERSITY	16	4.68
COLUMBIA UNIVERSITY	17	4.67
PENNSYLVANIA STATE UNIVERSITY—UNIVERSITY PARK	18	4.66
HARVARD UNIVERSITY	19	4.63
UNIVERSITY OF CALIFORNIA—SAN DIEGO	20	4.60
NORTHWESTERN UNIVERSITY	21	4.57
RICE UNIVERSITY	22	4.55
RENSSELAER POLYTECHNIC INSTITUTE	23	4.50
UNIVERSITY OF WASHINGTON	24	4.48
UNIVERSITY OF CALIFORNIA—LOS ANGELES	25	4.47
UNIVERSITY OF CALIFORNIA—DAVIS	26	4.46
CASE WESTERN RESERVE UNIVERSITY	27	4.44
TEXAS A&M UNIVERSITY—COLLEGE STATION	28	4.42
UNIVERSITY OF SOUTHERN CALIFORNIA	29	4.41
UNIVERSITY OF FLORIDA	30	4.40
NORTH CAROLINA STATE UNIVERSITY	31	4.39
UNIVERSITY OF VIRGINIA	32	4.37
UNIVERSITY OF ARIZONA	33	4.36
IOWA STATE UNIVERSITY	34	4.35
UNIVERSITY OF UTAH	35	4.34
UNIVERSITY OF DELAWARE	36	4.33
UNIVERSITY OF MARYLAND—COLLEGE PARK	37	4.32
LEHIGH UNIVERSITY	38	4.31
UNIVERSITY OF CINCINNATI	39	4.29
UNIVERSITY OF NOTRE DAME	40	4.28

WASHINGTON UNIVERSITY	41	4.26
UNIVERSITY OF HOUSTON	42	4.25
YALE UNIVERSITY	43	4.24
JOHNS HOPKINS UNIVERSITY	44	4.23
MICHIGAN STATE UNIVERSITY	45	4.22
UNIVERSITY OF MASSACHUSETTS—AMHERST	46	4.21
COLORADO SCHOOL OF MINES	47	4.20
LOUISIANA STATE UNIVERSITY—BATON ROUGE	48	4.19
UNIVERSITY OF TENNESSEE—KNOXVILLE	49	4.17
DREXEL UNIVERSITY	50	4.15

A RATING OF GRADUATE SCHOOLS IN ENGINEERING

INSTITUTION (IN ALPHABETICAL ORDER)	RANK	SCORE
UNIVERSITY OF AKRON College of Engineering Akron, OH	104	3.50
UNIVERSITY OF ALABAMA College of Engineering Tuscaloosa, AL	90	3.71
UNIVERSITY OF ALABAMA—BIRMINGHAM School of Engineering Birmingham, AL	133	3.11
UNIVERSITY OF ALABAMA—HUNTSVILLE College of Engineering Huntsville, AL	116	3.31
ARIZONA STATE UNIVERSITY College of Engineering and Applied Sciences Tempe, AZ	51	4.12
UNIVERSITY OF ARIZONA College of Engineering and Mines Tucson, AZ	33	4.36
UNIVERSITY OF ARKANSAS College of Engineering Fayetteville, AR	73	3.88
AUBURN UNIVERSITY College of Engineering Auburn University, AL	70	3.93
BOSTON UNIVERSITY College of Engineering Boston, MA	92	3.67
BRIGHAM YOUNG UNIVERSITY College of Engineering and Technology Provo, UT	131	3.14
BROWN UNIVERSITY School of Engineering Providence, RI	58	4.08
CALIFORNIA INSTITUTE OF TECHNOLOGY Programs in Engineering and Applied Sciences Pasadena, CA	5	4.88

Very Strong = 4.51-4.99   Strong = 4.01-4.49   Good = 3.61-3.99   Acceptable = 3.01-3.59

UNIVERSITY OF CALIFORNIA—BERKELEY 2 4.91
College of Engineering
Berkeley, CA

UNIVERSITY OF CALIFORNIA—DAVIS 26 4.46
College of Engineering
Davis, CA

UNIVERSITY OF CALIFORNIA—IRVINE 93 3.66
School of Engineering
Irvine, CA

UNIVERSITY OF CALIFORNIA—LOS ANGELES 25 4.47
School of Engineering and Applied Science
Los Angeles, CA

UNIVERSITY OF CALIFORNIA—SAN DIEGO 20 4.60
La Jolla, CA

UNIVERSITY OF CALIFORNIA—SANTA BARBARA 78 3.83
College of Engineering
Santa Barbara, CA

CARNEGIE MELLON UNIVERSITY 14 4.71
Carnegie Institute of Technology
Pittsburgh, PA

CASE WESTERN RESERVE UNIVERSITY 27 4.44
Case School of Engineering
Cleveland, OH

CATHOLIC UNIVERSITY OF AMERICA 99 3.60
School of Engineering and Architecture
Washington, D.C.

UNIVERSITY OF CENTRAL FLORIDA 128 3.18
College of Engineering
Orlando, FL

UNIVERSITY OF CINCINNATI 39 4.29
College of Engineering
Cincinnati, OH

CITY COLLEGE OF THE CITY UNIVERSITY OF NEW YORK 85 3.76
Department of Engineering
New York, NY

CLARKSON UNIVERSITY 86 3.75
School of Engineering
Potsdam, NY

Very Strong = 4.51-4.99   Strong = 4.01-4.49   Good = 3.61-3.99   Acceptable = 3.01-3.59

CLEMSON UNIVERSITY   71   3.91
College of Engineering
Clemson, SC

CLEVELAND STATE UNIVERSITY   127   3.19
Fenn College of Engineering
Cleveland, OH

COLORADO SCHOOL OF MINES   47   4.20
Division of Engineering
Golden, CO

COLORADO STATE UNIVERSITY   67   3.98
College of Engineering
Fort Collins, CO

UNIVERSITY OF COLORADO—BOULDER   60   4.06
College of Engineering and Applied Science
Boulder, CO

UNIVERSITY OF COLORADO—DENVER   137   3.04
College of Engineering and Applied Science
Denver, CO

COLUMBIA UNIVERSITY   17   4.67
School of Engineering and Applied Science
New York, NY

UNIVERSITY OF CONNECTICUT   103   3.53
School of Engineering
Storrs, CT

CORNELL UNIVERSITY   6   4.86
College of Engineering
Ithaca, NY

DARTMOUTH COLLEGE   66   4.00
Thayer School of Engineering
Hanover, NH

UNIVERSITY OF DAYTON   101   3.56
College of Engineering
Dayton, OH

UNIVERSITY OF DELAWARE   36   4.33
College of Engineering
Newark, DE

UNIVERSITY OF DETROIT MERCY   134   3.10
College of Engineering and Science
Detroit, MI

Very Strong = 4.51-4.99   Strong = 4.01-4.49   Good = 3.61-3.99   Acceptable = 3.01-3.59

DREXEL UNIVERSITY College of Engineering Philadelphia, PA	50	4.15
DUKE UNIVERSITY School of Engineering Durham, NC	65	4.01
FLORIDA ATLANTIC UNIVERSITY College of Engineering Boca Raton, FL	136	3.06
FLORIDA INSTITUTE OF TECHNOLOGY College of Engineering Melbourne, FL	138	3.02
UNIVERSITY OF FLORIDA College of Engineering Gainesville, FL	30	4.40
GEORGE WASHINGTON UNIVERSITY School of Engineering and Applied Sciences Washington, D.C.	87	3.74
GEORGIA INSTITUTE OF TECHNOLOGY College of Engineering Atlanta, GA	7	4.84
HARVARD UNIVERSITY Division of Applied Sciences Cambridge, MA	19	4.63
UNIVERSITY OF HAWAII—MANOA College of Engineering Honolulu, HI	125	3.21
UNIVERSITY OF HOUSTON Cullen College of Engineering Houston, TX	42	4.25
HOWARD UNIVERSITY School of Engineering Washington, D.C.	135	3.09
UNIVERSITY OF IDAHO College of Engineering Moscow, ID	118	3.28
ILLINOIS INSTITUTE OF TECHNOLOGY Armour College of Engineering Chicago, IL	81	3.80

Very Strong = 4.51-4.99 Strong = 4.01-4.49 Good = 3.61-3.99 Acceptable = 3.01-3.59

UNIVERSITY OF ILLINOIS—CHICAGO   107   3.44
College of Engineering
Chicago, IL

UNIVERSITY OF ILLINOIS—URBANA-CHAMPAIGN   3   4.90
College of Engineering
Urbana, IL

IOWA STATE UNIVERSITY   34   4.35
College of Engineering
Ames, IA

UNIVERSITY OF IOWA   59   4.07
College of Engineering
Iowa City, IA

JOHNS HOPKINS UNIVERSITY   44   4.23
G.W.C. Whiting School of Engineering
Baltimore, MD

KANSAS STATE UNIVERSITY   77   3.84
College of Engineering
Manhattan, KS

UNIVERSITY OF KANSAS   55   4.15
School of Engineering
Lawrence, KS

UNIVERSITY OF KENTUCKY   79   3.82
School of Engineering and School of Mines and Metallurgy
Lexington, KY

LEHIGH UNIVERSITY   38   4.31
College of Engineering and Applied Science
Bethlehem, PA

LOUISIANA STATE UNIVERSITY—BATON ROUGE   48   4.19
College of Engineering
Baton Rouge, LA

LOUISIANA TECH UNIVERSITY   110   3.39
College of Engineering
Ruston, LA

UNIVERSITY OF MAINE   119   3.27
College of Engineering and Sciences
Orono, ME

MARQUETTE UNIVERSITY   132   3.12
College of Engineering
Milwaukee, WI

Very Strong = 4.51-4.99   Strong = 4.01-4.49   Good = 3.61-3.99   Acceptable = 3.01-3.59

UNIVERSITY OF MARYLAND—COLLEGE PARK
College of Engineering
College Park, MD

37   4.32

MASSACHUSETTS INSTITUTE OF TECHNOLOGY
School of Engineering
Cambridge, MA

1   4.93

UNIVERSITY OF MASSACHUSETTS—AMHERST
College of Engineering
Amherst, MA

46   4.21

UNIVERSITY OF MASSACHUSETTS—LOWELL
James B. Francis College of Engineering
Lowell, MA

108   3.42

UNIVERSITY OF MIAMI
College of Engineering
Coral Gables, FL

112   3.37

MICHIGAN STATE UNIVERSITY
College of Engineering
East Lansing, MI

45   4.22

MICHIGAN TECHNOLOGICAL UNIVERSITY
College of Engineering
Houghton, MI

84   3.77

UNIVERSITY OF MICHIGAN—ANN ARBOR
College of Engineering
Ann Arbor, MI

10   4.79

UNIVERSITY OF MINNESOTA—TWIN CITIES
Graduate School
Minneapolis, MN

12   4.75

MISSISSIPPI STATE UNIVERSITY
College of Engineering
Mississippi State, MS

88   3.73

UNIVERSITY OF MISSISSIPPI
School of Engineering
University, MS

121   3.25

UNIVERSITY OF MISSOURI—COLUMBIA
College of Engineering
Columbia, MO

61   4.05

UNIVERSITY OF MISSOURI—ROLLA
School of Engineering
Rolla, MO

57   4.09

Very Strong = 4.51-4.99   Strong = 4.01-4.49   Good = 3.61-3.99   Acceptable = 3.01-3.59

MONTANA STATE UNIVERSITY—BOZEMAN   120   3.26
College of Engineering
Bozeman, MT

UNIVERSITY OF NEBRASKA—LINCOLN   91   3.69
College of Engineering and Technology
Lincoln, NE

UNIVERSITY OF NEW HAMPSHIRE   113   3.36
College of Engineering & Physical Sciences
Durham, NH

NEW MEXICO STATE UNIVERSITY   129   3.17
College of Engineering
Las Cruces, NM

UNIVERSITY OF NEW MEXICO   80   3.81
School of Engineering
Albuquerque, NM

NORTH CAROLINA STATE UNIVERSITY   31   4.39
College of Engineering
Raleigh, NC

NORTH DAKOTA STATE UNIVERSITY   124   3.22
College of Engineering & Architecture
Fargo, ND

NORTHWESTERN UNIVERSITY   21   4.57
Robert R. McCormick School of Engineering and Applied Sciences
Evanston, IL

UNIVERSITY OF NOTRE DAME   40   4.28
College of Engineering
Notre Dame, IN

OHIO STATE UNIVERSITY—COLUMBUS   15   4.69
College of Engineering
Columbus, OH

OHIO UNIVERSITY   111   3.38
College of Engineering and Technology
Athens, OH

OKLAHOMA STATE UNIVERSITY   69   3.95
College of Engineering, Architecture, and Technology
Stillwater, OK

UNIVERSITY OF OKLAHOMA   75   3.86
College of Engineering
Norman, OK

Very Strong = 4.51-4.99   Strong = 4.01-4.49   Good = 3.61-3.99   Acceptable = 3.01-3.59

OLD DOMINION UNIVERSITY	122	3.24
College of Engineering and Technology		
Norfolk, VA		
OREGON STATE UNIVERSITY	83	3.78
College of Engineering		
Corvallis, OR		
PENNSYLVANIA STATE UNIVERSITY—UNIVERSITY PARK	18	4.66
College of Engineering		
University Park, PA		
UNIVERSITY OF PENNSYLVANIA	11	4.77
School of Engineering and Applied Sciences		
Philadelphia, PA		
UNIVERSITY OF PITTSBURGH	52	4.14
School of Engineering		
Pittsburgh, PA		
POLYTECHNIC UNIVERSITY	62	4.04
Brooklyn, NY		
PRINCETON UNIVERSITY	16	4.68
School of Engineering and Applied Science		
Princeton, NJ		
PURDUE UNIVERSITY—WEST LAFAYETTE	8	4.83
School of Engineering		
West Lafayette, IN		
RENSSELAER POLYTECHNIC INSTITUTE	23	4.50
Troy, NY		
UNIVERSITY OF RHODE ISLAND	115	3.32
College of Engineering		
Kingston, RI		
RICE UNIVERSITY	22	4.55
George R. Brown School of Engineering		
Houston, TX		
UNIVERSITY OF ROCHESTER	63	4.03
School of Engineering		
Rochester, NY		
RUTGERS UNIVERSITY—NEW BRUNSWICK	56	4.10
College of Engineering		
New Brunswick, NJ		
UNIVERSITY OF SOUTH CAROLINA—COLUMBIA	109	3.40
College of Engineering		
Columbia, SC		

Very Strong = 4.51-4.99   Strong = 4.01-4.49   Good = 3.61-3.99   Acceptable = 3.01-3.59

SOUTH DAKOTA SCHOOL OF MINES & TECHNOLOGY   130   3.15
Graduate Engineering Program
Rapid City, SD

UNIVERSITY OF SOUTHERN CALIFORNIA   29   4.41
School of Engineering
Los Angeles, CA

SOUTHERN ILLINOIS UNIVERSITY—CARBONDALE   117   3.29
College of Engineering and Technology
Carbondale, IL

SOUTHERN METHODIST UNIVERSITY   96   3.63
School of Engineering and Applied Science
Dallas, TX

STANFORD UNIVERSITY   4   4.89
School of Engineering and Applied Sciences
Stanford, CA

STATE UNIVERSITY OF NEW YORK AT BUFFALO   53   4.13
School of Engineering and Applied Sciences
Buffalo, NY

STATE UNIVERSITY OF NEW YORK AT STONY BROOK   72   3.89
College of Engineering & Applied Science
Stony Brook, NY

STEVENS INSTITUTE OF TECHNOLOGY   68   3.96
School of Engineering
Hoboken, NJ

SYRACUSE UNIVERSITY   64   4.02
L. C. Smith College of Engineering and Computer Science
Syracuse, NY

UNIVERSITY OF TENNESSEE—KNOXVILLE   49   4.17
College of Engineering
Knoxville, TN

TEXAS A&M UNIVERSITY—COLLEGE STATION   28   4.42
College of Engineering
College Station, TX

TEXAS TECH UNIVERSITY   74   3.87
College of Engineering
Lubbock, TX

UNIVERSITY OF TEXAS—ARLINGTON   102   3.54
College of Engineering
Arlington, TX

Very Strong = 4.51-4.99   Strong = 4.01-4.49   Good = 3.61-3.99   Acceptable = 3.01-3.59

UNIVERSITY OF TEXAS—AUSTIN   9   4.80
College of Engineering
Austin, TX

UNIVERSITY OF TOLEDO   126   3.20
College of Engineering
Toledo, OH

TUFTS UNIVERSITY   97   3.62
College of Engineering
Medford, MA

TULANE UNIVERSITY   98   3.60
School of Engineering
New Orleans, LA

UNIVERSITY OF TULSA   106   3.45
College of Engineering and Applied Sciences
Tulsa, OK

UTAH STATE UNIVERSITY   76   3.85
College of Engineering
Logan, UT

UNIVERSITY OF UTAH   35   4.34
College of Engineering
Salt Lake City, UT

VANDERBILT UNIVERSITY   82   3.79
School of Engineering
Nashville, TN

UNIVERSITY OF VERMONT   139   3.00
College of Engineering and Mathematics
Burlington, VT

VIRGINIA POLYTECHNIC INSTITUTE AND STATE UNIVERSITY   54   4.12
College of Engineering
Blacksburg, VA

UNIVERSITY OF VIRGINIA   32   4.37
School of Engineering and Applied Science
Charlottesville, VA

WASHINGTON STATE UNIVERSITY   89   3.72
College of Engineering and Architecture
Pullman, WA

WASHINGTON UNIVERSITY   41   4.26
School of Engineering and Applied Science
St. Louis, MO

Very Strong = 4.51-4.99   Strong = 4.01-4.49   Good = 3.61-3.99   Acceptable = 3.01-3.59

UNIVERSITY OF WASHINGTON   24   4.48
College of Engineering
Seattle, WA

WAYNE STATE UNIVERSITY   94   3.65
College of Engineering
Detroit, MI

WEST VIRGINIA UNIVERSITY   105   3.48
College of Engineering
Morgantown, WV

WICHITA STATE UNIVERSITY   123   3.23
College of Engineering
Wichita, KS

UNIVERSITY OF WISCONSIN—MADISON   13   4.73
College of Engineering
Madison, WI

UNIVERSITY OF WISCONSIN—MILWAUKEE   95   3.64
College of Engineering & Applied Science
Milwaukee, WI

WORCESTER POLYTECHNIC INSTITUTE   100   3.58
Worcester, MA

UNIVERSITY OF WYOMING   114   3.34
College of Engineering
Laramie, WY

YALE UNIVERSITY   43   4.24
Graduate School of Arts and Sciences
New Haven, CT

Very Strong = 4.51-4.99   Strong = 4.01-4.49   Good = 3.61-3.99   Acceptable = 3.01-3.59

Part VI

THE GOURMAN REPORT
BUSINESS SCHOOLS

THE TOP 10 EMBA/MANAGEMENT SCHOOLS

A RATING OF EMBA/MANAGEMENT SCHOOLS

THE TOP 25 MBA/MANAGEMENT SCHOOLS

A RATING OF MBA/MANAGEMENT SCHOOLS

THE TOP 10 EMBA/MANAGEMENT SCHOOLS

INSTITUTION	RANK	SCORE
UNIVERSITY OF PENNSYLVANIA	1	4.90
UNIVERSITY OF CHICAGO	2	4.89
COLUMBIA UNIVERSITY	3	4.87
UNIVERSITY OF CALIFORNIA—LOS ANGELES	4	4.85
INDIANA UNIVERSITY—BLOOMINGTON	5	4.84
NORTHWESTERN UNIVERSITY	6	4.81
UNIVERSITY OF ILLINOIS—URBANA-CHAMPAIGN	7	4.75
NEW YORK UNIVERSITY	8	4.71
UNIVERSITY OF PITTSBURGH	9	4.70
UNIVERSITY OF TEXAS—AUSTIN	10	4.67

A RATING OF EMBA/MANAGEMENT SCHOOLS

INSTITUTION (IN ALPHABETICAL ORDER)	RANK	SCORE
UNIVERSITY OF CALIFORNIA—LOS ANGELES John E. Anderson Graduate School of Management Los Angeles, CA	4	4.85
UNIVERSITY OF CHICAGO Graduate School of Business Chicago, IL	2	4.89
COLUMBIA UNIVERSITY Graduate School of Business New York, NY	3	4.87
DUKE UNIVERSITY Fuqua School of Business Durham, NC	11	4.62
UNIVERSITY OF ILLINOIS—URBANA-CHAMPAIGN College of Commerce and Business Administration Champaign, IL	7	4.75
INDIANA UNIVERSITY—BLOOMINGTON Graduate School of Business Bloomington, IN	5	4.84
NEW YORK UNIVERSITY Leonard N. Stern School of Business New York, NY	8	4.71
NORTHWESTERN UNIVERSITY J.L. Kellogg Graduate School of Management Evanston, IL	6	4.81
UNIVERSITY OF PENNSYLVANIA The Wharton School Philadelphia, PA	1	4.90
UNIVERSITY OF PITTSBURGH Joseph M. Katz Graduate School of Business Pittsburgh, PA	9	4.70
PURDUE UNIVERSITY—WEST LAFAYETTE Krannert Graduate School of Management West Lafayette, IN	12	4.57
UNIVERSITY OF SOUTHERN CALIFORNIA Graduate School of Business Administration Los Angeles, CA	13	4.49
UNIVERSITY OF TEXAS—AUSTIN Graduate School of Business Austin, TX	10	4.67

Very Strong = 4.51-4.99   Strong = 4.01-4.49   Good = 3.61-3.99   Acceptable = 3.01-3.59

THE TOP 25 MBA/MANAGEMENT SCHOOLS

INSTITUTION	RANK	SCORE
HARVARD UNIVERSITY	1	4.94
UNIVERSITY OF PENNSYLVANIA	2	4.93
STANFORD UNIVERSITY	3	4.92
MASSACHUSETTS INSTITUTE OF TECHNOLOGY	4	4.91
UNIVERSITY OF CHICAGO	5	4.90
COLUMBIA UNIVERSITY	6	4.89
NORTHWESTERN UNIVERSITY	7	4.88
UNIVERSITY OF CALIFORNIA—LOS ANGELES	8	4.87
UNIVERSITY OF CALIFORNIA—BERKELEY	9	4.86
UNIVERSITY OF VIRGINIA	10	4.85
INDIANA UNIVERSITY—BLOOMINGTON	11	4.84
UNIVERSITY OF PITTSBURGH	12	4.83
DUKE UNIVERSITY	13	4.82
CORNELL UNIVERSITY	14	4.81
NEW YORK UNIVERSITY	15	4.80
DARTMOUTH COLLEGE	16	4.79
CARNEGIE MELLON UNIVERSITY	17	4.78
UNIVERSITY OF MICHIGAN—ANN ARBOR	18	4.77
UNIVERSITY OF ILLINOIS—URBANA-CHAMPAIGN	19	4.76
UNIVERSITY OF NORTH CAROLINA—CHAPEL HILL	20	4.75
UNIVERSITY OF TEXAS—AUSTIN	21	4.74
PURDUE UNIVERSITY—WEST LAFAYETTE	22	4.73
UNIVERSITY OF WASHINGTON	23	4.72
UNIVERSITY OF SOUTHERN CALIFORNIA	24	4.71
TEXAS A&M UNIVERSITY—COLLEGE STATION	25	4.70

Very Strong = 4.51-4.99   Strong = 4.01-4.49   Good = 3.61-3.99   Acceptable = 3.01-3.59

A RATING OF MBA/MANAGEMENT SCHOOLS

INSTITUTION (IN ALPHABETICAL ORDER)	RANK	SCORE
ARIZONA STATE UNIVERSITY College of Business Tempe, AZ	45	4.32
UNIVERSITY OF CALIFORNIA—BERKELEY Walter A. Haas School of Business Berkeley, CA	9	4.86
UNIVERSITY OF CALIFORNIA—LOS ANGELES John E. Anderson Graduate School of Management Los Angeles, CA	8	4.87
CARNEGIE MELLON UNIVERSITY Graduate School of Industrial Administration Pittsburgh, PA	17	4.78
CASE WESTERN RESERVE UNIVERSITY Weatherhead School of Management Cleveland, OH	29	4.63
UNIVERSITY OF CHICAGO Graduate School of Business Chicago, IL	5	4.90
CITY UNIVERSITY OF NEW YORK—BARUCH COLLEGE School of Business New York, NY	32	4.57
COLUMBIA UNIVERSITY Graduate School of Business New York, NY	6	4.89
CORNELL UNIVERSITY Johnson Graduate School of Management Ithaca, NY	14	4.81
DARTMOUTH COLLEGE The Amos Tuck School of Business Administration Hanover, NH	16	4.79
DUKE UNIVERSITY Fuqua School of Business Durham, NC	13	4.82
EMORY UNIVERSITY Goizueta Business School Atlanta, GA	48	4.24

Very Strong = 4.51-4.99   Strong = 4.01-4.49   Good = 3.61-3.99   Acceptable = 3.01-3.59

UNIVERSITY OF FLORIDA 39 4.43
University of Florida Business School
Gainesville, FL

GEORGE WASHINGTON UNIVERSITY 36 4.50
School of Business & Public Management
Washington, D.C.

GEORGIA INSTITUTE OF TECHNOLOGY 49 4.21
DuPree School of Management
Atlanta, GA

HARVARD UNIVERSITY 1 4.94
Graduate School of Business Administration
Boston, MA

UNIVERSITY OF HOUSTON 40 4.41
College of Business Administration
Houston, TX

UNIVERSITY OF ILLINOIS—URBANA-CHAMPAIGN 19 4.76
College of Commerce and Business Administration
Champaign, IL

INDIANA UNIVERSITY—BLOOMINGTON 11 4.84
Graduate School of Business
Bloomington, IN

UNIVERSITY OF IOWA 31 4.58
Iowa Business School
Iowa City, IA

LEHIGH UNIVERSITY 38 4.46
College of Business and Economics
Bethlehem, PA

MASSACHUSETTS INSTITUTE OF TECHNOLOGY 4 4.91
Sloan School of Management
Cambridge, MA

MICHIGAN STATE UNIVERSITY 26 4.68
Eli Broad Graduate School of Management
East Lansing, MI

UNIVERSITY OF MICHIGAN—ANN ARBOR 18 4.77
University of Michigan Business School
Ann Arbor, MI

UNIVERSITY OF MINNESOTA—TWIN CITIES 28 4.65
Curtis L. Carlson School of Management
Minneapolis, MN

Very Strong = 4.51-4.99   Strong = 4.01-4.49   Good = 3.61-3.99   Acceptable = 3.01-3.59

NEW YORK UNIVERSITY
Leonard N. Stern School of Business
New York, NY

15   4.80

UNIVERSITY OF NORTH CAROLINA—CHAPEL HILL
Kenan-Flagler Business School
Chapel Hill, NC

20   4.75

NORTHWESTERN UNIVERSITY
J.L. Kellogg Graduate School of Management
Evanston, IL

7   4.88

UNIVERSITY OF NOTRE DAME
College of Business Administration
Notre Dame, IN

42   4.38

OHIO STATE UNIVERSITY—COLUMBUS
Fisher College of Business
Columbus, OH

35   4.51

UNIVERSITY OF OREGON
Graduate School of Management-College of Business
Eugene, OR

44   4.33

PENNSYLVANIA STATE UNIVERSITY—UNIVERSITY PARK
Mary Jean and Frank P. Smeal College of Business Administration
University Park, PA

34   4.52

UNIVERSITY OF PENNSYLVANIA
The Wharton School
Philadelphia, PA

2   4.93

UNIVERSITY OF PITTSBURGH
Joseph M. Katz Graduate School of Business
Pittsburgh, PA

12   4.83

PURDUE UNIVERSITY—WEST LAFAYETTE
Krannert Graduate School of Management
West Lafayette, IN

22   4.73

UNIVERSITY OF ROCHESTER
William E. Simon Graduate School of Business Administration
Rochester, NY

37   4.48

UNIVERSITY OF SOUTH CAROLINA—COLUMBIA
College of Business Administration
Columbia, SC

50   4.18

UNIVERSITY OF SOUTHERN CALIFORNIA
Graduate School of Business Administration
Los Angeles, CA

24   4.71

Very Strong = 4.51-4.99   Strong = 4.01-4.49   Good = 3.61-3.99   Acceptable = 3.01-3.59

SOUTHERN METHODIST UNIVERSITY   46   4.30
Edwin L. Cox School of Business
Dallas, TX

STANFORD UNIVERSITY   3   4.92
Stanford Graduate School of Business
Stanford, CA

STATE UNIVERSITY OF NEW YORK AT BUFFALO   41   4.40
School of Management
Buffalo, NY

SYRACUSE UNIVERSITY   47   4.26
School of Management
Syracuse, NY

TEXAS A&M UNIVERSITY—COLLEGE STATION   25   4.70
College of Business Administration
College Station, TX

UNIVERSITY OF TEXAS—AUSTIN   21   4.74
Graduate School of Business
Austin, TX

TULANE UNIVERSITY   33   4.54
A.B. Freeman School of Business
New Orleans, LA

UNIVERSITY OF UTAH   43   4.36
David Eccles School of Business
Salt Lake City, UT

UNIVERSITY OF VIRGINIA   10   4.85
Darden Graduate School of Business Administration
Charlottesville, VA

WASHINGTON UNIVERSITY   30   4.61
John M. Olin School of Business
St. Louis, MO

UNIVERSITY OF WASHINGTON   23   4.72
Graduate School of Business Administration
Seattle, WA

UNIVERSITY OF WISCONSIN—MADISON   27   4.67
Business School
Madison, WI

Very Strong = 4.51-4.99   Strong = 4.01-4.49   Good = 3.61-3.99   Acceptable = 3.01-3.59

Part VII

THE GOURMAN REPORT DOCTORAL PROGRAMS IN MANAGEMENT

THE TOP 25 DOCTORAL PROGRAMS IN BUSINESS AND MANAGEMENT

A RATING OF DOCTORAL PROGRAMS IN BUSINESS AND MANAGEMENT

THE TOP 25 DOCTORAL PROGRAMS IN BUSINESS AND MANAGEMENT

INSTITUTION	RANK	SCORE
HARVARD UNIVERSITY	1	4.94
UNIVERSITY OF PENNSYLVANIA	2	4.93
STANFORD UNIVERSITY	3	4.92
MASSACHUSETTS INSTITUTE OF TECHNOLOGY	4	4.91
COLUMBIA UNIVERSITY	5	4.90
UNIVERSITY OF CHICAGO	6	4.89
NORTHWESTERN UNIVERSITY	7	4.88
INDIANA UNIVERSITY—BLOOMINGTON	8	4.87
UNIVERSITY OF CALIFORNIA—BERKELEY	9	4.86
UNIVERSITY OF CALIFORNIA—LOS ANGELES	10	4.85
UNIVERSITY OF MICHIGAN—ANN ARBOR	11	4.84
UNIVERSITY OF PITTSBURGH	12	4.83
NEW YORK UNIVERSITY	13	4.82
UNIVERSITY OF TEXAS—AUSTIN	14	4.81
CORNELL UNIVERSITY	15	4.80
UNIVERSITY OF VIRGINIA	16	4.79
PURDUE UNIVERSITY—WEST LAFAYETTE	17	4.78
UNIVERSITY OF NORTH CAROLINA—CHAPEL HILL	18	4.77
CARNEGIE MELLON UNIVERSITY	19	4.76
DUKE UNIVERSITY	20	4.75
UNIVERSITY OF WASHINGTON	21	4.74
UNIVERSITY OF ILLINOIS—URBANA-CHAMPAIGN	22	4.73
TEXAS A&M UNIVERSITY—COLLEGE STATION	23	4.72
UNIVERSITY OF SOUTHERN CALIFORNIA	24	4.71
OHIO STATE UNIVERSITY—COLUMBUS	25	4.70

A RATING OF DOCTORAL PROGRAMS IN BUSINESS AND MANAGEMENT

INSTITUTION (IN ALPHABETICAL ORDER)	RANK	SCORE
ARIZONA STATE UNIVERSITY College of Business Tempe, AZ	40	4.41
UNIVERSITY OF ARIZONA Karl Eller Graduate School of Management Tucson, AZ	49	4.20
UNIVERSITY OF CALIFORNIA—BERKELEY Walter A. Haas School of Business Berkeley, CA	9	4.86
UNIVERSITY OF CALIFORNIA—LOS ANGELES John E. Anderson Graduate School of Management Los Angeles, CA	10	4.85
CARNEGIE MELLON UNIVERSITY Graduate School of Industrial Administration Pittsburgh, PA	19	4.76
CASE WESTERN RESERVE UNIVERSITY Weatherhead School of Management Cleveland, OH	28	4.65
UNIVERSITY OF CHICAGO Graduate School of Business Chicago, IL	6	4.89
CITY UNIVERSITY OF NEW YORK—BARUCH COLLEGE School of Business New York, NY	31	4.58
UNIVERSITY OF COLORADO—BOULDER Graduate School of Business Administration Boulder, CO	44	4.30
COLUMBIA UNIVERSITY Graduate School of Business New York, NY	5	4.90
CORNELL UNIVERSITY Johnson Graduate School of Management Ithaca, NY	15	4.80
DUKE UNIVERSITY Fuqua School of Business Durham, NC	20	4.75

Very Strong = 4.51-4.99   Strong = 4.01-4.49   Good = 3.61-3.99   Acceptable = 3.01-3.59

UNIVERSITY OF FLORIDA University of Florida Business School Gainesville, FL	37	4.47
GEORGE WASHINGTON UNIVERSITY School of Business & Public Management Washington, D.C.	35	4.49
GEORGIA INSTITUTE OF TECHNOLOGY DuPree School of Management Atlanta, GA	46	4.26
HARVARD UNIVERSITY Graduate School of Business Administration Boston, MA	1	4.94
UNIVERSITY OF HOUSTON College of Business Administration Houston, TX	38	4.44
UNIVERSITY OF ILLINOIS—URBANA-CHAMPAIGN College of Commerce and Business Administration Champaign, IL	22	4.73
INDIANA UNIVERSITY—BLOOMINGTON Graduate School of Business Bloomington, IN	8	4.87
UNIVERSITY OF IOWA Iowa Business School Iowa City, IA	27	4.66
LEHIGH UNIVERSITY College of Business and Economics Bethlehem, PA	34	4.53
LOUISIANA STATE UNIVERSITY—BATON ROUGE College of Business Administration Baton Rouge, LA	47	4.22
MASSACHUSETTS INSTITUTE OF TECHNOLOGY Sloan School of Management Cambridge, MA	4	4.91
MICHIGAN STATE UNIVERSITY Eli Broad Graduate School of Management East Lansing, MI	29	4.62
UNIVERSITY OF MICHIGAN—ANN ARBOR University of Michigan Business School Ann Arbor, MI	11	4.84

Very Strong = 4.51-4.99   Strong = 4.01-4.49   Good = 3.61-3.99   Acceptable = 3.01-3.59

UNIVERSITY OF MINNESOTA—TWIN CITIES Curtis L. Carlson School of Management Minneapolis, MN	30	4.60
NEW YORK UNIVERSITY Leonard N. Stern School of Business New York, NY	13	4.82
UNIVERSITY OF NORTH CAROLINA—CHAPEL HILL Kenan-Flagler Business School Chapel Hill, NC	18	4.77
NORTHWESTERN UNIVERSITY J.L. Kellogg Graduate School of Management Evanston, IL	7	4.88
OHIO STATE UNIVERSITY—COLUMBUS Fisher College of Business Columbus, OH	25	4.70
UNIVERSITY OF OREGON Graduate School of Management-College of Business Eugene, OR	43	4.32
PENNSYLVANIA STATE UNIVERSITY—UNIVERSITY PARK Mary Jean and Frank P. Smeal College of Business Administration University Park, PA	32	4.55
UNIVERSITY OF PENNSYLVANIA The Wharton School Philadelphia, PA	2	4.93
UNIVERSITY OF PITTSBURGH Joseph M. Katz Graduate School of Business Pittsburgh, PA	12	4.83
PURDUE UNIVERSITY—WEST LAFAYETTE Krannert Graduate School of Management West Lafayette, IN	17	4.78
UNIVERSITY OF ROCHESTER William E. Simon Graduate School of Business Administration Rochester, NY	36	4.48
UNIVERSITY OF SOUTH CAROLINA—COLUMBIA College of Business Administration Columbia, SC	48	4.21
UNIVERSITY OF SOUTHERN CALIFORNIA Graduate School of Business Administration Los Angeles, CA	24	4.71

Very Strong = 4.51-4.99   Strong = 4.01-4.49   Good = 3.61-3.99   Acceptable = 3.01-3.59

STANFORD UNIVERSITY
Stanford Graduate School of Business
Stanford, CA
3   4.92

STATE UNIVERSITY OF NEW YORK AT BUFFALO
School of Management
Buffalo, NY
39   4.43

SYRACUSE UNIVERSITY
School of Management
Syracuse, NY
45   4.27

TEXAS A&M UNIVERSITY—COLLEGE STATION
College of Business Administration
College Station, TX
23   4.72

UNIVERSITY OF TEXAS—AUSTIN
Graduate School of Business
Austin, TX
14   4.81

TULANE UNIVERSITY
A.B. Freeman School of Business
New Orleans, LA
42   4.36

UNIVERSITY OF UTAH
David Eccles School of Business
Salt Lake City, UT
41   4.40

VANDERBILT UNIVERSITY
Owen Graduate School of Management
Nashville, TN
50   4.19

UNIVERSITY OF VIRGINIA
Darden Graduate School of Business Administration
Charlottesville, VA
16   4.79

WASHINGTON UNIVERSITY
John M. Olin School of Business
St. Louis, MO
33   4.54

UNIVERSITY OF WASHINGTON
Graduate School of Business Administration
Seattle, WA
21   4.74

UNIVERSITY OF WISCONSIN—MADISON
Business School
Madison, WI
26   4.68

Very Strong = 4.51-4.99   Strong = 4.01-4.49   Good = 3.61-3.99   Acceptable = 3.01-3.59

Part VIII

THE GOURMAN REPORT
CRIMINAL JUSTICE PROGRAMS

CRIMINAL JUSTICE/CRIMINOLOGY GRADUATE PROGRAMS

CRIMINAL JUSTICE/CRIMINOLOGY GRADUATE PROGRAMS

INSTITUTION (IN ALPHABETICAL ORDER)	CITY / STATE
UNIVERSITY OF ALABAMA Department of Criminal Justice	Tuscaloosa, AL
UNIVERSITY OF ALABAMA—BIRMINGHAM Department of Justice Sciences	Birmingham, AL
ALBANY STATE UNIVERSITY Department of Criminal Justice	Albany, GA
AMERICAN INTERNATIONAL COLLEGE Department of Criminal Justice Studies	Springfield, MA
AMERICAN UNIVERSITY Department of Justice, Law, and Society	Washington, D.C.
ARIZONA STATE UNIVERSITY	Tempe, AZ
UNIVERSITY OF ARKANSAS—LITTLE ROCK Department of Criminal Justice	Little Rock, AK
ARMSTRONG STATE COLLEGE School of Graduate Studies	Savannah, GA
AUBURN UNIVERSITY—MONTGOMERY Department of Justice and Public Safety	Montgomery, AL
UNIVERSITY OF BALTIMORE Program in Criminal Justice	Baltimore, MD
BOSTON UNIVERSITY Program in Criminal Justice	Boston, MA
CALIFORNIA STATE UNIVERSITY—FRESNO Department of Criminology	Fresno, CA
CALIFORNIA STATE UNIVERSITY—LONG BEACH Department of Criminal Justice	Long Beach, CA
CALIFORNIA STATE UNIVERSITY—LOS ANGELES Department of Criminal Justice	Los Angeles, CA
CALIFORNIA STATE UNIVERSITY—SACRAMENTO Division of Criminal Justice	Sacramento, CA
CALIFORNIA STATE UNIVERSITY—SAN BERNARDINO Department of Criminal Justice	San Bernardino, CA

INSTITUTION (IN ALPHABETICAL ORDER)	CITY / STATE
UNIVERSITY OF CALIFORNIA—IRVINE Department of Criminology, Law and Society	Irvine, CA
UNIVERSITY OF CENTRAL FLORIDA Program in Criminal Justice	Orlando, FL
CENTRAL MISSOURI STATE UNIVERSITY Department of Criminal Justice	Warrensburg, MO
UNIVERSITY OF CENTRAL OKLAHOMA Department of Sociology	Edmond, OK
UNIVERSITY OF CENTRAL TEXAS Division of Social and Behavioral Sciences	Killeen, TX
CHICAGO STATE UNIVERSITY Department of Criminal Justice	Chicago, IL
UNIVERSITY OF CINCINNATI Division of Criminal Justice	Cincinnati, OH
CITY UNIVERSITY OF NEW YORK— GRADUATE SCHOOL AND UNIVERSITY CENTER Program in Criminal Justice	New York, NY
CLAREMONT GRADUATE SCHOOL	Claremont, CA
CLARK ATLANTA UNIVERSITY Department of Criminal Justice	Atlanta, GA
UNIVERSITY OF DELAWARE Department of Sociology and Criminal Justice	Newark, DE
UNIVERSITY OF DETROIT MERCY Program in Criminal Justice	Detroit, MI
EAST TENNESSEE STATE UNIVERSITY Department of Criminal Justice and Criminology	Johnson City, TN
EASTERN KENTUCKY UNIVERSITY Program in Criminal Justice	Richmond, KY
EASTERN MICHIGAN UNIVERSITY Program in Criminology and Criminal Justice	Ypsilanti, MI
FLORIDA INTERNATIONAL UNIVERSITY Department of Criminal Justice	Miami, FL
FLORIDA STATE UNIVERSITY School of Criminology and Criminal Justice	Tallahassee, FL

INSTITUTION (IN ALPHABETICAL ORDER)	CITY / STATE
GEORGE WASHINGTON UNIVERSITY Program in Criminal Justice	Washington, D.C.
GEORGIA STATE UNIVERSITY Department of Criminal Justice	Atlanta, GA
GRAMBLING STATE UNIVERSITY Program in Criminal Justice	Grambling, LA
ILLINOIS STATE UNIVERSITY Department of Criminal Justice Sciences	Normal, IL
UNIVERSITY OF ILLINOIS—CHICAGO Department of Criminal Justice	Chicago, IL
INDIANA STATE UNIVERSITY Department of Criminology	Terre Haute, IN
INDIANA UNIVERSITY OF PENNSYLVANIA Department of Criminology	Indiana, PA
INDIANA UNIVERSITY—BLOOMINGTON Department of Criminal Justice	Bloomington, IN
INDIANA UNIVERSITY NORTHWEST Division of Public and Environmental Affairs	Gary, IN
INDIANA UNIVERSITY—PURDUE UNIVERSITY—INDIANAPOLIS Graduate Program in Public Affairs	Indianapolis, IN
JACKSONVILLE STATE UNIVERSITY College of Criminal Justice	Jacksonville, AL
JERSEY CITY STATE COLLEGE Department of Criminal Justice	Jersey City, NJ
CITY UNIVERSITY OF NEW YORK— JOHN JAY COLLEGE OF CRIMINAL JUSTICE Programs in Criminal Justice	New York, NY
KENT STATE UNIVERSITY Department of Criminal Justice Studies	Kent, OH
LONG ISLAND UNIVERSITY—C.W. POST Department of Criminal Justice	Brookville, NY
LOUISIANA STATE UNIVERSITY—BATON ROUGE	Baton Rouge, LA
UNIVERSITY OF LOUISVILLE Department of Justice Administration	Louisville, KY
MARSHALL UNIVERSITY Department of Criminal Justice	Huntington, WV

INSTITUTION (IN ALPHABETICAL ORDER)	CITY / STATE
UNIVERSITY OF MARYLAND—COLLEGE PARK Department of Criminology and Criminal Justice	College Park, MD
UNIVERSITY OF MASSACHUSETTS—LOWELL Department of Criminal Justice	Lowell, MA
UNIVERSITY OF MEMPHIS Department of Criminology and Criminal Justice	Memphis, TN
MICHIGAN STATE UNIVERSITY School of Criminal Justice	East Lansing, MI
MIDDLE TENNESSEE STATE UNIVERSITY Department of Criminal Justice Administration	Murfreesboro, TN
UNIVERSITY OF MISSOURI—KANSAS CITY Program in Administration of Justice	Kansas City, MO
MOREHEAD STATE UNIVERSITY	Morehead, KY
UNIVERSITY OF NEBRASKA—OMAHA Department of Criminal Justice	Omaha, NE
UNIVERSITY OF NEW HAVEN Program in Criminal Justice	West Haven, CT
NEW MEXICO STATE UNIVERSITY Department of Criminal Justice	Las Cruces, NM
NORTH CAROLINA CENTRAL UNIVERSITY Department of Criminal Justice	Durham, NC
UNIVERSITY OF NORTH CAROLINA—CHARLOTTE Department of Criminal Justice	Charlotte, NC
UNIVERSITY OF NORTH FLORIDA Department of Sociology/Criminal Justice	Jacksonville, FL
NORTHEAST LOUISIANA UNIVERSITY Program in Criminal Justice	Monroe, LA
NORTHEASTERN UNIVERSITY Graduate School of Criminal Justice	Boston, MA
OHIO STATE UNIVERSITY—COLUMBUS	Columbus, OH
OKLAHOMA CITY UNIVERSITY Program in Criminal Justice Administration	Oklahoma City, OK
OKLAHOMA STATE UNIVERSITY	Stillwater, OK
PENNSYLVANIA STATE UNIVERSITY—UNIVERSITY PARK Program in Crime, Law and Justice	University Park, PA

INSTITUTION (IN ALPHABETICAL ORDER)	CITY / STATE
PORTLAND STATE UNIVERSITY Department of Administration of Justice	Portland, OR
RADFORD UNIVERSITY Department of Criminal Justice	Radford, VA
RUTGERS UNIVERSITY—NEWARK Program in Criminal Justice	Newark, NJ
ST. CLOUD STATE UNIVERSITY Department of Criminal Justice	St. Cloud, MN
SAINT JOSEPH'S UNIVERSITY Program in Criminal Justice	Philadelphia, PA
SAM HOUSTON STATE UNIVERSITY College of Criminal Justice	Huntsville, TX
SAN JOSE STATE UNIVERSITY Department of Administration of Justice	San Jose, CA
SHIPPENSBURG UNIVERSITY OF PENNSYLVANIA Department of Criminal Justice	Shippensburg, PA
UNIVERSITY OF SOUTH CAROLINA—COLUMBIA College of Criminal Justice	Columbia, SC
UNIVERSITY OF SOUTH FLORIDA Department of Criminology	Tampa, FL
SOUTHEAST MISSOURI STATE UNIVERSITY Program in Administration Science	Cape Girardeau, MO
SOUTHERN ILLINOIS UNIVERSITY—CARBONDALE Administration of Justice Program	Carbondale, IL
UNIVERSITY OF SOUTHERN MISSISSIPPI Department of Criminal Justice	Hattiesburg, MS
SOUTHWEST TEXAS STATE UNIVERSITY Department of Criminal Justice	San Marcos, TX
STATE UNIVERSITY OF NEW YORK AT ALBANY School of Criminal Justice	Albany, NY
STATE UNIVERSITY OF NEW YORK AT BUFFALO Department of Criminal Justice	Buffalo, NY
TEMPLE UNIVERSITY Department of Criminal Justice	Philadelphia, PA
TENNESSEE STATE UNIVERSITY Department of Criminal Justice	Nashville, TN

INSTITUTION (IN ALPHABETICAL ORDER)	CITY / STATE
UNIVERSITY OF TENNESSEE—CHATTANOOGA Program in Criminal Justice	Chattanooga, TN
UNIVERSITY OF TEXAS—ARLINGTON Program in Criminal Justice	Arlington, TX
UNIVERSITY OF TEXAS—TYLER	Tyler, TX
VALDOSTA STATE UNIVERSITY Program in Criminal Justice	Valdosta, GA
VILLANOVA UNIVERSITY Program in Human Organization Science, Criminal Justice Administration Option	Villanova, PA
VIRGINIA COMMONWEALTH UNIVERSITY Department of Criminal Justice	Richmond, VA
WASHINGTON STATE UNIVERSITY Program in Criminal Justice	Pullman, WA
WAYNE STATE UNIVERSITY Department of Criminal Justice	Detroit, MI
WESTCHESTER UNIVERSITY OF PENNSYLVANIA Department of Criminal Justice	Westchester, PA
WESTERN ILLINOIS UNIVERSITY Department of Law Enforcement and Justice Administration	Macomb, IL
WESTERN MICHIGAN UNIVERSITY	Kalamazoo, MI
WESTFIELD STATE COLLEGE Department of Criminal Justice	Westfield, MA
WICHITA STATE UNIVERSITY Department of Administration of Justice	Wichita, KS
UNIVERSITY OF WISCONSIN—MILWAUKEE Program in Criminal Justice	Milwaukee, WI
XAVIER UNIVERSITY Department of Criminal Justice	Cincinnati, OH
YOUNGSTOWN STATE UNIVERSITY Department of Criminal Justice	Youngstown, OH

Part IX
THE GOURMAN REPORT
DEPARTMENTS OF GRADUATE
EDUCATION

DEPARTMENTS OF GRADUATE EDUCATION
A RATING OF DEPARTMENTS OF EDUCATION

DEPARTMENTS OF GRADUATE EDUCATION

INSTITUTION	RANK	SCORE
University of Michigan—Ann Arbor	1	0.92
Harvard University	2	0.91
Cornell University	3	0.88
Stanford University	4	0.87
Indiana University—Bloomington	5	0.86
University of Illinois—Urbana-Champaign	6	0.82
University of Minnesota—Twin Cities	7	0.81
New York University	8	0.80
Columbia University—Teachers College	9	0.79
Northwestern University	9	0.79
Ohio State University—Columbus	9	0.79
Michigan State University	10	0.78
University of Iowa	11	0.77
University of Illinois—Chicago	12	0.76
University of Pennsylvania	13	0.74
Arizona State University	14	0.73
Temple University	14	0.73
University of Wisconsin—Madison	14	0.73
University of Pittsburgh	15	0.72
Johns Hopkins University	16	0.71
Syracuse University	16	0.71
Purdue University—West Lafayette	17	0.70
Boston University	18	0.68
University of Washington	18	0.68
George Washington University	19	0.67
University of Connecticut	20	0.66
Wayne State University	20	0.66
University of Colorado—Boulder	21	0.65
Rutgers University—New Brunswick	21	0.65
State University of New York at Buffalo	21	0.65
University of Texas—Austin	21	0.65
University of North Carolina—Chapel Hill	22	0.64
University of Cincinnati	23	0.62
Florida State University	23	0.62
University of Georgia	23	0.62
University of Kansas	23	0.62
University of Rochester	23	0.62
University of Florida	24	0.61
Pennsylvania State University—University Park	24	0.61

Southern Illinois University—Carbondale	24	0.61
Texas A&M University—College Station	24	0.61
Washington University	24	0.61
American University	25	0.60
University of Oregon	25	0.60
University of Southern California	25	0.60
University of Utah	25	0.60

A RATING OF DEPARTMENTS OF EDUCATION

INSTITUTION	Overall Academic Score	Administration	Library Resources
ABILENE CHRISTIAN UNIVERSITY Abilene, TX	0.38	0.35	0.31
ADAMS STATE COLLEGE Alamosa, CO	0.39	0.36	0.32
ADELPHI UNIVERSITY Garden City, NY	0.45	0.37	0.34
ALABAMA A&M UNIVERSITY Normal, AL	0.31	0.32	0.28
ALABAMA STATE UNIVERSITY Montgomery, AL	0.30	0.31	0.27
ALASKA PACIFIC UNIVERSITY Anchorage, AK	0.31	0.29	0.25
ALBANY STATE COLLEGE Albany, GA	0.29	0.28	0.22
ALCORN STATE UNIVERSITY Lorman, MS	0.28	0.27	0.19
ALFRED UNIVERSITY Alfred, NY	0.32	0.30	0.31
AMERICAN INTERNATIONAL COLLEGE Springfield, MA	0.31	0.30	0.30
AMERICAN UNIVERSITY Washington, D.C.	0.60	0.53	0.49
ANDREWS UNIVERSITY Berrien Springs, MI	0.37	0.36	0.30
ANGELO STATE UNIVERSITY San Angelo, TX	0.41	0.40	0.34
APPALACHIAN STATE UNIVERSITY Boone, NC	0.41	0.39	0.32
ARIZONA STATE UNIVERSITY Tempe, AZ	0.73	0.68	0.78
ARKANSAS STATE UNIVERSITY State University, AR	0.32	0.31	0.31
ARKANSAS TECH UNIVERSITY Russellville, AR	0.33	0.32	0.28

Very Strong = 4.51-4.99   Strong = 4.01-4.49   Good = 3.61-3.99   Acceptable Plus = 3.01-3.59
Adequate = 2.51-2.99   Marginal = 2.01-2.49   Not Sufficient for Graduate Programs = 0.

INSTITUTION	Overall Academic Score	Administration	Library Resources
AUBURN UNIVERSITY Auburn, AL	0.52	0.51	0.46
AUBURN UNIVERSITY—MONTGOMERY Montgomery, AL	0.28	0.29	0.28
AUSTIN PEAY STATE UNIVERSITY Clarksville, TN	0.34	0.33	0.29
AZUSA PACIFIC UNIVERSITY Azusa, CA	0.35	0.34	0.30
BALL STATE UNIVERSITY Muncie, IN	0.51	0.46	0.41
BARRY UNIVERSITY Miami Shores, FL	0.33	0.31	0.31
BAYLOR UNIVERSITY Waco, TX	0.51	0.50	0.45
BEMIDJI STATE UNIVERSITY Bemidji, MN	0.36	0.37	0.37
BLOOMSBURG UNIVERSITY OF PENNSYLVANIA Bloomsburg, PA	0.39	0.37	0.35
BOISE STATE UNIVERSITY Boise, ID	0.38	0.39	0.36
BOSTON COLLEGE Chestnut Hill, MA	0.48	0.46	0.43
BOSTON UNIVERSITY Boston, MA	0.68	0.64	0.56
BOWIE STATE UNIVERSITY Bowie, MD	0.26	0.25	0.19
BOWLING GREEN STATE UNIVERSITY Bowling Green, OH	0.52	0.48	0.49
BRADLEY UNIVERSITY Peoria, IL	0.50	0.47	0.49
BRIDGEWATER STATE COLLEGE Bridgewater, MA	0.39	0.36	0.38
BRIGHAM YOUNG UNIVERSITY Provo, UT	0.54	0.52	0.51

Very Strong = 4.51-4.99   Strong = 4.01-4.49   Good = 3.61-3.99   Acceptable Plus = 3.01-3.59
Adequate = 2.51-2.99   Marginal = 2.01-2.49   Not Sufficient for Graduate Programs = 0.

INSTITUTION	Overall Academic Score	Administration	Library Resources
BUCKNELL UNIVERSITY Lewisburg, PA	0.34	0.33	0.33
BUTLER UNIVERSITY Indianapolis, IN	0.47	0.45	0.48
CALIFORNIA LUTHERAN UNIVERSITY Thousand Oaks, CA	0.46	0.44	0.47
CALIFORNIA POLYTECHNIC STATE UNIVERSITY—SAN LUIS OBISPO San Luis Obispo, CA	0.49	0.51	0.49
CALIFORNIA STATE POLYTECHNIC UNIVERSITY—POMONA Pomona, CA	0.46	0.48	0.41
CALIFORNIA STATE UNIVERSITY—BAKERSFIELD Bakersfield, CA	0.45	0.46	0.29
CALIFORNIA STATE UNIVERSITY—CHICO Chico, CA	0.48	0.49	0.48
CALIFORNIA STATE UNIVERSITY—DOMINGUEZ HILLS Carson, CA	0.49	0.46	0.47
CALIFORNIA STATE UNIVERSITY—FRESNO Fresno, CA	0.52	0.49	0.48
CALIFORNIA STATE UNIVERSITY—FULLERTON Fullerton, CA	0.51	0.48	0.38
CALIFORNIA STATE UNIVERSITY—HAYWARD Hayward, CA	0.47	0.46	0.42
CALIFORNIA STATE UNIVERSITY—LONG BEACH Long Beach, CA	0.47	0.42	0.46
CALIFORNIA STATE UNIVERSITY—LOS ANGELES Los Angeles, CA	0.38	0.37	0.39
CALIFORNIA STATE UNIVERSITY—NORTHRIDGE Northridge, CA	0.48	0.40	0.41
CALIFORNIA STATE UNIVERSITY—SACRAMENTO Sacramento, CA	0.48	0.49	0.45
CALIFORNIA STATE UNIVERSITY—SAN BERNARDINO San Bernardino, CA	0.49	0.50	0.46

Very Strong = 4.51-4.99   Strong = 4.01-4.49   Good = 3.61-3.99   Acceptable Plus = 3.01-3.59
Adequate = 2.51-2.99   Marginal = 2.01-2.49   Not Sufficient for Graduate Programs = 0.

INSTITUTION	Overall Academic Score	Administration	Library Resources
CALIFORNIA STATE UNIVERSITY—STANISLAUS Turlock, CA	0.45	0.46	0.37
CALIFORNIA UNIVERSITY OF PENNSYLVANIA California, PA	0.38	0.36	0.35
CANISIUS COLLEGE Buffalo, NY	0.36	0.35	0.37
CATHOLIC UNIVERSITY OF AMERICA Washington, D.C.	0.54	0.49	0.52
CENTRAL CONNECTICUT STATE UNIVERSITY New Britain, CT	0.45	0.42	0.41
CENTRAL MICHIGAN UNIVERSITY Mount Pleasant, MI	0.47	0.46	0.38
CENTRAL MISSOURI STATE UNIVERSITY Warrensburg, MO	0.45	0.42	0.39
CENTRAL STATE UNIVERSITY Edmond, OK	0.32	0.28	0.26
CENTRAL WASHINGTON UNIVERSITY Ellensburg, WA	0.43	0.39	0.37
CHAPMAN UNIVERSITY Orange, CA	0.41	0.39	0.35
CHEYNEY UNIVERSITY OF PENNSYLVANIA Cheyney, PA	0.37	0.35	0.34
CHICAGO STATE UNIVERSITY Chicago, IL	0.38	0.40	0.38
UNIVERSITY OF CINCINNATI Cincinnati, OH	0.62	0.61	0.60
CITY UNIVERSITY OF NEW YORK— BARUCH COLLEGE New York, NY	0.34	0.33	0.32
CITY UNIVERSITY OF NEW YORK— BROOKLYN COLLEGE Brooklyn, NY	0.49	0.45	0.48
CITY UNIVERSITY OF NEW YORK—CITY COLLEGE New York, NY	0.52	0.46	0.46

Very Strong = 4.51-4.99   Strong = 4.01-4.49   Good = 3.61-3.99   Acceptable Plus = 3.01-3.59
Adequate = 2.51-2.99   Marginal = 2.01-2.49   Not Sufficient for Graduate Programs = 0.

INSTITUTION	Overall Academic Score	Administration	Library Resources
CITY UNIVERSITY OF NEW YORK—COLLEGE OF STATEN ISLAND Staten Island, NY	0.32	0.31	0.31
CITY UNIVERSITY OF NEW YORK—HUNTER COLLEGE New York, NY	0.51	0.47	0.48
CITY UNIVERSITY OF NEW YORK—LEHMAN COLLEGE Bronx, NY	0.34	0.33	0.32
CITY UNIVERSITY OF NEW YORK—QUEENS COLLEGE Flushing, NY	0.51	0.46	0.49
CLAREMONT GRADUATE SCHOOL Claremont, CA	0.44	0.46	0.36
CLARION UNIVERSITY OF PENNSYLVANIA Clarion, PA	0.36	0.35	0.34
CLARK UNIVERSITY Worcester, MA	0.46	0.45	0.41
CLEMSON UNIVERSITY Clemson, SC	0.49	0.44	0.47
CLEVELAND STATE UNIVERSITY Cleveland, OH	0.44	0.43	0.45
COLORADO STATE UNIVERSITY Fort Collins, CO	0.50	0.46	0.47
UNIVERSITY OF COLORADO—BOULDER Boulder, CO	0.65	0.66	0.65
UNIVERSITY OF COLORADO—COLORADO SPRINGS Colorado Springs, CO	0.31	0.29	0.22
UNIVERSITY OF COLORADO—DENVER Denver, CO	0.41	0.40	0.36
COLUMBIA UNIVERSITY—TEACHERS COLLEGE New York, NY	0.79	0.75	0.80
UNIVERSITY OF CONNECTICUT Storrs, CT	0.66	0.65	0.64

Very Strong = 4.51-4.99   Strong = 4.01-4.49   Good = 3.61-3.99   Acceptable Plus = 3.01-3.59
Adequate = 2.51-2.99   Marginal = 2.01-2.49   Not Sufficient for Graduate Programs = 0.

INSTITUTION	Overall Academic Score	Administration	Library Resources
CORNELL UNIVERSITY Ithaca, NY	0.88	0.83	0.81
CREIGHTON UNIVERSITY Omaha, NE	0.41	0.39	0.37
UNIVERSITY OF DALLAS Irving, TX	0.31	0.29	0.27
UNIVERSITY OF DAYTON Dayton, OH	0.32	0.35	0.31
UNIVERSITY OF DELAWARE Newark, DE	0.49	0.46	0.45
DELTA STATE UNIVERSITY Cleveland, MS	0.27	0.26	0.22
UNIVERSITY OF DENVER Denver, CO	0.53	0.51	0.50
DEPAUL UNIVERSITY Chicago, IL	0.49	0.46	0.48
UNIVERSITY OF DETROIT MERCY Detroit, MI	0.36	0.37	0.36
UNIVERSITY OF THE DISTRICT OF COLUMBIA Washington, D.C.	0.20	0.21	0.16
DRAKE UNIVERSITY Des Moines, IA	0.47	0.45	0.48
DRURY COLLEGE Springfield, MO	0.27	0.28	0.28
DUQUESNE UNIVERSITY Pittsburgh, PA	0.45	0.43	0.41
EAST CAROLINA UNIVERSITY Greenville, NC	0.42	0.41	0.42
EAST CENTRAL UNIVERSITY Ada, OK	0.39	0.37	0.31
EAST STROUDSBURG UNIVERSITY OF PENNSYLVANIA East Stroudsburg, PA	0.37	0.35	0.38
EAST TENNESSEE STATE UNIVERSITY Johnson City, TN	0.39	0.38	0.39

Very Strong = 4.51-4.99   Strong = 4.01-4.49   Good = 3.61-3.99   Acceptable Plus = 3.01-3.59
Adequate = 2.51-2.99   Marginal = 2.01-2.49   Not Sufficient for Graduate Programs = 0.

INSTITUTION	Overall Academic Score	Administration	Library Resources
EAST TEXAS STATE UNIVERSITY Commerce, TX	0.37	0.36	0.38
EASTERN CONNECTICUT STATE UNIVERSITY Willimantic, CT	0.41	0.39	0.38
EASTERN ILLINOIS UNIVERSITY Charleston, IL	0.43	0.41	0.39
EASTERN KENTUCKY UNIVERSITY Richmond, KY	0.44	0.38	0.38
EASTERN MICHIGAN UNIVERSITY Ypsilanti, MI	0.45	0.43	0.41
EASTERN NEW MEXICO UNIVERSITY Portales, NM	0.43	0.38	0.39
EASTERN WASHINGTON UNIVERSITY Cheney, WA	0.47	0.43	0.41
EDINBORO UNIVERSITY OF PENNSYLVANIA Edinboro, PA	0.35	0.34	0.36
EMPORIA STATE UNIVERSITY Emporia, KS	0.39	0.35	0.37
UNIVERSITY OF EVANSVILLE Evansville, IN	0.34	0.36	0.35
FAIRFIELD UNIVERSITY Fairfield, CT	0.39	0.35	0.38
FAIRLEIGH DICKINSON UNIVERSITY—TEANECK- HACKENSACK CAMPUS Teaneck, NJ	0.46	0.42	0.40
FAYETTEVILLE STATE UNIVERSITY Fayetteville, NC	0.36	0.33	0.35
FLORIDA A&M UNIVERSITY Tallahassee, FL	0.31	0.30	0.33
FLORIDA ATLANTIC UNIVERSITY Boca Raton, FL	0.32	0.31	0.32
FLORIDA INTERNATIONAL UNIVERSITY Miami, FL	0.31	0.30	0.31
FLORIDA STATE UNIVERSITY Tallahassee, FL	0.62	0.58	0.60

Very Strong = 4.51-4.99   Strong = 4.01-4.49   Good = 3.61-3.99   Acceptable Plus = 3.01-3.59
Adequate = 2.51-2.99   Marginal = 2.01-2.49   Not Sufficient for Graduate Programs = 0.

INSTITUTION	Overall Academic Score	Administration	Library Resources
UNIVERSITY OF FLORIDA Gainesville, FL	0.61	0.60	0.58
FORDHAM UNIVERSITY Bronx, NY	0.56	0.52	0.53
FORT HAYS UNIVERSITY Hays, KS	0.38	0.36	0.32
FRAMINGHAM STATE COLLEGE Framingham, MA	0.39	0.35	0.34
FROSTBURG STATE UNIVERSITY Frostburg, MD	0.28	0.25	0.26
GANNON UNIVERSITY Erie, PA	0.29	0.28	0.28
GEORGE MASON UNIVERSITY Fairfax, VA	0.32	0.33	0.34
GEORGE WASHINGTON UNIVERSITY Washington, D.C.	0.67	0.63	0.62
GEORGIA COLLEGE Milledgeville, GA	0.30	0.27	0.29
GEORGIA SOUTHERN UNIVERSITY Statesboro, GA	0.30	0.26	0.28
GEORGIA STATE UNIVERSITY Atlanta, GA	0.41	0.35	0.36
UNIVERSITY OF GEORGIA Athens, GA	0.62	0.61	0.62
GONZAGA UNIVERSITY Spokane, WA	0.48	0.47	0.47
GOVERNORS STATE UNIVERSITY University Park, IL	0.38	0.39	0.39
GRAND VALLEY STATE UNIVERSITY Allendale, MI	0.37	0.36	0.37
HAMPTON UNIVERSITY Hampton, VA	0.28	0.26	0.22
HARDIN-SIMMONS UNIVERSITY Abilene, TX	0.36	0.34	0.34

Very Strong = 4.51-4.99   Strong = 4.01-4.49   Good = 3.61-3.99   Acceptable Plus = 3.01-3.59
Adequate = 2.51-2.99   Marginal = 2.01-2.49   Not Sufficient for Graduate Programs = 0.

INSTITUTION	Overall Academic Score	Administration	Library Resources
UNIVERSITY OF HARTFORD West Hartford, CT	0.31	0.28	0.29
HARVARD UNIVERSITY Cambridge, MA	0.91	0.89	0.90
UNIVERSITY OF HAWAII—MANOA Honolulu, HI	0.36	0.35	0.33
HENDERSON STATE UNIVERSITY Arkadelphia, AR	0.27	0.26	0.28
HOFSTRA UNIVERSITY Hempstead, NY	0.50	0.45	0.49
UNIVERSITY OF HOUSTON—CLEAR LAKE Houston, TX	0.27	0.28	0.26
UNIVERSITY OF HOUSTON Houston, TX	0.49	0.50	0.49
HOWARD UNIVERSITY Washington, D.C.	0.35	0.33	0.34
HUMBOLDT STATE UNIVERSITY Arcata, CA	0.36	0.35	0.33
IDAHO STATE UNIVERSITY Pocatello, ID	0.37	0.34	0.36
UNIVERSITY OF IDAHO Moscow, ID	0.41	0.43	0.43
ILLINOIS STATE UNIVERSITYL Normal, I	0.49	0.45	0.46
UNIVERSITY OF ILLINOIS—CHICAGO Chicago, IL	0.76	0.72	0.75
UNIVERSITY OF ILLINOIS—SPRINGFIELD Springfield, IL	0.32	0.31	0.31
UNIVERSITY OF ILLINOIS—URBANA-CHAMPAIGN Urbana, IL	0.82	0.84	0.84
INDIANA STATE UNIVERSITY Terre Haute, IN	0.48	0.44	0.47
INDIANA UNIVERSITY OF PENNSYLVANIA Indiana, PA	0.38	0.35	0.35

Very Strong = 4.51-4.99   Strong = 4.01-4.49   Good = 3.61-3.99   Acceptable Plus = 3.01-3.59
Adequate = 2.51-2.99   Marginal = 2.01-2.49   Not Sufficient for Graduate Programs = 0.

INSTITUTION	Overall Academic Score	Administration	Library Resources
INDIANA UNIVERSITY—BLOOMINGTON Bloomington, IN	0.86	0.85	0.91
INDIANA UNIVERSITY—PURDUE UNIVERSITY FORT WAYNE Fort Wayne, IN	0.49	0.45	0.39
INDIANA UNIVERSITY—PURDUE UNIVERSITY INDIANAPOLIS Indianapolis, IN	0.50	0.49	0.48
INDIANA UNIVERSITY—SOUTH BEND South Bend, IN	0.40	0.41	0.45
IOWA STATE UNIVERSITY Ames, IA	0.58	0.57	0.59
UNIVERSITY OF IOWA Iowa City, IA	0.77	0.79	0.80
JACKSON STATE UNIVERSITY Jackson, MS	0.29	0.25	0.18
JACKSONVILLE STATE UNIVERSITY Jacksonville, AL	0.30	0.24	0.19
JACKSONVILLE UNIVERSITY Jacksonville, FL	0.39	0.35	0.30
JAMES MADISON UNIVERSITY Harrisonburg, VA	0.36	0.32	0.35
JERSEY CITY STATE COLLEGE Jersey City, NJ	0.37	0.36	0.36
JOHN CARROLL UNIVERSITY University Heights, OH	0.30	0.31	0.30
JOHNS HOPKINS UNIVERSITY Baltimore, MD	0.71	0.68	0.70
KANSAS STATE UNIVERSITY Manhattan, KS	0.58	0.57	0.56
UNIVERSITY OF KANSAS Lawrence, KS	0.62	0.63	0.64
KEAN COLLEGE OF NEW JERSEY Union, NJ	0.39	0.36	0.34

Very Strong = 4.51-4.99   Strong = 4.01-4.49   Good = 3.61-3.99   Acceptable Plus = 3.01-3.59
Adequate = 2.51-2.99   Marginal = 2.01-2.49   Not Sufficient for Graduate Programs = 0.

INSTITUTION	Overall Academic Score	Administration	Library Resources
KEENE STATE COLLEGE Keene, NH	0.27	0.25	0.20
KENT STATE UNIVERSITY Kent, OH	0.51	0.50	0.50
UNIVERSITY OF KENTUCKY Lexington, KY	0.49	0.48	0.48
KUTZTOWN UNIVERSITY OF PENNSYLVANIA Kutztown, PA	0.36	0.33	0.31
LAMAR UNIVERSITY Beaumont, TX	0.37	0.34	0.33
LEHIGH UNIVERSITY Bethlehem, PA	0.40	0.42	0.41
LOMA LINDA UNIVERSITY Loma Linda, CA	0.36	0.35	0.35
LONG ISLAND UNIVERSITY—BROOKLYN Brooklyn, NY	0.35	0.36	0.30
LONG ISLAND UNIVERSITY—C.W. POST Greenvale, NY	0.43	0.41	0.41
LOUISIANA STATE UNIVERSITY AND AGRICULTURAL AND MECHANICAL COLLEGE Baton Rouge, LA	0.57	0.55	0.58
LOUISIANA STATE UNIVERSITY—SHREVEPORT Shreveport, LA	0.31	0.32	0.29
LOUISIANA TECH UNIVERSITY Ruston, LA	0.32	0.33	0.30
UNIVERSITY OF LOUISVILLE Louisville, KY	0.42	0.41	0.40
LOYOLA COLLEGE (MD) Baltimore, MD	0.29	0.28	0.26
LOYOLA MARYMOUNT UNIVERSITY Los Angeles, CA	0.40	0.39	0.36
LOYOLA UNIVERSITY NEW ORLEANS New Orleans, LA	0.39	0.38	0.35
LOYOLA UNIVERSITY OF CHICAGO Chicago, IL	0.42	0.40	0.41

Very Strong = 4.51-4.99   Strong = 4.01-4.49   Good = 3.61-3.99   Acceptable Plus = 3.01-3.59
Adequate = 2.51-2.99   Marginal = 2.01-2.49   Not Sufficient for Graduate Programs = 0.

INSTITUTION	Overall Academic Score	Administration	Library Resources
LYNCHBURG COLLEGE Lynchburg, VA	0.31	0.28	0.30
UNIVERSITY OF MAINE Orono, ME	0.33	0.34	0.34
MANKATO STATE UNIVERSITY Mankato, MN	0.32	0.29	0.29
MANSFIELD UNIVERSITY OF PENNSYLVANIA Mansfield, PA	0.36	0.35	0.37
MARQUETTE UNIVERSITY Milwaukee, WI	0.50	0.49	0.47
MARSHALL UNIVERSITY Huntington, WV	0.38	0.36	0.35
UNIVERSITY OF MARYLAND—BALTIMORE COUNTY Baltimore, MD	0.27	0.25	0.19
UNIVERSITY OF MARYLAND—COLLEGE PARK College Park, MD	0.58	0.61	0.63
UNIVERSITY OF MASSACHUSETTS—AMHERST Amherst, MA	0.48	0.49	0.50
UNIVERSITY OF MASSACHUSETTS—BOSTON Boston, MA	0.30	0.29	0.25
UNIVERSITY OF MASSACHUSETTS—LOWELL Lowell, MA	0.30	0.28	0.29
UNIVERSITY OF MEMPHIS Memphis, TN	0.49	0.48	0.47
MERCER UNIVERSITY Macon, GA	0.28	0.26	0.26
MERCER UNIVERSITY—ATLANTA Atlanta, GA	0.25	0.25	0.23
MIAMI UNIVERSITY Oxford, OH	0.41	0.38	0.37
UNIVERSITY OF MIAMI Coral Gables, FL	0.33	0.34	0.33
MICHIGAN STATE UNIVERSITY East Lansing, MI	0.78	0.75	0.79

Very Strong = 4.51-4.99   Strong = 4.01-4.49   Good = 3.61-3.99   Acceptable Plus = 3.01-3.59
Adequate = 2.51-2.99   Marginal = 2.01-2.49   Not Sufficient for Graduate Programs = 0.

INSTITUTION	Overall Academic Score	Administration	Library Resources
UNIVERSITY OF MICHIGAN—ANN ARBOR Ann Arbor, MI	0.92	0.91	0.90
MIDDLE TENNESSEE STATE UNIVERSITY Murfreesboro, TN	0.46	0.43	0.45
MIDWESTERN STATE UNIVERSITY Wichita Falls, TX	0.40	0.38	0.39
MILLERSVILLE UNIVERSITY OF PENNSYLVANIA Millersville, PA	0.36	0.35	0.33
UNIVERSITY OF MINNESOTA—DULUTH Duluth, MN	0.28	0.29	0.25
UNIVERSITY OF MINNESOTA—TWIN CITIES Minneapolis, MN	0.81	0.83	0.84
MISSISSIPPI STATE UNIVERSITY Mississippi State, MS	0.46	0.44	0.41
UNIVERSITY OF MISSISSIPPI University, MS	0.41	0.44	0.44
UNIVERSITY OF MISSOURI—COLUMBIA Columbia, MO	0.59	0.61	0.61
UNIVERSITY OF MISSOURI—KANSAS CITY Kansas City, MO	0.49	0.50	0.48
UNIVERSITY OF MISSOURI—ST. LOUIS St. Louis, MO	0.26	0.27	0.27
MONTANA STATE UNIVERSITY—BILLINGS Billings, MT	0.20	0.17	0.15
MONTANA STATE UNIVERSITY—BOZEMAN Bozeman, MT	0.43	0.42	0.40
UNIVERSITY OF MONTANA Missoula, MT	0.31	0.33	0.33
MONTCLAIR STATE COLLEGE Upper Monclair, NJ	0.39	0.38	0.37
UNIVERSITY OF MONTEVALLO Montevallo, AL	0.28	0.24	0.21
MOORHEAD STATE UNIVERSITY Moorhead, MN	0.39	0.35	0.34

Very Strong = 4.51-4.99   Strong = 4.01-4.49   Good = 3.61-3.99   Acceptable Plus = 3.01-3.59
Adequate = 2.51-2.99   Marginal = 2.01-2.49   Not Sufficient for Graduate Programs = 0.

INSTITUTION	Overall Academic Score	Administration	Library Resources
MOREHEAD STATE UNIVERSITY Morehead, KY	0.31	0.30	0.30
MORGAN STATE UNIVERSITY Baltimore, MD	0.28	0.26	0.21
MURRAY STATE UNIVERSITY Murray, KY	0.31	0.30	0.29
NATIONAL-LOUIS UNIVERSITY Evanston, IL	0.40	0.38	0.41
UNIVERSITY OF NEBRASKA—KEARNEY Kearney, NE	0.27	0.22	0.23
UNIVERSITY OF NEBRASKA—LINCOLN Lincoln, NE	0.54	0.56	0.51
UNIVERSITY OF NEBRASKA—OMAHA Omaha, NE	0.30	0.29	0.25
UNIVERSITY OF NEVADA—LAS VEGAS Las Vegas, NV	0.33	0.34	0.32
UNIVERSITY OF NEVADA—RENO Reno, NV	0.31	0.33	0.31
UNIVERSITY OF NEW HAMPSHIRE Durham, NH	0.46	0.45	0.42
NEW MEXICO HIGHLANDS UNIVERSITY Las Vegas, NM	0.26	0.27	0.25
NEW MEXICO STATE UNIVERSITY Las Cruces, NM	0.42	0.41	0.41
UNIVERSITY OF NEW MEXICO Albuquerque, NM	0.49	0.50	0.49
UNIVERSITY OF NEW ORLEANS New Orleans, LA	0.30	0.31	0.29
NEW YORK UNIVERSITY New York, NY	0.80	0.78	0.83
NIAGARA UNIVERSITY Niagara University, NY	0.30	0.29	0.25
NICHOLLS STATE UNIVERSITY Thibodaux, LA	0.31	0.30	0.27

Very Strong = 4.51-4.99   Strong = 4.01-4.49   Good = 3.61-3.99   Acceptable Plus = 3.01-3.59
Adequate = 2.51-2.99   Marginal = 2.01-2.49   Not Sufficient for Graduate Programs = 0.

INSTITUTION	Overall Academic Score	Administration	Library Resources
NORFOLK STATE UNIVERSITY Norfolk, VA	0.29	0.28	0.20
NORTH ADAMS STATE COLLEGE North Adams, MA	0.30	0.30	0.29
UNIVERSITY OF NORTH ALABAMA Florence, AL	0.29	0.32	0.28
NORTH CAROLINA A&T STATE UNIVERSITY Greensboro, NC	0.25	0.26	0.21
NORTH CAROLINA CENTRAL UNIVERSITY Durham, NC	0.26	0.27	0.20
NORTH CAROLINA STATE UNIVERSITY Raleigh, NC	0.49	0.48	0.48
UNIVERSITY OF NORTH CAROLINA—CHAPEL HILL Chapel Hill, NC	0.64	0.65	0.63
UNIVERSITY OF NORTH CAROLINA—CHARLOTTE Charlotte, NC	0.32	0.33	0.35
UNIVERSITY OF NORTH CAROLINA—GREENSBORO Greensboro, NC	0.41	0.42	0.40
UNIVERSITY OF NORTH CAROLINA—WILMINGTON Wilmington, NC	0.20	0.19	0.15
NORTH DAKOTA STATE UNIVERSITY Fargo, ND	0.38	0.39	0.36
UNIVERSITY OF NORTH DAKOTA Grand Forks, ND	0.35	0.34	0.30
UNIVERSITY OF NORTH FLORIDA Jacksonville, FL	0.31	0.32	0.31
UNIVERSITY OF NORTH TEXAS Denton, TX	0.43	0.42	0.40
NORTHEAST LOUISIANA UNIVERSITY Monroe, LA	0.38	0.37	0.36
NORTHEAST MISSOURI STATE UNIVERSITY Kirksville, MO	0.32	0.31	0.31
NORTHEASTERN ILLINOIS UNIVERSITY Chicago, IL	0.43	0.42	0.43

Very Strong = 4.51-4.99   Strong = 4.01-4.49   Good = 3.61-3.99   Acceptable Plus = 3.01-3.59
Adequate = 2.51-2.99   Marginal = 2.01-2.49   Not Sufficient for Graduate Programs = 0.

INSTITUTION	Overall Academic Score	Administration	Library Resources
NORTHEASTERN STATE UNIVERSITY Tahlequah, OK	0.30	0.30	0.29
NORTHEASTERN UNIVERSITY Boston, MA	0.45	0.42	0.45
NORTHERN ARIZONA UNIVERSITY Flagstaff, AZ	0.35	0.36	0.35
UNIVERSITY OF NORTHERN COLORADO Greeley, CO	0.38	0.39	0.34
NORTHERN ILLINOIS UNIVERSITY DeKalb, IL	0.43	0.42	0.41
UNIVERSITY OF NORTHERN IOWA Cedar Falls, IA	0.33	0.34	0.32
NORTHERN KENTUCKY UNIVERSITY Highland Heights, KY	0.30	0.31	0.29
NORTHERN MICHIGAN UNIVERSITY Marquette, MI	0.39	0.40	0.39
NORTHERN MONTANA COLLEGE Havre, MT	0.18	0.15	0.12
NORTHERN STATE UNIVERSITY Aberdeen, SD	0.28	0.26	0.21
NORTHWEST MISSOURI STATE UNIVERSITY Maryville, MO	0.36	0.34	0.32
NORTHWESTERN OKLAHOMA STATE UNIVERSITY Alva, OK	0.29	0.31	0.28
NORTHWESTERN STATE UNIVERSITY OF LOUISIANA Natchitoches, LA	0.31	0.32	0.29
NORTHWESTERN UNIVERSITY Evanston, IL	0.79	0.82	0.83
NORWICH UNIVERSITY Northfield, VT	0.28	0.26	0.27
NOVA SOUTHEASTERN UNIVERSITY Fort Lauderdale, FL	0.32	0.30	0.31
OAKLAND UNIVERSITY Rochester, MI	0.29	0.30	0.23

Very Strong = 4.51-4.99   Strong = 4.01-4.49   Good = 3.61-3.99   Acceptable Plus = 3.01-3.59
Adequate = 2.51-2.99   Marginal = 2.01-2.49   Not Sufficient for Graduate Programs = 0.

INSTITUTION	Overall Academic Score	Administration	Library Resources
OHIO STATE UNIVERSITY—COLUMBUS Columbus, OH	0.79	0.81	0.80
OHIO UNIVERSITY Athens, OH	0.57	0.58	0.56
OKLAHOMA STATE UNIVERSITY Stillwater, OK	0.40	0.39	0.42
UNIVERSITY OF OKLAHOMA Norman, OK	0.58	0.59	0.58
OLD DOMINION UNIVERSITY Norfolk, VA	0.43	0.42	0.42
ORAL ROBERTS UNIVERSITY Tulsa, OK	0.25	0.23	0.18
OREGON STATE UNIVERSITY Corvallis, OR	0.59	0.58	0.57
UNIVERSITY OF OREGON Eugene, OR	0.60	0.64	0.63
PACE UNIVERSITY New York, NY	0.43	0.41	0.42
PACIFIC LUTHERAN UNIVERSITY Tacoma, WA	0.31	0.32	0.30
PACIFIC UNIVERSITY Forest Grove, OR	0.30	0.31	0.29
UNIVERSITY OF THE PACIFIC Stockton, CA	0.47	0.46	0.43
PENNSYLVANIA STATE UNIVERSITY—HARRISBURG Middletown, PA	0.22	0.21	0.19
PENNSYLVANIA STATE UNIVERSITY— UNIVERSITY PARK University Park, PA	0.61	0.62	0.64
UNIVERSITY OF PENNSYLVANIA Philadelphia, PA	0.74	0.66	0.70
PEPPERDINE UNIVERSITY Malibu, CA	0.38	0.34	0.31
PITTSBURG STATE UNIVERSITY Pittsburg, KS	0.32	0.32	0.28

Very Strong = 4.51-4.99   Strong = 4.01-4.49   Good = 3.61-3.99   Acceptable Plus = 3.01-3.59
Adequate = 2.51-2.99   Marginal = 2.01-2.49   Not Sufficient for Graduate Programs = 0.

INSTITUTION	Overall Academic Score	Administration	Library Resources
UNIVERSITY OF PITTSBURGH Pittsburgh, PA	0.72	0.73	0.71
PORTLAND STATE UNIVERSITY Portland, OR	0.34	0.35	0.33
UNIVERSITY OF PORTLAND Portland, OR	0.36	0.31	0.30
PRAIRIE VIEW A&M UNIVERSITY Prairie View, TX	0.26	0.22	0.20
UNIVERSITY OF PUGET SOUND Tacoma, WA	0.32	0.33	0.31
PURDUE UNIVERSITY—CALUMET Hammond, IN	0.31	0.32	0.25
PURDUE UNIVERSITY—WEST LAFAYETTE West Lafayette, IN	0.70	0.72	0.74
RADFORD UNIVERSITY Radford, VA	0.33	0.34	0.28
UNIVERSITY OF REDLANDS Redlands, CA	0.31	0.32	0.29
UNIVERSITY OF RHODE ISLAND Kingston, RI	0.36	0.34	0.33
UNIVERSITY OF RICHMOND Richmond, VA	0.34	0.33	0.30
UNIVERSITY OF ROCHESTER Rochester, NY	0.62	0.66	0.66
ROOSEVELT UNIVERSITY Chicago, IL	0.48	0.50	0.50
RUTGERS UNIVERSITY—NEW BRUNSWICK New Brunswick, NJ	0.65	0.68	0.67
SAGINAW VALLEY STATE UNIVERSITY University Center, MI	0.23	0.22	0.25
ST. BONAVENTURE UNIVERSITY St. Bonaventure, NY	0.30	0.31	0.30
ST. CLOUD STATE UNIVERSITY St. Cloud, MN	0.31	0.33	0.32

Very Strong = 4.51-4.99   Strong = 4.01-4.49   Good = 3.61-3.99   Acceptable Plus = 3.01-3.59
Adequate = 2.51-2.99   Marginal = 2.01-2.49   Not Sufficient for Graduate Programs = 0.

INSTITUTION	Overall Academic Score	Administration	Library Resources
ST. JOHN'S UNIVERSITY Jamaica, NY	0.44	0.43	0.41
ST. LOUIS UNIVERSITY St. Louis, MO	0.46	0.47	0.47
SAM HOUSTON STATE UNIVERSITY Huntsville, TX	0.32	0.32	0.31
SAMFORD UNIVERSITY Birmingham, AL	0.30	0.31	0.29
SAN DIEGO STATE UNIVERSITY San Diego, CA	0.45	0.44	0.41
UNIVERSITY OF SAN DIEGO San Diego, CA	0.31	0.30	0.29
SAN FRANCISCO STATE UNIVERSITY San Francisco, CA	0.45	0.44	0.45
UNIVERSITY OF SAN FRANCISCO San Francisco, CA	0.39	0.38	0.37
SAN JOSE STATE UNIVERSITY San Jose, CA	0.44	0.43	0.44
UNIVERSITY OF SANTA CLARA Santa Clara, CA	0.29	0.26	0.26
UNIVERSITY OF SCRANTON Scranton, PA	0.32	0.31	0.26
SEATTLE UNIVERSITY Seattle, WA	0.40	0.41	0.41
SETON HALL UNIVERSITY South Orange, NJ	0.39	0.43	0.42
SHIPPENSBURG UNIVERSITY OF PENNSYLVANIA Shippensburg, PA	0.35	0.34	0.31
SIMMONS COLLEGE Boston, MA	0.36	0.37	0.35
SLIPPERY ROCK UNIVERSITY OF PENNSYLVANIA Slippery Rock, PA	0.32	0.33	0.32
SMITH COLLEGE Northampton, MA	0.33	0.34	0.33

Very Strong = 4.51-4.99   Strong = 4.01-4.49   Good = 3.61-3.99   Acceptable Plus = 3.01-3.59
Adequate = 2.51-2.99   Marginal = 2.01-2.49   Not Sufficient for Graduate Programs = 0.

INSTITUTION	Overall Academic Score	Administration	Library Resources
SONOMA STATE UNIVERSITY Rohnert Park, CA	0.36	0.35	0.34
UNIVERSITY OF SOUTH ALABAMA Mobile, AL	0.34	0.32	0.31
UNIVERSITY OF SOUTH CAROLINA—COLUMBIA Columbia, SC	0.46	0.45	0.44
SOUTH DAKOTA STATE UNIVERSITY Brookings, SD	0.37	0.36	0.33
UNIVERSITY OF SOUTH DAKOTA Vermillion, SD	0.34	0.31	0.32
UNIVERSITY OF SOUTH FLORIDA Tampa, FL	0.32	0.34	0.32
SOUTHEAST MISSOURI STATE UNIVERSITY Cape Girardeau, MO	0.30	0.35	0.31
SOUTHEASTERN LOUISIANA UNIVERSITY Hammond, LA	0.32	0.29	0.30
UNIVERSITY OF SOUTHERN CALIFORNIA Los Angeles, CA	0.60	0.58	0.63
SOUTHERN CONNECTICUT STATE UNIVERSITY New Haven, CT	0.32	0.36	0.34
SOUTHERN ILLINOIS UNIVERSITY—CARBONDALE Carbondale, IL	0.61	0.65	0.66
SOUTHERN ILLINOIS UNIVERSITY—EDWARDSVILLE Edwardsville, IL	0.50	0.51	0.52
UNIVERSITY OF SOUTHERN MISSISSIPPI Hattiesburg, MS	0.33	0.33	0.30
SOUTHERN UNIVERSITY AND AGRICULTURAL AND MECHANICAL COLLEGE Baton Rouge, LA	0.28	0.27	0.28
SOUTHWEST MISSOURI STATE UNIVERSITY Springfield, MO	0.30	0.29	0.27
SOUTHWEST TEXAS STATE UNIVERSITY San Marcos, TX	0.32	0.31	0.30
UNIVERSITY OF SOUTHWESTERN LOUISIANA Lafayette, LA	0.34	0.32	0.31

Very Strong = 4.51-4.99   Strong = 4.01-4.49   Good = 3.61-3.99   Acceptable Plus = 3.01-3.59
Adequate = 2.51-2.99   Marginal = 2.01-2.49   Not Sufficient for Graduate Programs = 0.

INSTITUTION	Overall Academic Score	Administration	Library Resources
SOUTHWESTERN OKLAHOMA STATE UNIVERSITY Weatherford, OK	0.31	0.30	0.28
STANFORD UNIVERSITY Stanford, CA	0.87	0.90	0.89
STATE UNIVERSITY OF NEW YORK AT ALBANY Albany, NY	0.53	0.54	0.52
STATE UNIVERSITY OF NEW YORK AT BINGHAMTON Binghamton, NY	0.54	0.55	0.54
STATE UNIVERSITY OF NEW YORK AT BUFFALO Buffalo, NY	0.65	0.64	0.68
STATE UNIVERSITY OF NEW YORK COLLEGE AT BROCKPORT Brockport, NY	0.30	0.31	0.29
STATE UNIVERSITY OF NEW YORK COLLEGE AT BUFFALO Buffalo, NY	0.31	0.32	0.30
STATE UNIVERSITY OF NEW YORK COLLEGE AT CORTLAND Cortland, NY	0.29	0.31	0.31
STATE UNIVERSITY OF NEW YORK COLLEGE AT FREDONIA Fredonia, NY	0.34	0.33	0.32
STATE UNIVERSITY OF NEW YORK COLLEGE AT GENESEO Geneseo, NY	0.35	0.34	0.33
STATE UNIVERSITY OF NEW YORK COLLEGE AT NEW PALTZ New Paltz, NY	0.36	0.35	0.34
STATE UNIVERSITY OF NEW YORK COLLEGE AT ONEONTA Oneonta, NY	0.33	0.30	0.32
STATE UNIVERSITY OF NEW YORK COLLEGE AT OSWEGO Oswego, NY	0.34	0.29	0.33
STATE UNIVERSITY OF NEW YORK COLLEGE AT PLATTSBURGH Plattsburgh, NY	0.30	0.31	0.32

Very Strong = 4.51-4.99   Strong = 4.01-4.49   Good = 3.61-3.99   Acceptable Plus = 3.01-3.59
Adequate = 2.51-2.99   Marginal = 2.01-2.49   Not Sufficient for Graduate Programs = 0.

INSTITUTION	Overall Academic Score	Administration	Library Resources
STATE UNIVERSITY OF NEW YORK COLLEGE AT POTSDAM Potsdam, NY	0.35	0.33	0.35
STEPHEN F. AUSTIN STATE UNIVERSITY Nacogdoches, TX	0.36	0.34	0.32
STETSON UNIVERSITY DeLand, FL	0.30	0.29	0.30
SUFFOLK UNIVERSITY Boston, MA	0.35	0.31	0.34
SUL ROSS STATE UNIVERSITY Alpine, TX	0.30	0.29	0.30
SYRACUSE UNIVERSITY Syracuse, NY	0.71	0.74	0.76
TARLETON STATE UNIVERSITY Stephenville, TX	0.41	0.46	0.45
TEMPLE UNIVERSITY Philadelphia, PA	0.73	0.76	0.79
TENNESSEE STATE UNIVERSITY Nashville, TN	0.30	0.28	0.26
TENNESSEE TECHNOLOGICAL UNIVERSITY Cookeville, TN	0.29	0.30	0.24
UNIVERSITY OF TENNESSEE—CHATTANOOGA Chattanooga, TN	0.31	0.30	0.26
UNIVERSITY OF TENNESSEE—KNOXVILLE Knoxville, TN	0.48	0.49	0.47
UNIVERSITY OF TENNESSEE—MARTIN Martin, TN	0.29	0.29	0.22
TEXAS A&M INTERNATIONAL UNIVERSITY Laredo, TX	0.28	0.29	0.23
TEXAS A&M UNIVERSITY—COLLEGE STATION College Station, TX	0.61	0.63	0.62
TEXAS A&M UNIVERSITY—CORPUS CHRISTI Corpus, TX	0.21	0.20	0.20
TEXAS A&M UNIVERSITY—KINGSVILLE Kingsville, TX	0.22	0.21	0.18

Very Strong = 4.51-4.99   Strong = 4.01-4.49   Good = 3.61-3.99   Acceptable Plus = 3.01-3.59
Adequate = 2.51-2.99   Marginal = 2.01-2.49   Not Sufficient for Graduate Programs = 0.

INSTITUTION	Overall Academic Score	Administration	Library Resources
TEXAS CHRISTIAN UNIVERSITY Fort Worth, TX	0.30	0.33	0.33
TEXAS SOUTHERN UNIVERSITY Houston, TX	0.27	0.25	0.20
TEXAS TECH UNIVERSITY Lubbock, TX	0.48	0.45	0.48
TEXAS WOMAN'S UNIVERSITY Denton, TX	0.33	0.35	0.31
UNIVERSITY OF TEXAS—ARLINGTON Arlington, TX	0.20	0.18	0.17
UNIVERSITY OF TEXAS—AUSTIN Austin, TX	0.65	0.61	0.66
UNIVERSITY OF TEXAS—EL PASO El Paso, TX	0.30	0.25	0.24
UNIVERSITY OF TEXAS—PAN AMERICAN Edinburg, TX	0.21	0.22	0.20
UNIVERSITY OF TEXAS—PERMIAN BASIN Odessa, TX	0.19	0.18	0.16
UNIVERSITY OF TEXAS—SAN ANTONIO San Antonio, TX	0.28	0.27	0.20
UNIVERSITY OF TEXAS—TYLER Tyler, TX	0.22	0.23	0.22
UNIVERSITY OF TOLEDO Toledo, OH	0.34	0.35	0.33
TOWSON STATE UNIVERSITY Towson, MD	0.28	0.27	0.23
TRENTON STATE COLLEGE Trenton, NJ	0.34	0.34	0.31
TRINITY UNIVERSITY San Antonio, TX	0.30	0.31	0.28
TROY STATE UNIVERSITY Troy, AL	0.33	0.32	0.29
TUFTS UNIVERSITY Medford, MA	0.49	0.53	0.47

Very Strong = 4.51-4.99   Strong = 4.01-4.49   Good = 3.61-3.99   Acceptable Plus = 3.01-3.59
Adequate = 2.51-2.99   Marginal = 2.01-2.49   Not Sufficient for Graduate Programs = 0.

INSTITUTION	Overall Academic Score	Administration	Library Resources
TULANE UNIVERSITY New Orleans, LA	0.46	0.51	0.50
UNIVERSITY OF TULSA Tulsa, OK	0.33	0.36	0.34
TUSKEGEE UNIVERSITY Tuskegee Institute, AL	0.21	0.22	0.16
UNITED STATES INTERNATIONAL UNIVERSITY San Diego, CA	0.30	0.26	0.24
UTAH STATE UNIVERSITY Logan, UT	0.37	0.38	0.34
UNIVERSITY OF UTAH Salt Lake City, UT	0.60	0.59	0.61
VALDOSTA STATE COLLEGE Valdosta, GA	0.27	0.26	0.24
VANDERBILT UNIVERSITY Nashville, TN	0.52	0.50	0.50
UNIVERSITY OF VERMONT Burlington, VT	0.41	0.41	0.42
VILLANOVA UNIVERSITY Villanova, PA	0.30	0.31	0.28
VIRGINIA COMMONWEALTH UNIVERSITY Richmond, VA	0.48	0.47	0.47
VIRGINIA POLYTECHNIC INSTITUTE AND STATE UNIVERSITY Blackburg, VA	0.48	0.49	0.46
VIRGINIA STATE UNIVERSITY Petersburg, VA	0.20	0.21	0.15
UNIVERSITY OF VIRGINIA Charlottesville, VA	0.51	0.53	0.58
WAKE FOREST UNIVERSITY Winston-Salem, NC	0.30	0.31	0.30
WASHBURN UNIVERSITY OF TOPEKA Topeka, KS	0.27	0.25	0.24
WASHINGTON STATE UNIVERSITY Pullman, WA	0.57	0.58	0.56

Very Strong = 4.51-4.99   Strong = 4.01-4.49   Good = 3.61-3.99   Acceptable Plus = 3.01-3.59
Adequate = 2.51-2.99   Marginal = 2.01-2.49   Not Sufficient for Graduate Programs = 0.

INSTITUTION	Overall Academic Score	Administration	Library Resources
WASHINGTON UNIVERSITY St. Louis, MO	0.61	0.64	0.63
UNIVERSITY OF WASHINGTON Seattle, WA	0.68	0.69	0.71
WAYNE STATE UNIVERSITY Detroit, MI	0.66	0.68	0.69
UNIVERSITY OF WEST FLORIDA Pensacola, FL	0.29	0.30	0.30
WEST TEXAS A&M UNIVERSITY Canyon, TX	0.38	0.39	0.35
WEST VIRGINIA UNIVERSITY Morgantown, WV	0.44	0.45	0.47
WESTCHESTER UNIVERSITY OF PENNSYLVANIA Westchester, PA	0.36	0.33	0.30
WESTERN CAROLINA UNIVERSITY Cullowhee, NC	0.37	0.38	0.36
WESTERN ILLINOIS UNIVERSITY Macomb, IL	0.43	0.44	0.42
WESTERN KENTUCKY UNIVERSITY Bowling Green, KY	0.40	0.41	0.41
WESTERN MICHIGAN UNIVERSITY Kalamazoo, MI	0.45	0.46	0.46
WESTERN WASHINGTON UNIVERSITY Bellingham, WA	0.41	0.42	0.42
WICHITA STATE UNIVERSITY Wichita, KS	0.27	0.30	0.24
WIDENER UNIVERSITY Chester, PA	0.30	0.31	0.27
THE COLLEGE OF WILLIAM AND MARY Williamsburg, VA	0.43	0.44	0.43
WILLIAM PATERSON COLLEGE OF NEW JERSEY Wayne, NJ	0.31	0.32	0.28
WINONA STATE UNIVERSITY Winona, MN	0.32	0.30	0.29

Very Strong = 4.51-4.99   Strong = 4.01-4.49   Good = 3.61-3.99   Acceptable Plus = 3.01-3.59
Adequate = 2.51-2.99   Marginal = 2.01-2.49   Not Sufficient for Graduate Programs = 0.

INSTITUTION	Overall Academic Score	Administration	Library Resources
UNIVERSITY OF WISCONSIN—EAU CLAIRE Eau Claire, WI	0.29	0.29	0.25
UNIVERSITY OF WISCONSIN—LACROSSE LaCrosse, WI	0.27	0.26	0.22
UNIVERSITY OF WISCONSIN—MADISON Madison, WI	0.73	0.75	0.84
UNIVERSITY OF WISCONSIN—MILWAUKEE Milwaukee, WI	0.50	0.51	0.59
UNIVERSITY OF WISCONSIN—OSHKOSH Oshkosh, WI	0.26	0.27	0.24
UNIVERSITY OF WISCONSIN—PLATTEVILLE Platteville, WI	0.28	0.26	0.23
UNIVERSITY OF WISCONSIN—RIVER FALLS River Falls, WI	0.25	0.24	0.22
UNIVERSITY OF WISCONSIN—STEVENS POINT Stevens Point, WI	0.24	0.23	0.21
UNIVERSITY OF WISCONSIN—STOUT Menomonie, WI	0.21	0.22	0.19
UNIVERSITY OF WISCONSIN—SUPERIOR Superior, WI	0.23	0.21	0.20
UNIVERSITY OF WISCONSIN—WHITEWATER Whitewater, WI	0.26	0.24	0.21
WRIGHT STATE UNIVERSITY Dayton, OH	0.33	0.34	0.31
UNIVERSITY OF WYOMING Laramie, WY	0.36	0.37	0.35
XAVIER UNIVERSITY Cincinnati, OH	0.30	0.29	0.25
YESHIVA UNIVERSITY New York, NY	0.58	0.59	0.56
YOUNGSTOWN STATE UNIVERSITY Youngstown, OH	0.27	0.28	0.26

Very Strong = 4.51-4.99   Strong = 4.01-4.49   Good = 3.61-3.99   Acceptable Plus = 3.01-3.59
Adequate = 2.51-2.99   Marginal = 2.01-2.49   Not Sufficient for Graduate Programs = 0.

Part X
THE GOURMAN REPORT
U.S. GRADUATE SCHOOLS

THE TOP 50 QUALITY GRADUATE SCHOOLS IN THE UNITED STATES

THE TOP 50 QUALITY U.S. GRADUATE SCHOOLS

INSTITUTION	RANK	SCORE
HARVARD UNIVERSITY	1	4.94
UNIVERSITY OF CALIFORNIA—BERKELEY	2	4.93
UNIVERSITY OF MICHIGAN—ANN ARBOR	3	4.92
YALE UNIVERSITY	4	4.91
STANFORD UNIVERSITY	5	4.90
UNIVERSITY OF CHICAGO	6	4.89
PRINCETON UNIVERSITY	7	4.88
UNIVERSITY OF WISCONSIN—MADISON	8	4.87
UNIVERSITY OF CALIFORNIA—LOS ANGELES	9	4.86
CORNELL UNIVERSITY	10	4.85
COLUMBIA UNIVERSITY	11	4.84
CALIFORNIA INSTITUTE OF TECHNOLOGY	12	4.83
MASSACHUSETTS INSTITUTE OF TECHNOLOGY	13	4.82
UNIVERSITY OF PENNSYLVANIA	14	4.81
UNIVERSITY OF MINNESOTA—TWIN CITIES	15	4.80
NORTHWESTERN UNIVERSITY	16	4.79
UNIVERSITY OF ILLINOIS—URBANA-CHAMPAIGN	17	4.78
JOHNS HOPKINS UNIVERSITY	18	4.77
UNIVERSITY OF CALIFORNIA—SAN DIEGO	19	4.76
BROWN UNIVERSITY	20	4.75
DUKE UNIVERSITY	21	4.73
INDIANA UNIVERSITY—BLOOMINGTON	22	4.71
UNIVERSITY OF IOWA	23	4.69
UNIVERSITY OF NORTH CAROLINA—CHAPEL HILL	24	4.68
UNIVERSITY OF VIRGINIA	25	4.67
UNIVERSITY OF TEXAS—AUSTIN	26	4.65
UNIVERSITY OF WASHINGTON	27	4.63
WASHINGTON UNIVERSITY	28	4.61
CARNEGIE MELLON UNIVERSITY	29	4.58
UNIVERSITY OF CALIFORNIA—DAVIS	30	4.57
PURDUE UNIVERSITY—WEST LAFAYETTE	31	4.55
RENSSELAER POLYTECHNIC INSTITUTE	32	4.53
UNIVERSITY OF ROCHESTER	33	4.51
UNIVERSITY OF CALIFORNIA—SAN FRANCISCO	34	4.49
RICE UNIVERSITY	35	4.47
STATE UNIVERSITY OF NEW YORK AT STONY BROOK	36	4.45
PENNSYLVANIA STATE UNIVERSITY—UNIVERSITY PARK	37	4.43
UNIVERSITY OF PITTSBURGH	38	4.41
UNIVERSITY OF NOTRE DAME	39	4.40
VANDERBILT UNIVERSITY	40	4.37

UNIVERSITY OF CALIFORNIA—IRVINE	41	4.35
RUTGERS UNIVERSITY—NEW BRUNSWICK	42	4.33
GEORGIA INSTITUTE OF TECHNOLOGY	43	4.31
DARTMOUTH COLLEGE	44	4.30
CASE WESTERN RESERVE UNIVERSITY	45	4.27
OHIO STATE UNIVERSITY—COLUMBUS	46	4.24
TUFTS UNIVERSITY	47	4.22
STATE UNIVERSITY OF NEW YORK AT BUFFALO	48	4.18
TULANE UNIVERSITY	49	4.16
BRANDEIS UNIVERSITY	50	4.13

Part XI
THE GOURMAN REPORT

A RATING OF U.S. GRADUATE SCHOOLS

A Rating of United States Graduate Schools: Academic and Selective

INSTITUTION	Overall Academic Rating	INSTITUTION	Overall Academic Rating
AIR FORCE INSTITUTE OF TECHNOLOGY Wright-Patterson AFB, OH	2.80	UNIVERSITY OF ARKANSAS—LITTLE ROCK Little Rock, AR	2.19
UNIVERSITY OF AKRON Akron, OH	2.36	AUBURN UNIVERSITY Auburn, AL	3.59
ALABAMA A&M UNIVERSITY Normal, AL	2.10	BALL STATE UNIVERSITY Muncie, IN	2.30
UNIVERSITY OF ALABAMA University, AL	3.36	BAYLOR UNIVERSITY Waco, TX	3.61
UNIVERSITY OF ALABAMA—BIRMINGHAM Birmingham, AL	3.38	BLOOMSBURG UNIVERSITY OF PENNSYLVANIA Bloomsburg, PA	0.
UNIVERSITY OF ALABAMA—HUNTSVILLE Huntsville, AL	2.77	BOSTON COLLEGE Chestnut Hill, MA	2.48
UNIVERSITY OF ALASKA—ANCHORAGE Anchorage, AK	2.01	BOSTON UNIVERSITY Boston, MA	3.91
UNIVERSITY OF ALASKA—FAIRBANKS Fairbanks, AK	2.60	BOWLING GREEN STATE UNIVERSITY Bowling Green, OH	2.90
ALFRED UNIVERSITY Alfred, NY	3.10	BRADLEY UNIVERSITY Peoria, IL	2.40
AMERICAN UNIVERSITY Washington, D.C.	3.18	BRANDEIS UNIVERSITY Waltham, MA	4.13
APPALACHIAN STATE UNIVERSITY Boone, NC	2.01	BRIDGEWATER STATE COLLEGE Bridgewater, MA	0.
ARIZONA STATE UNIVERSITY Tempe, AZ	3.65	BRIGHAM YOUNG UNIVERSITY Provo, UT	2.70
UNIVERSITY OF ARIZONA Tucson, AZ	3.72	BROWN UNIVERSITY Providence, RI	4.75
ARKANSAS STATE UNIVERSITY State University, AR	2.02	BRYN MAWR COLLEGE Bryn Mawr, PA	3.30
UNIVERSITY OF ARKANSAS Fayetteville, AR	3.15	CALIFORNIA INSTITUTE OF TECHNOLOGY Pasadena, CA	4.83

Very Strong = 4.51-4.99   Strong = 4.01-4.49   Good = 3.61-3.99   Acceptable Plus = 3.01-3.59
Adequate = 2.51-2.99   Marginal = 2.01-2.49   Not Sufficient for Graduate Programs = 0.

INSTITUTION	Overall Academic Rating	INSTITUTION	Overall Academic Rating
CALIFORNIA POLYTECHNIC STATE UNIVERSITY—SAN LUIS OBISPO San Luis Obispo, CA	2.60	UNIVERSITY OF CALIFORNIA—DAVIS Davis, CA	4.57
CALIFORNIA STATE POLYTECHNIC UNIVERSITY—POMONA Pomona, CA	2.02	UNIVERSITY OF CALIFORNIA—IRVINE Irvine, CA	4.35
CALIFORNIA STATE UNIVERSITY—BAKERSFIELD Bakersfield, CA	0.	UNIVERSITY OF CALIFORNIA—LOS ANGELES Los Angeles, CA	4.86
CALIFORNIA STATE UNIVERSITY—CHICO Chico, CA	0.	UNIVERSITY OF CALIFORNIA—RIVERSIDE Riverside, CA	3.80
CALIFORNIA STATE UNIVERSITY— DOMINGUEZ HILLS Carson, CA	0.	UNIVERSITY OF CALIFORNIA—SAN DIEGO La Jolla, CA	4.76
CALIFORNIA STATE UNIVERSITY—FRESNO Fresno, CA	2.14	UNIVERSITY OF CALIFORNIA—SAN FRANCISCO San Francisco, CA	4.49
CALIFORNIA STATE UNIVERSITY—FULLERTON Fullerton, CA	2.13	UNIVERSITY OF CALIFORNIA—SANTA BARBARA Santa Barbara, CA	3.95
CALIFORNIA STATE UNIVERSITY—HAYWARD Hayward, CA	0.	UNIVERSITY OF CALIFORNIA—SANTA CRUZ Santa Cruz, CA	3.50
CALIFORNIA STATE UNIVERSITY—LONG BEACH Long Beach, CA	2.12	CARNEGIE MELLON UNIVERSITY Pittsburgh, PA	4.58
CALIFORNIA STATE UNIVERSITY—LOS ANGELES Los Angeles, CA	1.89	CASE WESTERN RESERVE UNIVERSITY Cleveland, OH	4.27
CALIFORNIA STATE UNIVERSITY—NORTHRIDGE Northridge, CA	1.90	CATHOLIC UNIVERSITY OF AMERICA Washington, D.C.	3.12
CALIFORNIA STATE UNIVERSITY—SACRAMENTO Sacramento, CA	2.15	CENTRAL CONNECTICUT STATE UNIVERSITY New Britain, CT	2.07
CALIFORNIA STATE UNIVERSITY—SAN BERNARDINO San Bernardino, CA	2.03	UNIVERSITY OF CENTRAL FLORIDA Orlando, FL	2.19
CALIFORNIA STATE UNIVERSITY—STANISLAUS Turlock, CA	0.	CENTRAL MICHIGAN UNIVERSITY Mount Pleasant, MI	2.09
CALIFORNIA UNIVERSITY OF PENNSYLVANIA California, PA	0.	CENTRAL MISSOURI STATE UNIVERSITY Warrensburg, MO	2.01
UNIVERSITY OF CALIFORNIA—BERKELEY Berkeley, CA	4.93	CHEYNEY UNIVERSITY OF PENNSYLVANIA Cheyney, PA	0.
		CHICAGO STATE UNIVERSITY Chicago, IL	0.

Very Strong = 4.51-4.99   Strong = 4.01-4.49   Good = 3.61-3.99   Acceptable Plus = 3.01-3.59
Adequate = 2.51-2.99   Marginal = 2.01-2.49   Not Sufficient for Graduate Programs = 0.

INSTITUTION	Overall Academic Rating	INSTITUTION	Overall Academic Rating
UNIVERSITY OF CHICAGO Chicago, IL	4.89	CLEMSON UNIVERSITY Clemson, SC	3.10
UNIVERSITY OF CINCINNATI Cincinnati, OH	3.52	CLEVELAND STATE UNIVERSITY Cleveland, OH	2.15
CITY UNIVERSITY OF NEW YORK—BARUCH COLLEGE New York, NY	3.08	COLORADO SCHOOL OF MINES Golden, CO	3.84
CITY UNIVERSITY OF NEW YORK—BROOKLYN COLLEGE New York, NY	3.10	COLORADO STATE UNIVERSITY Fort Collins, CO	2.95
CITY UNIVERSITY OF NEW YORK—CITY COLLEGE New York, NY	3.31	UNIVERSITY OF COLORADO—BOULDER Boulder, CO	3.73
CITY UNIVERSITY OF NEW YORK—COLLEGE OF STATEN ISLAND Staten Island, NY	0.	UNIVERSITY OF COLORADO—COLORADO SPRINGS Colorado Springs, CO	2.01
CITY UNIVERSITY OF NEW YORK—GRADUATE SCHOOL AND UNIVERSITY CENTER New York, NY	3.88	UNIVERSITY OF COLORADO—DENVER Denver, CO	3.06
CITY UNIVERSITY OF NEW YORK—HUNTER COLLEGE New York, NY	3.13	COLUMBIA UNIVERSITY New York, NY	4.84
CITY UNIVERSITY OF NEW YORK—LEHMAN COLLEGE Bronx, NY	2.68	COLUMBIA UNIVERSITY—TEACHERS COLLEGE New York, NY	3.32
CITY UNIVERSITY OF NEW YORK—QUEENS COLLEGE Flushing, NY	3.15	UNIVERSITY OF CONNECTICUT Storrs, CT	3.71
CLAREMONT GRADUATE SCHOOL Claremont, CA	3.52	THE COOPER UNION New York, NY	2.58
CLARION UNIVERSITY OF PENNSYLVANIA Clarion, PA	0.	CORNELL UNIVERSITY Ithaca, NY	4.85
CLARK UNIVERSITY Worcester, MA	3.55	CREIGHTON UNIVERSITY Omaha, NE	3.09
CLARKSON UNIVERSITY Potsdam, NY	2.76	UNIVERSITY OF DALLAS Irving, TX	2.12
		DARTMOUTH COLLEGE Hanover, NH	4.30
		UNIVERSITY OF DAYTON Dayton, OH	2.19
		UNIVERSITY OF DELAWARE Newark, DE	3.30

Very Strong = 4.51-4.99   Strong = 4.01-4.49   Good = 3.61-3.99   Acceptable Plus = 3.01-3.59
Adequate = 2.51-2.99   Marginal = 2.01-2.49   Not Sufficient for Graduate Programs = 0.

INSTITUTION	Overall Academic Rating	INSTITUTION	Overall Academic Rating
UNIVERSITY OF DENVER Denver, CO	3.55	EDINBORO UNIVERSITY OF PENNSYLVANIA Edinboro, PA	0.
DEPAUL UNIVERSITY Chicago, IL	2.89	EMORY UNIVERSITY Atlanta, GA	3.79
UNIVERSITY OF DETROIT MERCY Detroit, MI	2.33	EMPORIA STATE UNIVERSITY Emporia, KS	2.18
UNIVERSITY OF THE DISTRICT OF COLUMBIA Washington, D.C.	0.	FAIRLEIGH DICKINSON UNIVERSITY— FLORHAM-MADISON CAMPUS Madison, NJ	3.05
DRAKE UNIVERSITY Des Moines, IA	2.10	FAIRLEIGH DICKINSON UNIVERSITY— TEANECK-HACKENSACK CAMPUS Teaneck, NJ	3.06
DREXEL UNIVERSITY Philadelphia, PA	3.62	FLORIDA A&M UNIVERSITY Tallahassee, FL	2.12
DUKE UNIVERSITY Durham, NC	4.73	FLORIDA ATLANTIC UNIVERSITY Boca Raton, FL	2.04
DUQUESNE UNIVERSITY Pittsburgh, PA	2.14	FLORIDA INSTITUTE OF TECHNOLOGY Melbourne, FL	2.05
EAST CAROLINA UNIVERSITY Greenville, NC	2.53	FLORIDA INTERNATIONAL UNIVERSITY Miami, FL	2.06
EAST STROUDSBURG UNIVERSITY OF PENNSYLVANIA East Stroudsburg, PA	0.	FLORIDA STATE UNIVERSITY Tallahassee, FL	3.52
EAST TENNESSEE STATE UNIVERSITY Johnson City, TN	2.19	UNIVERSITY OF FLORIDA Gainesville, FL	3.89
EAST TEXAS STATE UNIVERSITY Commerce, TX	0.	FORDHAM UNIVERSITY Bronx, NY	3.37
EASTERN ILLINOIS UNIVERSITY Charleston, IL	2.06	FORT HAYS STATE UNIVERSITY Hays, KS	2.01
EASTERN KENTUCKY UNIVERSITY Richmond, KY	2.18	FRAMINGHAM STATE COLLEGE Framingham, MA	0.
EASTERN MICHIGAN UNIVERSITY Ypsilanti, MI	2.31	GEORGE MASON UNIVERSITY Fairfax, VA	2.13
EASTERN NEW MEXICO UNIVERSITY Portales, NM	2.04	GEORGE WASHINGTON UNIVERSITY Washington, D.C.	3.68
EASTERN WASHINGTON UNIVERSITY Cheney, WA	2.02		

Very Strong = 4.51-4.99   Strong = 4.01-4.49   Good = 3.61-3.99   Acceptable Plus = 3.01-3.59
Adequate = 2.51-2.99   Marginal = 2.01-2.49   Not Sufficient for Graduate Programs = 0.

INSTITUTION	Overall Academic Rating	INSTITUTION	Overall Academic Rating
GEORGETOWN UNIVERSITY Washington, D.C.	4.04	UNIVERSITY OF IDAHO Moscow, ID	3.05
GEORGIA INSTITUTE OF TECHNOLOGY Atlanta, GA	4.31	ILLINOIS INSTITUTE OF TECHNOLOGY Chicago, IL	2.54
GEORGIA SOUTHERN UNIVERSITY Statesboro, GA	2.11	ILLINOIS STATE UNIVERSITY Normal, IL	2.45
GEORGIA STATE UNIVERSITY Atlanta, GA	2.27	UNIVERSITY OF ILLINOIS—CHICAGO Chicago, IL	3.77
UNIVERSITY OF GEORGIA Athens, GA	3.51	UNIVERSITY OF ILLINOIS—SPRINGFIELD Springfield, IL	2.05
GOLDEN GATE UNIVERSITY San Francisco, CA	2.25	UNIVERSITY OF ILLINOIS—URBANA-CHAMPAIGN Urbana, IL	4.78
GONZAGA UNIVERSITY Spokane, WA	2.96	INDIANA STATE UNIVERSITY Terre Haute, IN	2.01
GRAND VALLEY STATE UNIVERSITY Allendale, MI	2.01	INDIANA UNIVERSITY OF PENNSYLVANIA Indiana, PA	0.
UNIVERSITY OF HARTFORD West Hartford, CT	2.55	INDIANA UNIVERSITY—BLOOMINGTON Bloomington, IN	4.71
HARVARD UNIVERSITY Cambridge, MA	4.94	INDIANA UNIVERSITY—KOKOMO Kokomo, IN	0.
UNIVERSITY OF HAWAII—MANOA Honolulu, HI	3.42	INDIANA UNIVERSITY NORTHWEST Gary, IN	0.
HOFSTRA UNIVERSITY Hempstead, NY	2.88	INDIANA UNIVERSITY–PURDUE UNIVERSITY Fort Wayne Fort Wayne, IN	2.04
UNIVERSITY OF HOUSTON—CLEAR LAKE Houston, TX	2.01	INDIANA UNIVERSITY–PURDUE UNIVERSITY INDIANAPOLIS Indianapolis, IN	3.98
UNIVERSITY OF HOUSTON Houston, TX	3.47	INDIANA UNIVERSITY—SOUTH BEND South Bend, IN	0.
HOWARD UNIVERSITY Washington, D.C.	2.68	INDIANA UNIVERSITY SOUTHEAST New Albany, IN	0.
HUMBOLDT STATE UNIVERSITY Arcata, CA	2.01	IOWA STATE UNIVERSITY Ames, IA	3.64
IDAHO STATE UNIVERSITY Pocatello, ID	2.28		

Very Strong = 4.51-4.99   Strong = 4.01-4.49   Good = 3.61-3.99   Acceptable Plus = 3.01-3.59
Adequate = 2.51-2.99   Marginal = 2.01-2.49   Not Sufficient for Graduate Programs = 0.

INSTITUTION	Overall Academic Rating	INSTITUTION	Overall Academic Rating
UNIVERSITY OF IOWA Iowa City, IA	4.69	LOYOLA UNIVERSITY OF CHICAGO Chicago, IL	3.14
JAMES MADISON UNIVERSITY Harrisonburg, VA	2.31	UNIVERSITY OF MAINE Orono, ME	3.19
JOHNS HOPKINS UNIVERSITY Baltimore, MD	4.77	MANKATO STATE UNIVERSITY Mankato, MN	2.09
KANSAS STATE UNIVERSITY Manhattan, KS	3.48	MANSFIELD UNIVERSITY OF PENNSYLVANIA Mansfield, PA	0.
UNIVERSITY OF KANSAS Lawrence, KS	3.99	MARQUETTE UNIVERSITY Milwaukee, WI	3.38
KENT STATE UNIVERSITY Kent, OH	2.70	MARSHALL UNIVERSITY Huntington, WV	2.45
UNIVERSITY OF KENTUCKY Lexington, KY	3.24	UNIVERSITY OF MARYLAND—COLLEGE PARK College Park, MD	3.80
KUTZTOWN UNIVERSITY OF PENNSYLVANIA Kutztown, PA	0.	UNIVERSITY OF MARYLAND—BALTIMORE Baltimore, MD	3.79
LAMAR UNIVERSITY Beaumont, TX	2.02	MASSACHUSETTS INSTITUTE OF TECHNOLOGY Cambridge, MA	4.82
LEHIGH UNIVERSITY Bethlehem, PA	3.41	UNIVERSITY OF MASSACHUSETTS—AMHERST Amherst, MA	3.86
LOMA LINDA UNIVERSITY Loma Linda, CA	3.29	UNIVERSITY OF MASSACHUSETTS—BOSTON Boston, MA	2.20
LONG ISLAND UNIVERSITY—BROOKLYN Brooklyn, NY	3.27	UNIVERSITY OF MASSACHUSETTS—DARTMOUTH North Dartmouth, MA	2.11
LONG ISLAND UNIVERSITY—C.W. POST Brookville, NY	3.14	UNIVERSITY OF MASSACHUSETTS—LOWELL Lowell, MA	3.26
LOUISIANA STATE UNIVERSITY AND AGRICULTURAL AND MECHANICAL COLLEGE Baton Rouge, LA	3.61	UNIVERSITY OF MEMPHIS Memphis, TN	3.05
LOUISIANA STATE UNIVERSITY—SHREVEPORT Shreveport, LA	2.01	MERCER UNIVERSITY Macon, GA	2.45
LOUISIANA TECH UNIVERSITY Ruston, LA	2.18	MIAMI UNIVERSITY Oxford, OH	2.28
UNIVERSITY OF LOUISVILLE Louisville, KY	3.22	UNIVERSITY OF MIAMI Coral Gables, FL	2.99

Very Strong = 4.51-4.99   Strong = 4.01-4.49   Good = 3.61-3.99   Acceptable Plus = 3.01-3.59
Adequate = 2.51-2.99   Marginal = 2.01-2.49   Not Sufficient for Graduate Programs = 0.

INSTITUTION	Overall Academic Rating	INSTITUTION	Overall Academic Rating
MICHIGAN STATE UNIVERSITY East Lansing, MI	4.03	MONTANA TECH OF THE UNIVERSITY OF MONTANA Butte, MT	3.19
MICHIGAN TECHNOLOGICAL UNIVERSITY Houghton, MI	2.93	UNIVERSITY OF MONTANA Missoula, MT	3.30
UNIVERSITY OF MICHIGAN—ANN ARBOR Ann Arbor, MI	4.92	MONTCLAIR STATE UNIVERSITY Upper Montclair, NJ	2.78
UNIVERSITY OF MICHIGAN—DEARBORN Dearborn, MI	2.40	UNIVERSITY OF MONTEVALLO Montevallo, AL	0.
MIDDLE TENNESSEE STATE UNIVERSITY Murfreesboro, TN	2.16	MOORHEAD STATE UNIVERSITY Moorhead, MN	2.12
MILLERSVILLE UNIVERSITY OF PENNSYLVANIA Millersville, PA	0.	MOREHEAD STATE UNIVERSITY Morehead, KY	2.09
MILWAUKEE SCHOOL OF ENGINEERING Milwaukee, WI	2.62	MURRAY STATE UNIVERSITY Murray, KY	2.03
UNIVERSITY OF MINNESOTA—DULUTH Duluth, MN	2.60	NAVAL POSTGRADUATE SCHOOL Monterey, CA	2.85
UNIVERSITY OF MINNESOTA—TWIN CITIES Minneapolis, MN	4.80	UNIVERSITY OF NEBRASKA—KEARNEY Kearney, NE	2.68
MISSISSIPPI STATE UNIVERSITY Mississippi State, MS	2.91	UNIVERSITY OF NEBRASKA—LINCOLN Lincoln, NE	3.41
UNIVERSITY OF MISSISSIPPI University, MS	2.93	UNIVERSITY OF NEBRASKA—OMAHA Omaha, NE	3.27
UNIVERSITY OF MISSOURI—COLUMBIA Columbia, MO	3.79	UNIVERSITY OF NEVADA—LAS VEGAS Las Vegas, NV	2.45
UNIVERSITY OF MISSOURI—KANSAS CITY Kansas City, MO	3.36	UNIVERSITY OF NEVADA—RENO Reno, NV	2.57
UNIVERSITY OF MISSOURI—ROLLA Rolla, MO	3.51	UNIVERSITY OF NEW HAMPSHIRE Durham, NH	2.97
UNIVERSITY OF MISSOURI—ST. LOUIS St. Louis, MO	3.28	UNIVERSITY OF NEW HAVEN West Haven, CT	2.01
MONTANA STATE UNIVERSITY—BILLINGS Billings, MT	0.	NEW JERSEY INSTITUTE OF TECHNOLOGY Newark, NJ	2.88
MONTANA STATE UNIVERSITY—BOZEMAN Bozeman, MT	2.55	NEW MEXICO HIGHLANDS UNIVERSITY Las Vegas, NM	0.

Very Strong = 4.51-4.99   Strong = 4.01-4.49   Good = 3.61-3.99   Acceptable Plus = 3.01-3.59
Adequate = 2.51-2.99   Marginal = 2.01-2.49   Not Sufficient for Graduate Programs = 0.

INSTITUTION	Overall Academic Rating	INSTITUTION	Overall Academic Rating
NEW MEXICO INSTITUTE OF MINING & TECHNOLOGY Socorro, NM	2.95	UNIVERSITY OF NORTH FLORIDA Jacksonville, FL	2.01
NEW MEXICO STATE UNIVERSITY Las Cruces, NM	2.08	UNIVERSITY OF NORTH TEXAS Denton, TX	2.84
UNIVERSITY OF NEW MEXICO Albuquerque, NM	3.22	NORTHEAST LOUISIANA UNIVERSITY Monroe, LA	2.04
UNIVERSITY OF NEW ORLEANS New Orleans, LA	2.49	NORTHEASTERN ILLINOIS UNIVERSITY Chicago, IL	2.01
NEW SCHOOL FOR SOCIAL RESEARCH New York, NY	3.07	NORTHEASTERN UNIVERSITY Boston, MA	2.47
NEW YORK INSTITUTE OF TECHNOLOGY Old Westbury, NY	2.04	NORTHERN ARIZONA UNIVERSITY Flagstaff, AZ	2.10
NEW YORK UNIVERSITY New York, NY	4.02	UNIVERSITY OF NORTHERN COLORADO Greeley, CO	2.01
NORTH ADAMS STATE COLLEGE North Adams, MA	0.	NORTHERN ILLINOIS UNIVERSITY DeKalb, IL	2.51
NORTH CAROLINA A&T STATE UNIVERSITY Greensboro, NC	2.11	UNIVERSITY OF NORTHERN IOWA Cedar Falls, IA	2.04
NORTH CAROLINA CENTRAL UNIVERSITY Durham, NC	2.01	NORTHERN MICHIGAN UNIVERSITY Marquette, MI	2.12
NORTH CAROLINA STATE UNIVERSITY Raleigh, NC	3.42	NORTHERN MONTANA COLLEGE Havre, MT	0.
UNIVERSITY OF NORTH CAROLINA—CHAPEL HILL Chapel Hill, NC	4.68	NORTHWESTERN STATE UNIVERSITY OF LOUISIANA Natchitoches, LA	2.06
UNIVERSITY OF NORTH CAROLINA—CHARLOTTE Charlotte, NC	2.34	NORTHWESTERN UNIVERSITY Evanston, IL	4.79
UNIVERSITY OF NORTH CAROLINA—GREENSBORO Greensboro, NC	2.32	UNIVERSITY OF NOTRE DAME Notre Dame, IN	4.40
NORTH DAKOTA STATE UNIVERSITY Fargo, ND	3.01	NOVA SOUTHEASTERN UNIVERSITY Fort Lauderdale, FL	2.28
UNIVERSITY OF NORTH DAKOTA Grand Forks, ND	3.06	OAKLAND UNIVERSITY Rochester, NY	3.23
		OHIO STATE UNIVERSITY—COLUMBUS Columbus, OH	4.24

Very Strong = 4.51-4.99   Strong = 4.01-4.49   Good = 3.61-3.99   Acceptable Plus = 3.01-3.59
Adequate = 2.51-2.99   Marginal = 2.01-2.49   Not Sufficient for Graduate Programs = 0.

INSTITUTION	Overall Academic Rating	INSTITUTION	Overall Academic Rating
OHIO UNIVERSITY Athens, OH	3.06	PURDUE UNIVERSITY—CALUMET Hammond, IN	2.01
OKLAHOMA STATE UNIVERSITY Stillwater, OK	2.84	PURDUE UNIVERSITY—WEST LAFAYETTE West Lafayette, IN	4.55
UNIVERSITY OF OKLAHOMA Norman, OK	3.31	PURDUE UNIVERSITY—NORTH CENTRAL Westville, IN	0.
OLD DOMINION UNIVERSITY Norfolk, VA	2.59	RADFORD UNIVERSITY Radford, VA	2.19
OREGON STATE UNIVERSITY Corvallis, OR	3.69	RENSSELAER POLYTECHNIC INSTITUTE Troy, NY	4.51
UNIVERSITY OF OREGON Eugene, OR	3.80	UNIVERSITY OF RHODE ISLAND Kingston, RI	2.86
PACE UNIVERSITY New York, NY	2.27	RICE UNIVERSITY Houston, TX	4.47
UNIVERSITY OF THE PACIFIC Stockton, CA	2.81	UNIVERSITY OF RICHMOND Richmond, VA	2.02
PENNSYLVANIA STATE UNIVERSITY— UNIVERSITY PARK University Park, PA	4.43	ROCHESTER INSTITUTE OF TECHNOLOGY Rochester, NY	2.11
UNIVERSITY OF PENNSYLVANIA Philadelphia, PA	4.81	UNIVERSITY OF ROCHESTER Rochester, NY	4.51
PEPPERDINE UNIVERSITY Malibu, CA	0.	ROCKEFELLER UNIVERSITY New York, NY	4.02
UNIVERSITY OF PITTSBURGH Pittsburgh, PA	(4.41)	ROOSEVELT UNIVERSITY Chicago, IL	2.60
POLYTECHNIC UNIVERSITY Brooklyn, NY	3.21	ROSE-HULMAN INSTITUTE OF TECHNOLOGY Terre Haute, IN	2.51
PORTLAND STATE UNIVERSITY Portland, OR	2.07	RUTGERS UNIVERSITY—NEW BRUNSWICK New Brunswick, NJ	4.33
UNIVERSITY OF PORTLAND Portland, OR	2.01	RUTGERS UNIVERSITY—NEWARK Newark, NJ	2.74
PRATT INSTITUTE Brooklyn, NY	2.60	ST. CLOUD STATE UNIVERSITY St. Cloud, MN	2.01
PRINCETON UNIVERSITY Princeton, NJ	4.88	ST. JOHN'S UNIVERSITY Jamaica, NY	2.50

Very Strong = 4.51-4.99   Strong = 4.01-4.49   Good = 3.61-3.99   Acceptable Plus = 3.01-3.59
Adequate = 2.51-2.99   Marginal = 2.01-2.49   Not Sufficient for Graduate Programs = 0.

INSTITUTION	Overall Academic Rating	INSTITUTION	Overall Academic Rating
ST. LOUIS UNIVERSITY St. Louis, MO	3.31	UNIVERSITY OF SOUTH CAROLINA Columbia, SC	3.27
SAM HOUSTON STATE UNIVERSITY Huntsville, TX	2.11	SOUTH DAKOTA SCHOOL OF MINES & TECHNOLOGY Rapid City, SD	3.15
SAMFORD UNIVERSITY Birmingham, AL	2.10	SOUTH DAKOTA STATE UNIVERSITY Brookings, SD	2.49
SAN DIEGO STATE UNIVERSITY San Diego, CA	2.20	UNIVERSITY OF SOUTH DAKOTA Vermillion, SD	2.96
UNIVERSITY OF SAN DIEGO San Diego, CA	2.01	UNIVERSITY OF SOUTH FLORIDA Tampa, FL	3.20
SAN FRANCISCO STATE UNIVERSITY San Francisco, CA	2.19	SOUTHEAST MISSOURI STATE UNIVERSITY Cape Giradeau, MO	2.01
UNIVERSITY OF SAN FRANCISCO San Francisco, CA	2.11	SOUTHEASTERN LOUISIANA UNIVERSITY Hammond, LA	2.01
SAN JOSE STATE UNIVERSITY San Jose, CA	2.18	UNIVERSITY OF SOUTHERN CALIFORNIA Los Angeles, CA	3.84
UNIVERSITY OF SANTA CLARA Santa Clara, CA	2.47	SOUTHERN CONNECTICUT STATE UNIVERSITY New Haven, CT	2.05
SEATTLE UNIVERSITY Seattle, WA	2.52	SOUTHERN ILLINOIS UNIVERSITY—CARBONDALE Carbondale, IL	3.27
SETON HALL UNIVERSITY South Orange, NJ	2.50	SOUTHERN ILLINOIS UNIVERSITY— EDWARDSVILLE Edwardsville, IL	2.12
SHIPPENSBURG UNIVERSITY OF PENNSYLVANIA Shippensburg, PA	0.	SOUTHERN METHODIST UNIVERSITY Dallas, TX	3.28
SIMMONS COLLEGE Boston, MA	2.33	UNIVERSITY OF SOUTHERN MISSISSIPPI Hattiesburg, MS	2.36
SLIPPERY ROCK UNIVERSITY OF PENNSYLVANIA Slippery Rock, PA	0.	SOUTHERN UNIVERSITY AND AGRICULTURAL AND MECHANICAL COLLEGE Baton Rouge, LA	2.01
SMITH COLLEGE Northhampton, MA	2.67	SOUTHWEST MISSOURI STATE UNIVERSITY Springfield, MO	2.16
SONOMA STATE UNIVERSITY Rohnert Park, CA	0.	SOUTHWEST TEXAS STATE UNIVERSITY San Marcos, TX	2.21
UNIVERSITY OF SOUTH ALABAMA Mobile, AL	2.38		

Very Strong = 4.51-4.99   Strong = 4.01-4.49   Good = 3.61-3.99   Acceptable Plus = 3.01-3.59
Adequate = 2.51-2.99   Marginal = 2.01-2.49   Not Sufficient for Graduate Programs = 0.

INSTITUTION	Overall Academic Rating	INSTITUTION	Overall Academic Rating
UNIVERSITY OF SOUTHWESTERN LOUISIANA Lafayette, LA	2.21	STATE UNIVERSITY OF NEW YORK COLLEGE AT OSWEGO Oswego, NY	0.
STANFORD UNIVERSITY Stanford, CA	4.90	STATE UNIVERSITY OF NEW YORK COLLEGE AT PLATTSBURGH Plattsburgh, NY	0.
STATE UNIVERSITY OF NEW YORK AT ALBANY Albany, NY	3.92	STATE UNIVERSITY OF NEW YORK COLLEGE AT POTSDAM Potsdam, NY	0.
STATE UNIVERSITY OF NEW YORK AT BINGHAMTON Binghamton, NY	3.98	STATE UNIVERSITY OF NEW YORK COLLEGE OF ENVIRONMENTAL SCIENCE AND FORESTRY Syracuse, NY	3.80
STATE UNIVERSITY OF NEW YORK AT BUFFALO Buffalo, NY	4.18	STEPHEN F. AUSTIN STATE UNIVERSITY Nacogdoches, TX	2.19
STATE UNIVERSITY OF NEW YORK AT STONY BROOK Stony Brook, NY	4.45	STEVENS INSTITUTE OF TECHNOLOGY Hoboken, NJ	3.31
STATE UNIVERSITY OF NEW YORK COLLEGE AT BROCKPORT Brockport, NY	0.	SUFFOLK UNIVERSITY Boston, MA	2.12
STATE UNIVERSITY OF NEW YORK COLLEGE AT BUFFALO Buffalo, NY	0.	SYRACUSE UNIVERSITY Syracuse, NY	3.78
STATE UNIVERSITY OF NEW YORK COLLEGE AT CORTLAND Cortland, NY	0.	TARLETON STATE UNIVERSITY Stephenville, TX	2.02
STATE UNIVERSITY OF NEW YORK COLLEGE AT FREDONIA Fredonia, NY	0.	TEMPLE UNIVERSITY Philadelphia, PA	3.20
		TENNESSEE STATE UNIVERSITY Nashville, TN	2.01
STATE UNIVERSITY OF NEW YORK COLLEGE AT GENESEO Geneseo, NY	0.	TENNESSEE TECHNOLOGICAL UNIVERSITY Cookeville, TN	2.10
STATE UNIVERSITY OF NEW YORK COLLEGE AT NEW PALTZ New Paltz, NY	0.	UNIVERSITY OF TENNESSEE—CHATTANOOGA Chattanooga, TN	2.02
		UNIVERSITY OF TENNESSEE—KNOXVILLE Knoxville, TN	3.60
STATE UNIVERSITY OF NEW YORK COLLEGE AT ONEONTA Oneonta, NY	0.	UNIVERSITY OF TENNESSEE—MARTIN Martin, TN	2.01
		TEXAS A&M INTERNATIONAL UNIVERSITY Laredo, TX	0.

Very Strong = 4.51-4.99   Strong = 4.01-4.49   Good = 3.61-3.99   Acceptable Plus = 3.01-3.59
Adequate = 2.51-2.99   Marginal = 2.01-2.49   Not Sufficient for Graduate Programs = 0.

INSTITUTION	Overall Academic Rating	INSTITUTION	Overall Academic Rating
TEXAS A&M UNIVERSITY—COLLEGE STATION College Station, TX	3.71	TRUMAN STATE UNIVERSITY Kirksville, MO	2.12
TEXAS A&M UNIVERSITY—CORPUS CHRISTI Corpus Christi, TX	0.	TUFTS UNIVERSITY Medford, MA	4.22
TEXAS A&M UNIVERSITY—KINGSVILLE Kingsville, TX	0.	TULANE UNIVERSITY New Orleans, LA	4.16
TEXAS CHRISTIAN UNIVERSITY Fort Worth, TX	2.90	UNIVERSITY OF TULSA Tulsa, OK	2.64
TEXAS SOUTHERN UNIVERSITY Houston, TX	2.15	TUSKEGEE UNIVERSITY Tuskegee Institute, AL	2.40
TEXAS TECH UNIVERSITY Lubbock, TX	3.01	UTAH STATE UNIVERSITY Logan, UT	2.96
TEXAS WOMAN'S UNIVERSITY Denton, TX	2.79	UNIVERSITY OF UTAH Salt Lake City, UT	3.96
UNIVERSITY OF TEXAS—ARLINGTON Arlington, TX	2.29	VANDERBILT UNIVERSITY Nashville, TN	4.37
UNIVERSITY OF TEXAS—AUSTIN Austin, TX	4.65	UNIVERSITY OF VERMONT Burlington, VT	2.97
UNIVERSITY OF TEXAS—BROWNSVILLE Brownsville, TX	0.	VILLANOVA UNIVERSITY Villanova, PA	0.
UNIVERSITY OF TEXAS—DALLAS Richardson, TX	3.31	VIRGINIA COMMONWEALTH UNIVERSITY Richmond, VA	3.11
UNIVERSITY OF TEXAS—EL PASO El Paso, TX	2.05	VIRGINIA POLYTECHNIC INSTITUTE AND STATE UNIVERSITY Blacksburg, VA	3.59
UNIVERSITY OF TEXAS—PAN AMERICAN Edinburg, TX	0.	UNIVERSITY OF VIRGINIA Charlottesville, VA	4.67
UNIVERSITY OF TEXAS—PERMIAN BASIN Odessa, TX	0.	WAKE FOREST UNIVERSITY Winston-Salem, NC	2.89
UNIVERSITY OF TEXAS—SAN ANTONIO San Antonio, TX	2.39	WASHINGTON STATE UNIVERSITY Pullman, WA	3.40
UNIVERSITY OF TEXAS—TYLER Tyler, TX	0.	WASHINGTON UNIVERSITY St. Louis, MO	4.61
UNIVERSITY OF TOLEDO Toledo, OH	2.56	UNIVERSITY OF WASHINGTON Seattle, WA	4.63

Very Strong = 4.51-4.99   Strong = 4.01-4.49   Good = 3.61-3.99   Acceptable Plus = 3.01-3.59
Adequate = 2.51-2.99   Marginal = 2.01-2.49   Not Sufficient for Graduate Programs = 0.

INSTITUTION	Overall Academic Rating	INSTITUTION	Overall Academic Rating
WAYNE STATE UNIVERSITY Detroit, MI	3.40	UNIVERSITY OF WISCONSIN—LACROSSE LaCrosse, WI	0.
WESLEYAN UNIVERSITY Middletown, CT	2.37	UNIVERSITY OF WISCONSIN—MADISON Madison, WI	4.87
UNIVERSITY OF WEST FLORIDA Pensacola, FL	2.01	UNIVERSITY OF WISCONSIN—MILWAUKEE Milwaukee, WI	3.43
WEST TEXAS A&M UNIVERSITY Canyon, TX	2.01	UNIVERSITY OF WISCONSIN—OSHKOSH Oshkosh, WI	0.
WEST VIRGINIA UNIVERSITY Morgantown, WV	3.19	UNIVERSITY OF WISCONSIN—PARKSIDE Kenosha, WI	0.
WESTCHESTER UNIVERSITY OF PENNSYLVANIA Westchester, PA	0.	UNIVERSITY OF WISCONSIN—PLATTEVILLE Platteville, WI	0.
WESTERN ILLINOIS UNIVERSITY Macomb, IL	2.08	UNIVERSITY OF WISCONSIN—RIVER FALLS River Falls, WI	0.
WESTERN KENTUCKY UNIVERSITY Bowling Green, KY	2.15	UNIVERSITY OF WISCONSIN—STEVENS POINT Stevens Point, WI	0.
WESTERN MICHIGAN UNIVERSITY Kalamazoo, MI	2.52	UNIVERSITY OF WISCONSIN—STOUT Menomonie, WI	0.
WESTERN WASHINGTON UNIVERSITY Bellingham, WA	2.01	UNIVERSITY OF WISCONSIN—SUPERIOR Superior, WI	0.
WICHITA STATE UNIVERSITY Wichita, KS	2.05	UNIVERSITY OF WISCONSIN—WHITEWATER Whitewater, WI	0.
WIDENER UNIVERSITY Chester, PA	2.18	WORCESTER POLYTECHNIC INSTITUTE Worcester, MA	2.95
THE COLLEGE OF WILLIAM AND MARY Williamsburg, VA	2.51	WRIGHT STATE UNIVERSITY Dayton, OH	2.95
WILLIAM PATERSON COLLEGE OF NEW JERSEY Wayne, NJ	2.02	UNIVERSITY OF WYOMING Laramie, WY	3.11
WINONA STATE UNIVERSITY Winona, MN	2.01	YALE UNIVERSITY New Haven, CT	4.91
UNIVERSITY OF WISCONSIN—EAU CLAIRE Eau Claire, WI	0.	YESHIVA UNIVERSITY New York, NY	3.79
UNIVERSITY OF WISCONSIN—GREEN BAY Green Bay, WI	0.	YOUNGSTOWN STATE UNIVERSITY Youngstown, OH	1.68

Very Strong = 4.51-4.99   Strong = 4.01-4.49   Good = 3.61-3.99   Acceptable Plus = 3.01-3.59
Adequate = 2.51-2.99   Marginal = 2.01-2.49   Not Sufficient for Graduate Programs = 0.

Part XII

THE GOURMAN REPORT

A RATING OF GRADUATE RESEARCH LIBRARIES

A RATING OF GRADUATE RESEARCH LIBRARIES

INSTITUTION	RANK	SCORE
HARVARD UNIVERSITY	1	4.93
UNIVERSITY OF CALIFORNIA—BERKELEY	2	4.92
UNIVERSITY OF MICHIGAN—ANN ARBOR	3	4.91
YALE UNIVERSITY	4	4.90
STANFORD UNIVERSITY	5	4.89
UNIVERSITY OF CHICAGO	6	4.88
PRINCETON UNIVERSITY	7	4.87
UNIVERSITY OF WISCONSIN—MADISON	8	4.86
UNIVERSITY OF CALIFORNIA—LOS ANGELES	9	4.85
CORNELL UNIVERSITY	10	4.84
COLUMBIA UNIVERSITY	11	4.83
CALIFORNIA INSTITUTE OF TECHNOLOGY	12	4.82
MASSACHUSETTS INSTITUTE OF TECHNOLOGY	13	4.81
UNIVERSITY OF PENNSYLVANIA	14	4.80
UNIVERSITY OF MINNESOTA—TWIN CITIES	15	4.79
NORTHWESTERN UNIVERSITY	16	4.78
UNIVERSITY OF ILLINOIS—URBANA-CHAMPAIGN	17	4.77
JOHNS HOPKINS UNIVERSITY	18	4.76
UNIVERSITY OF CALIFORNIA—SAN DIEGO	19	4.75
BROWN UNIVERSITY	20	4.74
DUKE UNIVERSITY	21	4.73
INDIANA UNIVERSITY—BLOOMINGTON	22	4.70
UNIVERSITY OF IOWA	23	4.68
UNIVERSITY OF NORTH CAROLINA—CHAPEL HILL	24	4.67
UNIVERSITY OF VIRGINIA	25	4.66
UNIVERSITY OF TEXAS—AUSTIN	26	4.64
UNIVERSITY OF WASHINGTON	27	4.62
WASHINGTON UNIVERSITY	28	4.61
CARNEGIE MELLON UNIVERSITY	29	4.57
UNIVERSITY OF CALIFORNIA—DAVIS	30	4.56
PURDUE UNIVERSITY—WEST LAFAYETTE	31	4.54
RENSSELAER POLYTECHNIC INSTITUTE	32	4.52
UNIVERSITY OF ROCHESTER	33	4.50
UNIVERSITY OF CALIFORNIA—SAN FRANCISCO	34	4.48
RICE UNIVERSITY	35	4.46
STATE UNIVERSITY OF NEW YORK AT STONY BROOK	36	4.44
PENNSYLVANIA STATE UNIVERSITY—UNIVERSITY PARK	37	4.42
UNIVERSITY OF PITTSBURGH	38	4.41
UNIVERSITY OF NOTRE DAME	39	4.40
VANDERBILT UNIVERSITY	40	4.36

Very Strong = 4.51-4.99   Strong = 4.01-4.49   Good = 3.61-3.99   Acceptable Plus = 3.01-3.59
Adequate = 2.51-2.99   Marginal = 2.01-2.49   Not Sufficient for Graduate Programs = 0.

UNIVERSITY OF CALIFORNIA—IRVINE	41	4.34
RUTGERS UNIVERSITY—NEW BRUNSWICK	42	4.32
GEORGIA INSTITUTE OF TECHNOLOGY	43	4.30
DARTMOUTH COLLEGE	44	4.29
CASE WESTERN RESERVE UNIVERSITY	45	4.26
OHIO STATE UNIVERSITY—COLUMBUS	46	4.23
TUFTS UNIVERSITY	47	4.21
STATE UNIVERSITY OF NEW YORK AT BUFFALO	48	4.17
TULANE UNIVERSITY	49	4.15
BRANDEIS UNIVERSITY	50	4.11

Very Strong = 4.51-4.99 Strong = 4.01-4.49 Good = 3.61-3.99 Acceptable Plus = 3.01-3.59
Adequate = 2.51-2.99 Marginal = 2.01-2.49 Not Sufficient for Graduate Programs = 0.

Part XIII

THE GOURMAN REPORT LEADING INTERNATIONAL UNIVERSITIES

A RATING OF INTERNATIONAL UNIVERSITIES

A RATING OF INTERNATIONAL LAW SCHOOLS

A RATING OF INTERNATIONAL MEDICAL SCHOOLS

A RATING OF INTERNATIONAL UNIVERSITIES

INSTITUTION	COUNTRY	Rank	Score
UNIVERSITY OF PARIS I/PANTHÉON-SORBONNE	France	1	4.92
UNIVERSITY OF LAW, ECONOMICS AND SOCIAL SCIENCES/PARIS II	France	1	4.92
UNIVERSITY OF THE NEW SORBONNE/PARIS III	France	1	4.92
UNIVERSITY OF PARIS-SORBONNE/PARIS IV	France	1	4.92
UNIVERSITY OF RENÉ DESCARTES/PARIS V	France	1	4.92
UNIVERSITY PIERRE AND MARIE CURIE/PARIS VI	France	1	4.92
UNIVERSITY OF PARIS VII	France	1	4.92
UNIVERSITY OF VINCENNES AT SAINT-DENIS/PARIS VIII	France	1	4.92
UNIVERSITY PARIS-DAUPHINE/PARIS IX	France	1	4.92
UNIVERSITY OF PARIS X/NANTERRE	France	1	4.92
UNIVERSITY OF PARIS-SUD/PARIS XI	France	1	4.92
UNIVERSITY OF PARIS VAL-DE-MARNE/PARIS XII	France	1	4.92
UNIVERSITY OF PARIS-NORD/PARIS XIII	France	1	4.92
UNIVERSITY OF OXFORD	United Kingdom	2	4.91
UNIVERSITY OF CAMBRIDGE	United Kingdom	3	4.90
RUPERT CHARLES UNIVERSITY OF HEIDELBERG	Federal Republic of Germany	4	4.89
UNIVERSITY OF MONTPELLIER I	France	5	4.85
LANGUEDOC UNIVERSITY OF SCIENCE AND TECHNOLOGY/MONTPELLIER II	France	5	4.85
UNIVERSITY PAUL VALÉRY/MONTPELLIER III	France	5	4.85
LUDWIG MAXIMILIANS-UNIVERSITY OF MUNICH	Federal Republic of Germany	6	4.83
UNIVERSITY CLAUDE BERNARD/LYONS I	France	7	4.81
UNIVERSITY OF LYONS II	France	7	4.81
UNIVERSITY JEAN MOULIN/LYONS III	France	7	4.81
UNIVERSITY OF SCIENCE AND TECHNOLOGY/LILLE I	France	8	4.80

Very Strong = 4.51-4.99   Strong = 4.01-4.49   Good = 3.61-3.99   Acceptable Plus = 3.01-3.59
Adequate = 2.51-2.99   Marginal = 2.01-2.49   Not Sufficient for Graduate Programs = 0.

INSTITUTION	COUNTRY	Rank	Score
UNIVERSITY OF LAW AND HEALTH SCIENCES/LILLE II	France	8	4.80
UNIVERSITY OF HUMAN SCIENCES, LITERATURE AND ARTS/LILLE III	France	8	4.80
UNIVERSITY OF EDINBURGH	United Kingdom	9	4.79
UNIVERSITY OF VIENNA	Austria	10	4.77
UNIVERSITY OF PROVENCE/AIX-MARSEILLES I	France	11	4.75
UNIVERSITY OF AIX-MARSEILLES II	France	11	4.75
UNIVERSITY OF LAW, ECONOMICS AND SCIENCE/AIX-MARSEILLES III	France	11	4.75
FREE UNIVERSITY OF BRUSSELS	Belgium	12	4.73
UNIVERSITY OF ZÜRICH	Switzerland	13	4.71
GEORG AUGUST UNIVERSITY OF GÖTTINGEN	Federal Republic of Germany	14	4.70
UNIVERSITY OF BORDEAUX I TALENCE	France	15	4.68
UNIVERSITY OF BORDEAUX II	France	15	4.68
UNIVERSITY OF BORDEAUX III	France	15	4.68
UNIVERSITY OF NANCY I	France	16	4.65
UNIVERSITY OF NANCY II	France	16	4.65
UNIVERSITY OF TORONTO	Canada	17	4.64
McGILL UNIVERSITY	Canada	18	4.61
UNIVERSITY OF GENEVA	Switzerland	19	4.59
EBERHARD KARL UNIVERSITY OF TÜBINGEN	Federal Republic of Germany	20	4.56
FRIEDRICH ALEXANDER UNIVERSITY OF ERLANGEN-NUREMBERG	Federal Republic of Germany	21	4.54
UNIVERSITY 'JOSEPH FOURIER'/GRENOBLE I	France	22	4.53
UNIVERSITY PIERRE MENDÊS FRANCE/GRENOBLE II	France	22	4.53
UNIVERSITY STENDHAL/GRENOBLE III	France	22	4.53
UNIVERSITY OF BURGUNDY DIJON	France	23	4.52
UNIVERSITY OF MARBURG	Federal Republic of Germany	24	4.49

Very Strong = 4.51-4.99   Strong = 4.01-4.49   Good = 3.61-3.99   Acceptable Plus = 3.01-3.59
Adequate = 2.51-2.99   Marginal = 2.01-2.49   Not Sufficient for Graduate Programs = 0.

INSTITUTION	COUNTRY	Rank	Score
UNIVERSITY OF RENNES I	France	25	4.45
UNIVERSITY OF HAUTE-BRETAGNE/RENNES II	France	25	4.45
UNIVERSITY OF SOCIAL SCIENCES/TOULOUSE I	France	25	4.45
UNIVERSITY OF TOULOUSE-LE-MIRAIL/TOULOUSE II	France	25	4.45
UNIVERSITY PAUL SABATIER/TOULOUSE III	France	26	4.44
UNIVERSITY OF ROUEN-HAUTE-NORMANDIE	France	27	4.42
UNIVERSITY OF CLERMONT-FERRAND I	France	28	4.41
RHENISH FRIEDRICH-WILHELM	Federal Republic of Germany	29	4.36
UNIVERSITY OF BONN	Federal Republic of Germany	30	4.35
UNIVERSITY OF COLOGNE	Federal Republic of Germany	30	4.35
UNIVERSITY OF NICE	France	31	4.33
THE HEBREW UNIVERSITY OF JERUSALEM	Israel	32	4.32
JOHANN WOLFGANG GOETHE	Federal Republic of Germany	33	4.30
UNIVERSITY OF FRANKFURT	Federal Republic of Germany	33	4.30
CATHOLIC UNIVERSITY OF LOUVAIN	Belgium	34	4.24
STOCKHOLM UNIVERSITY	Sweden	35	4.20
UNIVERSITY OF MÜNSTER	Federal Republic of Germany	36	4.17
UNIVERSITY OF COPENHAGEN	Denmark	37	4.16
JOHANNES GUTENBERG UNIVERSITY OF MAINZ	Federal Republic of Germany	38	4.15
BAYERISCHE JULIUS-MAXIMILIANS UNIVERSITY OF WÜRZBURG	Federal Republic of Germany	39	4.14
UNIVERSITY OF FRANCHE-COMTÉ BESANÇON	France	40	4.13
UNIVERSITY OF AMSTERDAM	Netherlands	41	4.12
UNIVERSITY OF LONDON	United Kingdom	42	4.11

Very Strong = 4.51-4.99   Strong = 4.01-4.49   Good = 3.61-3.99   Acceptable Plus = 3.01-3.59
Adequate = 2.51-2.99   Marginal = 2.01-2.49   Not Sufficient for Graduate Programs = 0.

INSTITUTION	COUNTRY	Rank	Score
UNIVERSITY OF TOKYO	Japan	43	4.10
UNIVERSITY OF NANTES	France	44	4.09
UNIVERSITY OF POITIERS	France	45	4.08
UNIVERSITY OF ORLÉANS	France	46	4.07
UNIVERSITY OF CAEN	France	47	4.05
UNIVERSITY OF BOLOGNA	Italy	48	4.04
UNIVERSITY OF MADRID	Spain	49	4.03

Very Strong = 4.51-4.99   Strong = 4.01-4.49   Good = 3.61-3.99   Acceptable Plus = 3.01-3.59
Adequate = 2.51-2.99   Marginal = 2.01-2.49   Not Sufficient for Graduate Programs = 0.

A RATING OF INTERNATIONAL LAW SCHOOLS

INSTITUTION	COUNTRY	Rank	Score
UNIVERSITY OF PARIS I/PANTHÉON-SORBONNE	France	1	4.92
UNIVERSITY OF LAW, ECONOMICS AND SOCIAL SCIENCES/PARIS II	France	1	4.92
UNIVERSITY OF PARIS X/NANTERRE	France	1	4.92
UNIVERSITY OF PARIS VAL-DE-MARNE/PARIS XII	France	1	4.92
UNIVERSITY OF PARIS-NORD/PARIS XIII	France	1	4.92
UNIVERSITY OF OXFORD	United Kingdom	2	4.91
UNIVERSITY OF CAMBRIDGE	United Kingdom	3	4.90
RUPERT CHARLES UNIVERSITY OF HEIDELBERG	Federal Republic of Germany	4	4.87
UNIVERSITY JEAN MOULIN/LYONS III	France	5	4.86
LUDWIG MAXIMILIANS-UNIVERSITY OF MUNICH	Federal Republic of Germany	6	4.83
UNIVERSITY OF MONTPELLIER I	France	7	4.82
FREE UNIVERSITY OF BRUSSELS	Belgium	8	4.81
GEORG AUGUST UNIVERSITY OF GÖTTINGEN	Federal Republic of Germany	9	4.78
FRIEDRICH ALEXANDER UNIVERSITY OF ERLANGEN-NUREMBERG	Federal Republic of Germany	10	4.77
UNIVERSITY OF AIX-MARSEILLES II	France	11	4.76
UNIVERSITY OF EDINBURGH	United Kingdom	12	4.75
UNIVERSITY OF BORDEAUX I TALENCE	France	13	4.74
RHENISH FRIEDRICH-WILHELM UNIVERSITY OF BONN	Federal Republic of Germany	14	4.73
UNIVERSITY OF LAW AND HEALTH SCIENCES/LILLE II	France	15	4.72
UNIVERSITY OF BURGUNDY DIJON	France	16	4.71
UNIVERSITY OF NANCY II	France	17	4.68
UNIVERSITY OF FRANCHE-COMTÉ BESANÇON	France	18	4.66
UNIVERSITY PIERRE MENDÊS FRANCE/GRENOBLE II	France	19	4.64
UNIVERSITY OF CLERMONT-FERRAND I	France	20	4.62
UNIVERSITY OF ROUEN-HAUTE-NORMANDIE	France	21	4.60
UNIVERSITY OF RHEIMS CHAMPAGNE-ARDENNES	France	22	4.58
UNIVERSITY OF COLOGNE	Federal Republic of Germany	23	4.57
UNIVERSITY OF RENNES I	France	24	4.55
UNIVERSITY OF VIENNA	Austria	25	4.54
CHRISTIAN ALBRECHT UNIVERSITY OF KIEL	Federal Republic of Germany	26	4.51

Very Strong = 4.51-4.99   Strong = 4.01-4.49   Good = 3.61-3.99   Acceptable Plus = 3.01-3.59
Adequate = 2.51-2.99   Marginal = 2.01-2.49   Not Sufficient for Graduate Programs = 0.

STOCKHOLM UNIVERSITY	Sweden	27	4.49
UNIVERSITY OF NICE	France	28	4.48
UNIVERSITY OF CAEN	France	29	4.47
UNIVERSITY OF POITIERS	France	30	4.44
UNIVERSITY OF SOCIAL SCIENCES/TOULOUSE I	France	31	4.42
UNIVERSITY OF LIMOGES	France	32	4.40
UNIVERSITY OF NANTES	France	33	4.39
UNIVERSITY OF COPENHAGEN	Denmark	34	4.38
JOHANNES GUTENBERG UNIVERSITY OF MAINZ	Federal Republic of Germany	35	4.35
UNIVERSITY OF ORLÉANS	France	36	4.34
JEAN MONNET UNIVERSITY SAINT-ETIENNE	France	37	4.33
UNIVERSITY OF TOKYO	Japan	38	4.32
ALBERT LUDWIG UNIVERSITY OF FREIBURG IM BREISGAU	Federal Republic of Germany	39	4.31
EBERHARD KARL UNIVERSITY OF TÜBINGEN	Federal Republic of Germany	40	4.30
UNIVERSITY OF INNSBRUCK	Austria	41	4.29
UNIVERSITY OF MÜNSTER	Federal Republic of Germany	42	4.27
BAYERISCHE JULIUS-MAXIMILIANS UNIVERSITY OF WÜRZBURG	Federal Republic of Germany	43	4.26
THE UNIVERSITY OF DUBLIN-TRINITY COLLEG	Elreland	44	4.25
THE HEBREW UNIVERSITY OF JERUSALEM	Israel	45	4.23
UNIVERSITY OF MADRID	Spain	46	4.22
UNIVERSITY OF MARBURG	Federal Republic of Germany	47	4.20
UNIVERSITY OF GENEVA	Switzerland	48	4.19
UNIVERSITY OF LONDON	United Kingdom	49	4.16
UNIVERSITY OF FRIBOURG	Switzerland	50	4.15
UNIVERSITY OF ROME I 'LA SAPIENZA'	Italy	51	4.14
UNIVERSITY OF AMSTERDAM	Netherlands	52	4.12
NATIONAL AND CAPODISTRIAN UNIVERSITY OF ATHENS	Greece	53	4.05

Very Strong = 4.51-4.99   Strong = 4.01-4.49   Good = 3.61-3.99   Acceptable Plus = 3.01-3.59
Adequate = 2.51-2.99   Marginal = 2.01-2.49   Not Sufficient for Graduate Programs = 0.

A RATING OF INTERNATIONAL MEDICAL SCHOOLS

INSTITUTION	COUNTRY	Rank	Score
UNIVERSITY RENÉ DESCARTES/PARIS V	France	1	4.92
UNIVERSITY PIERRE AND MARIE CURIE/PARIS VI	France	1	4.92
UNIVERSITY OF PARIS VII	France	1	4.92
UNIVERSITY OF PARIS-SUD/PARIS XI	France	1	4.92
UNIVERSITY OF PARIS VAL-DE-MARNE/PARIS XII	France	1	4.92
UNIVERSITY OF PARIS-NORD/PARIS XIII	France	1	4.92
UNIVERSITY OF OXFORD	United Kingdom	2	4.91
UNIVERSITY OF CAMBRIDGE	United Kingdom	3	4.90
RUPERT CHARLES UNIVERSITY OF HEIDELBERG	Federal Republic of Germany	4	4.89
LUDWIG MAXIMILIANS-UNIVERSITY OF MUNICH	Federal Republic of Germany	5	4.88
UNIVERSITY CLAUDE BERNARD/LYONS I	France	6	4.87
UNIVERSITY OF VIENNA	Austria	7	4.86
UNIVERSITY OF MONTPELLIER I	France	8	4.84
UNIVERSITY OF ZÜRICH	Switzerland	9	4.82
GEORG AUGUST UNIVERSITY OF GÖTTINGEN	Federal Republic of Germany	10	4.81
UNIVERSITY OF EDINBURGH	United Kingdom	11	4.80
UNIVERSITY OF LAW AND HEALTH SCIENCES/LILLE II	France	12	4.78
FREE UNIVERSITY OF BRUSSELS	Belgium	13	4.77
UNIVERSITY OF BURGUNDY DIJON	France	14	4.73
CATHOLIC FACULTIES OF LILLE/FACULTÉ LIBRE DE MÉDICINE	France	15	4.72
UNIVERSITY OF GENEVA	Switzerland	16	4.71
KEIO UNIVERSITY	Japan	17	4.67
FRIEDRICH ALEXANDER UNIVERSITY OF	Federal Republic of Germany	18	4.66
ERLANGEN-NUREMBERG	Federal Republic of Germany	18	4.66
TOKYO MEDICAL COLLEGE	Japan	19	4.63
UNIVERSITY OF AIX-MARSEILLES II	France	20	4.59
UNIVERSITY OF NANCY I	France	21	4.57
UNIVERSITY OF NICE	France	22	4.56
UNIVERSITY OF RHEIMS CHAMPAGNE-ARDENNES	France	23	4.55
UNIVERSITY OF CLERMONT-FERRAND I	France	24	4.54

Very Strong = 4.51-4.99   Strong = 4.01-4.49   Good = 3.61-3.99   Acceptable Plus = 3.01-3.59
Adequate = 2.51-2.99   Marginal = 2.01-2.49   Not Sufficient for Graduate Programs = 0.

UNIVERSITY OF RENNES I	France	25	4.53
UNIVERSITY OF ROUEN-HAUTE-NORMANDIE	France	26	4.52
UNIVERSITY OF BORDEAUX II	France	27	4.46
RHENISH FRIEDRICH-WILHELM UNIVERSITY OF BONN	Federal Republic of Germany	28	4.37
BAYERISCHE JULIUS-MAXIMILIANS UNIVERSITY OF WÜRZBURG	Federal Republic of Germany	29	4.36
THE HEBREW UNIVERSITY OF JERUSALEM	Israel	30	4.33
UNIVERSITY OF LONDON	United Kingdom	31	4.32
CHARING CROSS AND WESTMINSTER MEDICAL SCHOOL	United Kingdom	31	4.32
KING'S COLLEGE LONDON	United Kingdom	31	4.32
THE LONDON HOSPITAL MEDICAL COLLEGE	United Kingdom	31	4.32
THE MIDDLESEX HOSPITAL MEDICAL SCHOOL	United Kingdom	31	4.32
ROYAL FREE HOSPITAL SCHOOL OF MEDICINE	United Kingdom	31	4.32
ST. BARTHOLOMEW'S HOSPITAL MEDICAL COLLEGE	United Kingdom	31	4.32
ST. GEORGE'S HOSPITAL MEDICAL SCHOOL	United Kingdom	31	4.32
ST. MARY'S HOSPITAL MEDICAL SCHOOL	United Kingdom	31	4.32
UNITED MEDICAL AND DENTAL SCHOOLS OF GUY'S AND ST. THOMAS'S HOSPITALS	United Kingdom	31	4.32
UNIVERSITY COLLEGE LONDON	United Kingdom	31	4.32
ALBERT LUDWIG UNIVERSITY OF FREIBURG IM BREISGAU	Federal Republic of Germany	32	4.31
UNIVERSITY OF HAMBURG	Federal Republic of Germany	33	4.30
UNIVERSITY OF PICARDIE AMIENS	France	34	4.29
UNIVERSITY OF FRANCHE-COMTÉ BESANÇON	France	35	4.28
UNIVERSITY 'JOSEPH FOURIER'/GRENOBLE I	France	36	4.27
UNIVERSITY OF MARBURG	Federal Republic of Germany	37	4.26
EBERHARD KARL UNIVERSITY OF TÜBINGEN	Federal Republic of Germany	38	4.25
UNIVERSITY OF POITIERS	France	39	4.24
UNIVERSITY OF LIMOGES	France	40	4.23
JEAN MONNET UNIVERSITY SAINT-ETIENNE	France	41	4.22
JOHANNES GUTENBERG UNIVERSITY OF MAINZ	Federal Republic of Germany	42	4.21
LOUIS PASTEUR UNIVERSITY/STRASBOURG I	France	43	4.20
UNIVERSITY OF CAEN	France	44	4.19
STOCKHOLM UNIVERSITY	Sweden	45	4.18

Very Strong = 4.51-4.99   Strong = 4.01-4.49   Good = 3.61-3.99   Acceptable Plus = 3.01-3.59
Adequate = 2.51-2.99   Marginal = 2.01-2.49   Not Sufficient for Graduate Programs = 0.

CATHOLIC UNIVERSITY OF LOUVAIN	Belgium	46	4.17
UNIVERSITY OF AMSTERDAM	Netherlands	47	4.16
ROYAL COLLEGE OF SURGEONS IN IRELAND	Ireland	48	4.15
LEIDEN UNIVERSITY	Netherlands	49	4.13
UNIVERSITY OF TOURS	France	50	4.12
UNIVERSITY PAUL SABATIER/TOULOUSE III	France	51	4.11
JOHANN WOLFGANG GOETHE UNIVERSITY OF FRANKFURT	Federal Republic of Germany	52	4.10
UNIVERSITY OF ANGERS	France	53	4.09
UNIVERSITY OF MÜNSTER	Federal Republic of Germany	54	4.08
UNIVERSITY OF NANTES	France	55	4.06

Very Strong = 4.51-4.99   Strong = 4.01-4.49   Good = 3.61-3.99   Acceptable Plus = 3.01-3.59
Adequate = 2.51-2.99   Marginal = 2.01-2.49   Not Sufficient for Graduate Programs = 0.

Part XIV
THE GOURMAN REPORT
APPENDICES

APPENDIX A
A LIST OF TABLES
TABLE 1
A RATING OF GRADUATE PROGRAMS IN THE UNITED STATES

FIELD OF STUDY	Selected Number of Institutions Granting Degree	Total Number of Programs (Curriculum) Evaluated	Total Number of Areas of Study Evaluated	Total Number of Faculty Areas Evaluated	Quality Institutions Listed in the Gourman Report
Aerospace Engineering	38	38	885	370	30
Agricultural Economics	74	74	801	166	34
Agricultural Engineering	39	39	658	143	32
Agricultural Sciences	104	104	2,412	638	32
Agronomy/Soil Sciences	69	69	977	202	26
Anthropology	72	72	964	138	31
Applied Mathematics	131	131	96	242	24
Applied Physics	44	44	407	88	11
Architecture	89	89	833	207	29
Art History	40	40	551	96	20
Astronomy	57	57	865	352	27
Biochemistry	201	201	1,011	450	30
Biomedical Engineering	43	43	736	223	26
Botany	110	110	911	210	40
Business Administration (EMB)[1] See Table 14.					
Business Administration (MBA)[2] See Table 15.					
Business Administration (Ph.D./DBA)[3] See Table 16.					
Cell Biology	184	184	912	214	35
Ceramic Sciences and Engineering	15	15	641	188	9
Chemical Engineering	98	98	933	207	50
Chemistry	173	173	1,016	450	40
City/Regional Planning	75	75	220	51	17
Civil Engineering	107	107	975	77	40
Classics	31	31	402	50	30
Comparative Literature	46	46	222	47	30
Computer Science	119	119	862	58	41
Drama/Theatre	190	190	1,613	268	32
Economics	113	113	998	303	40
Electrical Engineering	135	135	989	301	35

FIELD OF STUDY	Selected Number of Institutions Granting Degree	Total Number of Programs (Curriculum) Evaluated	Total Number of Areas of Study Evaluated	Total Number of Faculty Areas Evaluated	Quality Institutions Listed in the Gourman Report
English	131	131	990	338	37
Entomology	60	60	870	229	31
Environmental Engineering	82	82	691	214	10
Forestry	53	53	839	255	31
French	48	48	309	200	32
Geography	40	40	307	166	30
Geosciences	111	111	1,120	460	39
German	35	35	732	361	31
History	119	119	989	264	37
Horticulture	47	47	709	207	27
Industrial Engineering	44	44	971	211	30
Industrial/Labor Relations	49	49	310	48	8
Inorganic Chemistry	63	63	960	75	16
Journalism	100	100	914	312	22
Landscape Architecture	24	24	359	91	17
Library Science	56	56	864	322	20
Linguistics	43	43	630	209	32
Materials Science	72	72	910	355	36
Mathematics	145	145	1,119	840	47
Mechanical Engineering	117	117	994	219	36
Microbiology	194	194	2,866	631	40
Molecular Genetics	107	107	862	222	36
Music	71	71	840	232	36
Near and Middle Eastern Studies	25	25	244	80	13
Neurosciences	105	105	765	243	35
Nuclear Engineering	38	38	995	416	25
Nutrition	140	140	870	239	38
Occupational Therapy	52	52	978	224	20
Oceanography	30	30	430	120	24
Organic Chemistry	63	63	964	166	13
Petroleum Engineering	27	27	965	140 ·	14
Pharmacology	130	130	970	215	30
Philosophy	80	80	688	171	40
Physical Chemistry	65	65	793	87	16

FIELD OF STUDY	Selected Number of Institutions Granting Degree	Total Number of Programs (Curriculum) Evaluated	Total Number of Areas of Study Evaluated	Total Number of Faculty Areas Evaluated	Quality Institutions Listed in the Gourman Report
Physical Therapy	111	111	891	322	21
Physics	155	155	1,119	460	41
Physiology	148	148	828	261	30
Plant Pathology	44	44	560	208	30
Political Science	104	104	733	388	34
Psychology	190	190	1,114	640	40
Psychology—Child Development	48	48	333	86	14
Psychology—Clinical	258	258	851	78	24
Psychology—Cognitive	125	125	306	65	31
Psychology—Developmental	107	107	860	63	26
Psychology—Experimental (General)	135	135	1,122	427	16
Psychology—Industrial/Organizational	106	106	812	99	17
Psychology—Personality	60	60	627	128	18
Psychology—Sensation and Perception	55	55	361	77	24
Psychology—Social	118	118	991	234	32
Public Administration	60	60	608	211	19
Radio/TV/Film	73	73	541	112	10
Russian	26	26	158	49	10
Slavic Languages	31	31	404	50	16
Social Welfare/Social Work	169	169	941	485	31
Sociology	112	112	968	450	32
Spanish	61	61	444	100	30
Speech Pathology/Audiology	226	226	1,150	453	21
Statistics	71	71	984	366	30
Toxicology	85	85	573	88	34

TABLE 2 A Rating of Law Schools	International Law Schools	U.S.A. Law Schools
Selected Number of Law Schools Evaluated	543	175
Quality Law Schools Listed in the Gourman Report	53	175*
Total Number of Law Programs Evaluated	543	175
Total Number of Faculty Areas Evaluated	2,098	983
Total Number of Administrative Areas Evaluated	2,161	1,854
Total Number of Curriculum Areas Evaluated	3,002	1,833

*U.S.A. SCHOOLS OF LAW

Rating Categories	Numerical Range	Number of Institutions
Very Strong	4.6-5.0	20
Strong	4.0-4.5	23
Good	3.6-3.9	31
Acceptable Plus	3.0-3.5	43
Adequate	2.1-2.9	58
	TOTAL	**175**

TABLE 3 A Rating of Law Schools	Canadian Law Schools
Selected Number of Law Schools Evaluated	14
Quality Law Schools Listed in the Gourman Report	14
Total Number of Law Programs Evaluated	14
Total Number of Faculty Areas Evaluated	217
Total Number of Administrative Areas Evaluated	290
Total Number of Curriculum Areas Evaluated	253

TABLE 4 A Rating of Medical Schools	International Medical Schools	U.S.A. Medical Schools
Selected Number of Medical Schools Evaluated	712	125
Quality Medical Schools Listed in the Gourman Report	55	125*
Total Number of Medical Programs Evaluated	712	125
Total Number of Faculty Areas Evaluated	1,650	900
Total Number of Administrative Areas Evaluated	2,310	1,071
Total Number of Curriculum Areas Evaluated	5,898	4,680

*U.S.A. SCHOOLS OF MEDICINE

Rating Categories	Numerical Range	Number of Institutions
Very Strong	4.6-5.0	19
Strong	4.0-4.5	32
Good	3.6-3.9	29
Acceptable Plus	3.0-3.5	45
	TOTAL	**125**

TABLE 5 A Rating of Medical Schools	Canadian Medical Schools
Selected Number of Medical Schools Evaluated	16
Quality Medical Schools Listed in the Gourman Report	16
Total Number of Medical Programs Evaluated	16
Total Number of Faculty Areas Evaluated	225
Total Number of Administrative Areas Evaluated	612
Total Number of Curriculum Areas Evaluated	848

TABLE 6
A Rating of Dental Schools

	U.S.A. Dental Schools
Selected Number of Dental Schools Evaluated	54
Quality Dental Schools Listed in the Gourman Report	54
Total Number of Dental Programs Evaluated	54
Total Number of Curriculum Areas Evaluated	1,002
Total Number of Faculty Areas Evaluated	630
Total Number of Administrative Areas Evaluated	848

TABLE 7
A Rating of Dental Schools

	Canadian Dental Schools
Selected Number of Dental Schools Evaluated	10
Quality Dental Schools Listed in the Gourman Report	10
Total Number of Dental Programs Evaluated	10
Total Number of Curriculum Areas Evaluated	972
Total Number of Faculty Areas Evaluated	466
Total Number of Administrative Areas Evaluated	500

TABLE 8
A Rating of Nursing Schools

	U.S.A Nursing Schools
Selected Number of Nursing Schools Evaluated	73
Quality Nursing Schools Listed in the Gourman Report	73
Total Number of Nursing Programs Evaluated	73
Total Number of Curriculum Areas Evaluated	1,733
Total Number of Faculty Areas Evaluated	675
Total Number of Administrative Areas Evaluated	914

TABLE 9 A Rating of Optometry Schools	U.S.A. Optometry Schools
Selected Number of Optometry Schools Evaluated	17
Quality Optometry Schools Listed in the Gourman Report	17
Total Number of Optometry Programs Evaluated	17
Total Number of Curriculum Areas Evaluated	740
Total Number of Faculty Areas Evaluated	155
Total Number of Administrative Areas Evaluated	488

TABLE 10 A Rating of Pharmacy Schools	U.S.A Pharmacy Schools
Selected Number of Pharmacy Schools Evaluated	73
Quality Pharmacy Schools Listed in the Gourman Report	59
Total Number of Pharmacy Programs Evaluated	73
Total Number of Curriculum Areas Evaluated	3,115
Total Number of Faculty Areas Evaluated	860
Total Number of Administrative Areas Evaluated	939

TABLE 11 A Rating of Pharmacy Schools	Canadian Pharmacy Schools
Selected Number of Pharmacy Schools Evaluated	8
Quality Pharmacy Schools Listed in the Gourman Report	8
Total Number of Pharmacy Programs Evaluated	8
Total Number of Curriculum Areas Evaluated	711
Total Number of Faculty Areas Evaluated	153
Total Number of Administrative Areas Evaluated	322

	U.S.A. Public Health Schools
TABLE 12 **A Rating of Public Health Schools**	
Selected Number of Public Health Schools Evaluated	28
Quality Public Health Schools Listed in the Gourman Report	26
Total Number of Public Health Programs Evaluated	28
Total Number of Curriculum Areas Evaluated	462
Total Number of Faculty Areas Evaluated	325
Total Number of Administrative Areas Evaluated	422

	U.S.A. Veterinary Schools
TABLE 13 **A Rating of Veterinary Schools**	
Selected Number of Veterinary Schools Evaluated	27
Quality Veterinary Schools Listed in the Gourman Report	26
Total Number of Veterinary Programs Evaluated	27
Total Number of Curriculum Areas Evaluated	2,010
Total Number of Faculty Areas Evaluated	667
Total Number of Administrative Areas Evaluated	846

	U.S.A. Engineering Schools
TABLE 14 **A Rating of Engineering Schools**	
Number of Schools Evaluated	139
Number of Schools Listed in the Gourman Report	50
Total Number of Administrative Areas Evaluated	974
Total Number of Curriculum Areas Evaluated	1,001
Total Number of Faculty Areas Evaluated	732

TABLE 15 **A Rating of EMBA/Management Schools**	**U.S.A.** **EMBA/Management** **Schools**
Selected Number of Schools Evaluated	20
Quality of EMBA Schools Listed in the Gourman Report	13
Total Number of Administrative Areas Evaluated	61
Total Number of Curriculum Areas Evaluated	264
Total Number of Faculty Areas Evaluated	70

TABLE 16 **A Rating of MBA/Management Schools**	**U.S.A** **MBA/Management** **Schools**
Number of Schools Evaluated	528
Number of Schools Listed in the Gourman Report	50
Total Number of Administrative Areas Evaluated	1,976
Total Number of Curriculum Areas Evaluated	2,020
Total Number of Faculty Areas Evaluated	981

TABLE 17 **A Rating of Doctoral Business/Management Schools**	**U.S.A. Doctoral/** **Bus. Management** **Schools**
Number of Schools Evaluated	135
Number of Schools Listed in the Gourman Report	50
Total Number of Administrative Areas Evaluated	1,001
Total Number of Curriculum Areas Evaluated	988
Total Number of Faculty Areas Evaluated	980

APPENDIX B
UNITED STATES INSTITUTIONS OF LAW

STATE AND LAW SCHOOL

ALABAMA
University of Alabama
Samford University

ARIZONA
Arizona State University
University of Arizona

ARKANSAS
University of Arkansas
University of Arkansas—Little Rock

CALIFORNIA
University of California—Berkeley
University of California—Davis
University of California—Los Angeles
University of California—San Francisco
California Western
Golden Gate University
Loyola Marymount University
University of the Pacific
Pepperdine University
University of San Diego
University of San Francisco
Santa Clara University
University of Southern California
Southwestern University
Stanford University
Whittier College

COLORADO
University of Colorado—Boulder
University of Denver

CONNECTICUT
University of Connecticut
Quinnipiac College
Yale University

DELAWARE
Widener University

DISTRICT OF COLUMBIA
American University
Catholic University of America
District of Columbia School of Law
George Washington University
Georgetown University
Howard University

FLORIDA
Florida State University
University of Florida
University of Miami
Nova Southeastern University
Stetson University

GEORGIA
Emory University
Georgia State University
University of Georgia
Mercer University

HAWAII
University of Hawaii—Manoa

IDAHO
University of Idaho

ILLINOIS
University of Chicago
DePaul University
Illinois Institute of Technology
University of Illinois—Urbana-Champaign
The John Marshall Law School
Loyola University of Chicago
Northern Illinois University
Northwestern University
Southern Illinois University—Carbondale

INDIANA
Indiana University—Bloomington
Indiana University—Indianapolis
University of Notre Dame
Valparaiso University

IOWA
Drake University
University of Iowa

KANSAS
University of Kansas
Washburn University

KENTUCKY
University of Kentucky
University of Louisville
Northern Kentucky University

LOUISIANA
Louisiana State University—Baton Rouge
Loyola University New Orleans
Southern University—Baton Rouge
Tulane University

MAINE
University of Maine

MARYLAND
University of Baltimore
University of Maryland—Baltimore County

MASSACHUSETTS
Boston College
Boston University
Harvard University
New England School of Law
Northeastern University
Suffolk University
Western New England College

MICHIGAN
Detroit College of Law at Michigan State
  University
University of Detroit
University of Michigan—Ann Arbor
Thomas M. Cooley Law School
Wayne State University

MINNESOTA
Hamline University
University of Minnesota—Twin Cities
William Mitchell College of Law

MISSISSIPPI
Mississippi College
University of Mississippi

MISSOURI
University of Missouri—Columbia
University of Missouri—Kansas City
St. Louis University
Washington University

MONTANA
University of Montana

NEBRASKA
Creighton University
University of Nebraska—Lincoln

NEW HAMPSHIRE
Franklin Pierce Law Center

NEW JERSEY
Rutgers University—Camden
Rutgers University—Newark
Seton Hall University

NEW MEXICO
University of New Mexico

NEW YORK
Albany Law School of Union University
Brooklyn Law School
City University of New York—Queens College
Columbia University
Cornell University
Fordham University
Hofstra University
New York Law School
New York University
Pace University
St. John's University
State University of New York at Buffalo
Syracuse University
Touro College
Yeshiva University

NORTH CAROLINA
Campbell University
Duke University
North Carolina Central University
University of North Carolina—Chapel Hill
Wake Forest University

NORTH DAKOTA
University of North Dakota

OHIO
University of Akron
Capital University Law School
Case Western Reserve University
University of Cincinnati
Cleveland State University
University of Dayton
Ohio Northern University
Ohio State University—Columbus
University of Toledo

OKLAHOMA
Oklahoma City University
University of Oklahoma
University of Tulsa

OREGON
Lewis and Clark College
University of Oregon
Williamette University

PENNSYLVANIA
Dickinson School of Law
Duquesne University
University of Pennsylvania
University of Pittsburgh
Temple University
Villanova University
Widener University—Harrisburg

SOUTH CAROLINA
University of South Carolina—Columbia

SOUTH DAKOTA
University of South Dakota

TENNESSEE
The University of Memphis
University of Tennessee—Knoxville
Vanderbilt University

TEXAS
Baylor University
University of Houston
St. Mary's University
South Texas College of Law
Southern Methodist University
Texas Southern University
Texas Tech University
University of Texas—Austin

UTAH
Brigham Young University
University of Utah

VERMONT
Vermont Law School

VIRGINIA
George Mason University
University of Richmond
University of Virginia
Washington and Lee University
The College of William and Mary

WASHINGTON
Gonzaga University
Seattle University
University of Washington

WEST VIRGINIA
West Virginia University

WISCONSIN
Marquette University
University of Wisconsin—Madison

WYOMING
University of Wyoming

COMMONWEALTH OF PUERTO RICO
Catholic University of Puerto Rico
Inter American University of Puerto Rico
University of Puerto Rico

APPENDIX C
LAW SCHOOLS IN CANADA

PROVINCE AND LAW SCHOOL

ALBERTA
University of Alberta
University of Calgary

BRITISH COLUMBIA
University of British Columbia
University of Victoria

MANITOBA
University of Manitoba

NOVA SCOTIA
Dalhousie University

ONTARIO
University of Ottawa
Queen's University
University of Toronto
University of Western Ontario
University of Windsor
York University Osgoode Hall

QUEBEC
McGill University

SASKATCHEWAN
University of Saskatchewan

APPENDIX D
INTERNATIONAL INSTITUTIONS OF LAW

COUNTRY AND LAW SCHOOL

AUSTRIA
University of Innsbruck

University of Vienna

BELGIUM
Free University of Brussels

DENMARK
University of Copenhagen

FRANCE
University of Aix-Marseilles II

University of Franche-Comté Besançon

University of Bordeaux I Talence

University of Caen

University of Clermont-Ferrand I

University of Burgundy Dijon

University of Pierre Mendês France/Grenoble II

University of Law and Health Sciences/Lille II

University of Limoges

University Jean Moulin/Lyons III

University of Montpellier I

University of Nancy II

University of Nantes

University of Nice

University of Orléans

University of Paris I/Panthéon-Sorbonne

University of Law, Economics and Social Sciences/Paris II

University of Paris X/Nanterre

University of Paris Val-de-Marne/Paris XII

University of Paris-Nord/Paris XIII

University of Poitiers

University of Rheims Champagne-Ardennes

University of Rennes I

University of Rouen-Haute-Normandie

Jean Monnet University Saint-Etienne

University of Social Sciences/Toulouse I

FEDERAL REPUBLIC OF GERMANY
Rhenish Friedrich-Wilhelm University of Bonn

University of Cologne

Friedrich Alexander University of Erlangen-Nuremberg

Albert Ludwig University of Freiburg im Breisgau

Georg August University of Göttingen

Rupert Charles University of Heidelberg

Christian Albrecht University of Kiel

Johannes Gutenberg University of Mainz

University of Marburg

Ludwig Maximilians-University of Munich

University of Münster

Eberhard Karl University of Tübingen

Bayerische Julius-Maximilians University of Würzburg

GREECE
National and Capodistrian University of Athens

IRELAND
The University of Dublin-Trinity College

ISRAEL
The Hebrew University of Jerusalem

ITALY
University of Rome I 'La Sapienza'

JAPAN
University of Tokyo

NETHERLANDS
University of Amsterdam

SPAIN
University of Madrid

SWEDEN
Stockholm University

SWITZERLAND
University of Fribourg

University of Geneva

UNITED KINGDOM
University of Cambridge

University of Edinburgh

University of London

University of Oxford

APPENDIX E
UNITED STATES INSTITUTIONS OF MEDICINE

STATE AND MEDICAL SCHOOL

ALABAMA
University of Alabama—Birmingham
University of South Alabama

ARIZONA
University of Arizona

ARKANSAS
University of Arkansas for Medical Sciences

CALIFORNIA
Loma Linda University
University of California—Davis
University of California—Irvine
University of California—Los Angeles
University of California—San Diego
University of California—San Francisco
University of Southern California
Stanford University

COLORADO
University of Colorado—Denver

CONNECTICUT
University of Connecticut—Farmington
Yale University

DISTRICT OF COLUMBIA
George Washington University
Georgetown University
Howard University

FLORIDA
University of Florida
University of Miami
University of South Florida

GEORGIA
Emory University
Medical College of Georgia
Mercer University
Morehouse School of Medicine

HAWAII
University of Hawaii—Manoa

ILLINOIS
University of Chicago
University of Health Sciences
University of Illinois—Chicago
Loyola University of Chicago
Northwestern University
Rush Medical College of Rush University
Southern Illinois University—Springfield

INDIANA
Indiana University—Indianapolis

IOWA
University of Iowa

KANSAS
University of Kansas—Kansas City

KENTUCKY
University of Kentucky
University of Louisville

LOUISIANA
Louisiana State University—New Orleans
Louisiana State University—Shreveport
Tulane University

MARYLAND

Johns Hopkins University

University of Maryland—Baltimore County

Uniformed Services University of the Health
 Sciences

MASSACHUSETTS

Boston University

Harvard Medical School

University of Massachusetts—Worcester

Tufts University

MICHIGAN

Michigan State University

University of Michigan—Ann Arbor

Wayne State University

MINNESOTA

Mayo Medical School

University of Minnesota—Twin Cities

MISSISSIPPI

University of Mississippi—Jackson

MISSOURI

University of Missouri—Columbia

University of Missouri—Kansas City

St. Louis University

Washington University

NEBRASKA

Creighton University

University of Nebraska—Omaha

NEVADA

University of Nevada—Reno

NEW HAMPSHIRE

Dartmouth Medical School

NEW JERSEY

University of Medicine and Dentistry of New
 Jersey—Newark

University of Medicine and Dentistry of New
 Jersey—Piscataway

NEW MEXICO

University of New Mexico

NEW YORK

Albany Medical College

Albert Einstein College of Medicine of Yeshiva
 University

Columbia University

Cornell University Medical College

Mount Sinai

New York Medical College

New York University

University of Rochester

State University of New York at Buffalo

State University of New York at Stony Brook
 Health Sciences Center

State University of New York Health Science
 Center at Brooklyn

State University of New York Health Science
 Center at Syracuse

NORTH CAROLINA

Bowman Gray

Duke University

East Carolina University

University of North Carolina—Chapel Hill

NORTH DAKOTA

University of North Dakota

OHIO

Case Western Reserve University

University of Cincinnati

Medical College of Ohio

Northeastern Ohio Universities

Ohio State University—Columbus

Wright State University

OKLAHOMA

University of Oklahoma—Oklahoma City

OREGON

Oregon Health Sciences University

PENNSYLVANIA

Jefferson Medical College of Thomas Jefferson University

Pennsylvania State University—Hershey

University of Pennsylvania

University of Pittsburgh

Temple University

RHODE ISLAND

Brown University

SOUTH CAROLINA

Medical University of South Carolina

University of South Carolina—Columbia

SOUTH DAKOTA

University of South Dakota

TENNESSEE

East Tennessee State University

Meharry Medical College

University of Tennessee—Memphis

Vanderbilt University

TEXAS

Baylor College of Medicine

Texas A&M University—College Station

Texas Tech University Health Sciences Center

University of Texas—Dallas

University of Texas—Galveston

University of Texas—Houston

University of Texas Health Science Center at San Antonio

UTAH

University of Utah

VERMONT

University of Vermont

VIRGINIA

Eastern Virginia Medical School

Virginia Commonwealth University

University of Virginia

WASHINGTON

University of Washington

WEST VIRGINIA

West Virginia University

Marshall University

WISCONSIN

Medical College of Wisconsin

University of Wisconsin—Madison

COMMONWEALTH OF PUERTO RICO

Universidad Central del Caribe

Ponce School of Medicine

University of Puerto Rico—Medical Sciences Campus

APPENDIX F
MEDICAL SCHOOLS IN CANADA

PROVINCE AND MEDICAL SCHOOL

ALBERTA
University of Alberta
University of Calgary

BRITISH COLUMBIA
University of British Columbia

MANITOBA
University of Manitoba

NEWFOUNDLAND
Memorial University of Newfoundland

NOVA SCOTIA
Dalhousie University

ONTARIO
McMaster University
University of Ottawa
Queen's University
University of Toronto
University of Western Ontario

QUEBEC
Laval University
McGill University
University of Montreal
University of Sherbrooke

SASKATCHEWAN
University of Saskatchewan

APPENDIX G
INTERNATIONAL INSTITUTIONS OF MEDICINE

COUNTRY AND MEDICAL SCHOOL

AUSTRIA
University of Vienna

BELGIUM
Free University of Brussels
Catholic University of Louvain

FRANCE
University of Aix-Marseilles II
University of Picardie Amiens
University of Angers
University of Franche-Comté Besançon
University of Bordeaux II
University of Caen
University of Clermont-Ferrand I
University of Burgundy Dijon
University 'Joseph Fourier'/Grenoble I
Catholic Faculties of Lille/Faculté Libre de Médecine
University of Law and Health Sciences/Lille II
University of Limoges
University Claude Bernard/Lyons I
University of Montpellier I
University of Nancy I
University of Nantes
University of Nice
University René Descartes/Paris V
University Pierre and Marie Curie/Paris VI
University of Paris VII
University of Paris-Sud/Paris XI
University of Paris Val-de-Marne/Paris XII
University of Paris-Nord/Paris XIII
University of Poitiers

University of Rheims Champagne-Ardennes
University of Rennes I
University of Rouen-Haute-Normandie
Jean Monnet University Saint-Etienne
Louis Pasteur University/Strasbourg I
University Paul Sabatier/Toulouse III
University of Tours

FEDERAL REPUBLIC OF GERMANY
Rhenish Friedrich-Wilhelm University of Bonn
Friedrich Alexander University of Erlangen-Nuremberg
Johann Wolfgang Goethe University of Frankfurt
Albert Ludwig University of Freiburg im Breisgau
Georg August University of Göttingen
University of Hamburg
Rupert Charles University of Heidelberg
Johannes Gutenberg University of Mainz
University of Marburg
Ludwig Maximilians-University of Munich
University of Münster
Eberhard Karl University of Tübingen
Bayerische Julius-Maximilians University of Würzburg

IRELAND
Royal College of Surgeons in Ireland

ISRAEL
The Hebrew University of Jerusalem

JAPAN
Keio University
Tokyo Medical College

NETHERLANDS
University of Amsterdam
Leiden University

SWEDEN
Stockholm University

SWITZERLAND
University of Geneva
University of Zürich

UNITED KINGDOM
University of Cambridge
University of Edinburgh
University of London
Charing Cross and Westminster Medical School
King's College London
The London Hospital Medical College
The Middlesex Hospital Medical School
Royal Free Hospital School of Medicine
St. Bartholomew's Hospital Medical College
St. George's Hospital Medical School
St. Mary's Hospital Medical School
United Medical and Dental Schools of Guy's
and St. Thomas's Hospitals
University College London
University of Oxford

APPENDIX H
UNITED STATES INSTITUTIONS OF DENTISTRY

STATE AND DENTAL SCHOOL

ALABAMA
University of Alabama—Birmingham

CALIFORNIA
University of California—Los Angeles
University of California—San Francisco
Loma Linda University
University of the Pacific
University of Southern California

COLORADO
University of Colorado—Denver

CONNECTICUT
University of Connecticut—Farmington

DISTRICT OF COLUMBIA
Howard University

FLORIDA
University of Florida

GEORGIA
Medical College of Georgia

ILLINOIS
University of Illinois—Chicago
Northwestern University Dental School
Southern Illinois University—Alton

INDIANA
Indiana University—Indianapolis

IOWA
University of Iowa

KENTUCKY
University of Kentucky
University of Louisville

LOUISIANA
Louisiana State University—New Orleans

MARYLAND
The Baltimore College of Dental Surgery

MASSACHUSETTS
Boston University Medical Center
Harvard School of Dental Medicine
Tufts University

MICHIGAN
University of Detroit Mercy
University of Michigan—Ann Arbor

MINNESOTA
University of Minnesota—Twin Cities

MISSISSIPPI
University of Mississippi—Jackson

MISSOURI
University of Missouri—Kansas City

NEBRASKA
Creighton University
University of Nebraska Medical Center

NEW JERSEY
University of Medicine and Dentistry of New
   Jersey—Newark

NEW YORK
Columbia University
New York University
State University of New York at Buffalo
State University of New York at Stony Brook

NORTH CAROLINA
University of North Carolina—Chapel Hill

OHIO

Case Western Reserve University

Ohio State University—Columbus

OKLAHOMA

University of Oklahoma—Oklahoma City

OREGON

Oregon Health Sciences University

PENNSYLVANIA

University of Pennsylvania

University of Pittsburgh

Temple University

SOUTH CAROLINA

Medical University of South Carolina

TENNESSEE

Meharry Medical College

University of Tennessee—Memphis

TEXAS

Baylor College of Dentistry

University of Texas Health Science Center at Houston

University of Texas Health Science Center at San Antonio

VIRGINIA

Virginia Commonwealth University

WASHINGTON

University of Washington

WEST VIRGINIA

West Virginia University

WISCONSIN

Marquette University

COMMONWEALTH OF PUERTO RICO

University of Puerto Rico—Medical Sciences Campus

APPENDIX I
DENTAL SCHOOLS IN CANADA

PROVINCE AND DENTISTRY SCHOOL

ALBERTA
University of Alberta

BRITISH COLUMBIA
University of British Columbia

MANITOBA
University of Manitoba

NOVA SCOTIA
Dalhousie University

ONTARIO
University of Toronto
University of Western Ontario

QUEBEC
Université Laval
McGill University
Université de Montréal,

SASKATCHEWAN
University of Saskatchewan

APPENDIX J
UNITED STATES INSTITUTIONS OF NURSING

STATE AND NURSING SCHOOL

ALABAMA
University of Alabama—Birmingham

ARIZONA
Arizona State University
University of Arizona

ARKANSAS
University of Arkansas for Medical Sciences

CALIFORNIA
California State University—Fresno
California State University—Los Angeles
University of California—Los Angeles
University of California—San Francisco
Loma Linda University

COLORADO
University of Colorado Health Sciences Center

CONNECTICUT
University of Connecticut
Yale University

DELAWARE
University of Delaware

DISTRICT OF COLUMBIA
Catholic University of America

FLORIDA
University of Florida

GEORGIA
Emory University
Medical College of Georgia

ILLINOIS
DePaul University
University of Illinois—Chicago
Loyola University of Chicago
Northern Illinois University
Rush University

INDIANA
Indiana University—Purdue University—
  Indianapolis

IOWA
University of Iowa

KANSAS
University of Kansas—Kansas City

KENTUCKY
University of Kentucky

LOUISIANA
Louisiana State University Medical Center

MARYLAND
University of Maryland—Baltimore

MASSACHUSETTS
Boston College

MICHIGAN
University of Michigan—Ann Arbor
Wayne State University

MINNESOTA
University of Minnesota—Twin Cities

MISSISSIPPI
University of Southern Mississippi

MISSOURI

University of Missouri—Columbia

St. Louis University

NEBRASKA

University of Nebraska Medical Center

NEW JERSEY

Rutgers University—Newark

NEW YORK

Adelphi University

City University of New York—Hunter College

Columbia University

Columbia University—Teachers College

New York University

University of Rochester

Sage Graduate School

State University of New York at Binghamton

State University of New York at Buffalo

Syracuse University

NORTH CAROLINA

University of North Carolina—Chapel Hill

School of Public Health

OHIO

Case Western Reserve University

University of Cincinnati

Ohio State University—Columbus

OKLAHOMA

University of Oklahoma Health Sciences Center

OREGON

Oregon Health Sciences University

PENNSYLVANIA

Pennsylvania State University—University Park

University of Pennsylvania

University of Pittsburgh

SOUTH CAROLINA

University of South Carolina—Columbia

TENNESSEE

University of Tennessee—Memphis

Vanderbilt University

TEXAS

Texas Woman's University

University of Texas—Austin

University of Texas Health Science Center at Houston

University of Texas Health Science Center at San Antonio

UTAH

Brigham Young University

University of Utah

VIRGINIA

Virginia Commonwealth University

University of Virginia

WASHINGTON

University of Washington

WISCONSIN

Marquette University

University of Wisconsin—Madison

University of Wisconsin—Milwaukee

COMMONWEALTH OF PUERTO RICO

University of Puerto Rico—Medical Sciences Campus

APPENDIX K
UNITED STATES INSTITUTIONS OF OPTOMETRY

STATE AND OPTOMETRY SCHOOL

ALABAMA
University of Alabama—Birmingham

CALIFORNIA
University of California—Berkeley
Southern California College of Optometry

FLORIDA
Nova Southeastern University

ILLINOIS
Illinois College of Optometry

INDIANA
Indiana University—Bloomington

MASSACHUSETTS
New England College of Optometry

MICHIGAN
Ferris State University

MISSOURI
University of Missouri—St. Louis

NEW YORK
State University of New York College of
  Optometry

OHIO
Ohio State University—Columbus

OKLAHOMA
Northeastern State University

OREGON
Pacific University

PENNSYLVANIA
Pennsylvania College of Optometry

TENNESSEE
Southern College of Optometry

TEXAS
University of Houston

COMMONWEALTH OF PUERTO RICO
Inter American University of Puerto Rico—
  Metropolitan Campus

APPENDIX L
UNITED STATES INSTITUTIONS OF PHARMACY

STATE AND PHARMACY SCHOOL

ALABAMA
Auburn University

ARIZONA
University of Arizona

ARKANSAS
University of Arkansas for Medical Sciences

CALIFORNIA
University of California—San Francisco
University of the Pacific
University of Southern California

COLORADO
University of Colorado Health Sciences Center

CONNECTICUT
University of Connecticut

FLORIDA
Florida A&M University
University of Florida
Nova Southeastern University

GEORGIA
University of Georgia

IDAHO
Idaho State University

ILLINOIS
University of Illinois—Chicago

INDIANA
Butler University
Purdue University—West Lafayette

IOWA
University of Iowa

KANSAS
University of Kansas

KENTUCKY
University of Kentucky

MARYLAND
University of Maryland—Baltimore

MASSACHUSETTS
Massachusetts College of Pharmacy and Allied
  Health Sciences

MICHIGAN
Ferris State University
University of Michigan—Ann Arbor
Wayne State University

MINNESOTA
University of Minnesota—Twin Cities

MISSISSIPPI
University of Mississippi

MISSOURI
University of Missouri—Kansas City
St. Louis College of Pharmacy

NEBRASKA
Creighton University
University of Nebraska Medical Center

NEW JERSEY
Rutgers University—New Brunswick

NEW MEXICO
University of New Mexico

NEW YORK

Albany College of Pharmacy of Union
  University

Long Island University—Brooklyn Campus

St. John's University

State University of New York at Buffalo

NORTH CAROLINA

University of North Carolina—Chapel Hill

NORTH DAKOTA

North Dakota State University

OHIO

University of Cincinnati

Ohio State University—Columbus

OKLAHOMA

University of Oklahoma Health Sciences Center

OREGON

Oregon State University

PENNSYLVANIA

Duquesne University

Philadelphia College of Pharmacy and Science

University of Pittsburgh

Temple University

RHODE ISLAND

University of Rhode Island

SOUTH CAROLINA

Medical University of South Carolina

University of South Carolina—Columbia

TENNESSEE

University of Tennessee—Memphis

TEXAS

University of Houston

University of Texas—Austin

UTAH

University of Utah

VIRGINIA

Virginia Commonwealth University

WASHINGTON

Washington State University

University of Washington

WEST VIRGINIA

West Virginia University

WISCONSIN

University of Wisconsin—Madison

COMMONWEALTH OF PUERTO RICO

University of Puerto Rico—Medical Sciences
  Campus

APPENDIX O
UNITED STATES INSTITUTIONS OF VETERINARY MEDICINE

STATE AND VETERINARY SCHOOL

ALABAMA
Auburn University

CALIFORNIA
University of California—Davis

COLORADO
Colorado State University

FLORIDA
University of Florida

GEORGIA
University of Georgia

ILLINOIS
University of Illinois—Urbana-Champaign

INDIANA
Purdue University—West Lafayette

IOWA
Iowa State University of Science and Technology

KANSAS
Kansas State University

LOUISIANA
Louisiana State University—Baton Rouge

MASSACHUSETTS
Tufts University

MICHIGAN
Michigan State University

MINNESOTA
University of Minnesota—Twin Cities

MISSISSIPPI
Mississippi State University

MISSOURI
University of Missouri—Columbia

NEW YORK
Cornell University

NORTH CAROLINA
North Carolina State University

OHIO
Ohio State University—Columbus

OKLAHOMA
Oklahoma State University

OREGON
Oregon State University

PENNSYLVANIA
University of Pennsylvania

TENNESSEE
University of Tennessee—Knoxville

TEXAS
Texas A&M University—College Station

VIRGINIA
Virginia Polytechnic Institute and State University

WASHINGTON
Washington State University

WISCONSIN
University of Wisconsin—Madison

International

Hong Kong
4/F Sun Hung Kai Centre
30 Harbour Road, Wan Chai,
Hong Kong
Tel: (011)85-2-517-3016

Japan
Fuji Building 40, 15-14
Sakuragaokacho, Shibuya Ku,
Tokyo 150, Japan
Tel: (011)81-3-3463-1343

Korea
Tae Young Bldg, 944-24,
Daechi- Dong, Kangnam-Ku
The Princeton Review- ANC
Seoul, Korea 135-280,
South Korea
Tel: (011)82-2-554-7763

Mexico City
PR Mex S De RL De Cv
Guanajuato 228 Col. Roma
06700 Mexico D.F., Mexico
Tel: 525-564-9468

Montreal
666 Sherbrooke St.
West, Suite 202
Montreal, QC H3A 1E7 Canada
Tel: (514) 499-0870

Pakistan
1 Bawa Park - 90 Upper Mall
Lahore, Pakistan
Tel: (011)92-42-571-2315

Spain
Pza. Castilla, 3 - 5º A, 28046
Madrid, Spain

Tel: (011)341-323-4212

Taiwan
155 Chung Hsiao East Road
Section 4 - 4th Floor,
Taipei R.O.C., Taiwan
Tel: (011)886-2-751-1243

Thailand
Building One, 99 Wireless Road
Bangkok, Thailand 10330
Tel: (662) 256-7080

Toronto
1240 Bay Street, Suite 300
Toronto M5R 2A7 Canada
Tel: (800) 495-7737
Tel: (716) 839-4391

Vancouver
4212 University Way NE,
Suite 204
Seattle, WA 98105
Tel: (206) 548-1100

National (U.S.)

We have over 60 offices around the U.S. and
run courses in over 400 sites. For courses and
locations within the U.S. call 1 (800)
2/Review

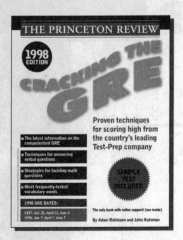